IMAGES
of America

CLINTON, FLEMINGTON AND LAMBERTVILLE

IMAGES
of America

CLINTON, FLEMINGTON AND LAMBERTVILLE

Compiled by
Sally A. Freedman

ARCADIA
PUBLISHING

ISBN 978-0-7385-1269-3

Published by Arcadia Publishing
Charleston, South Carolina

Printed in the United States of America

Library of Congress Catalog Card Number: Applied for

For all general information contact Arcadia Publishing at:
Telephone 843-853-2070
Fax 843-853-0044
E-mail sales@arcadiapublishing.com
For customer service and orders:
Toll-Free 1-888-313-2665

Visit us on the Internet at www.arcadiapublishing.com

Contents

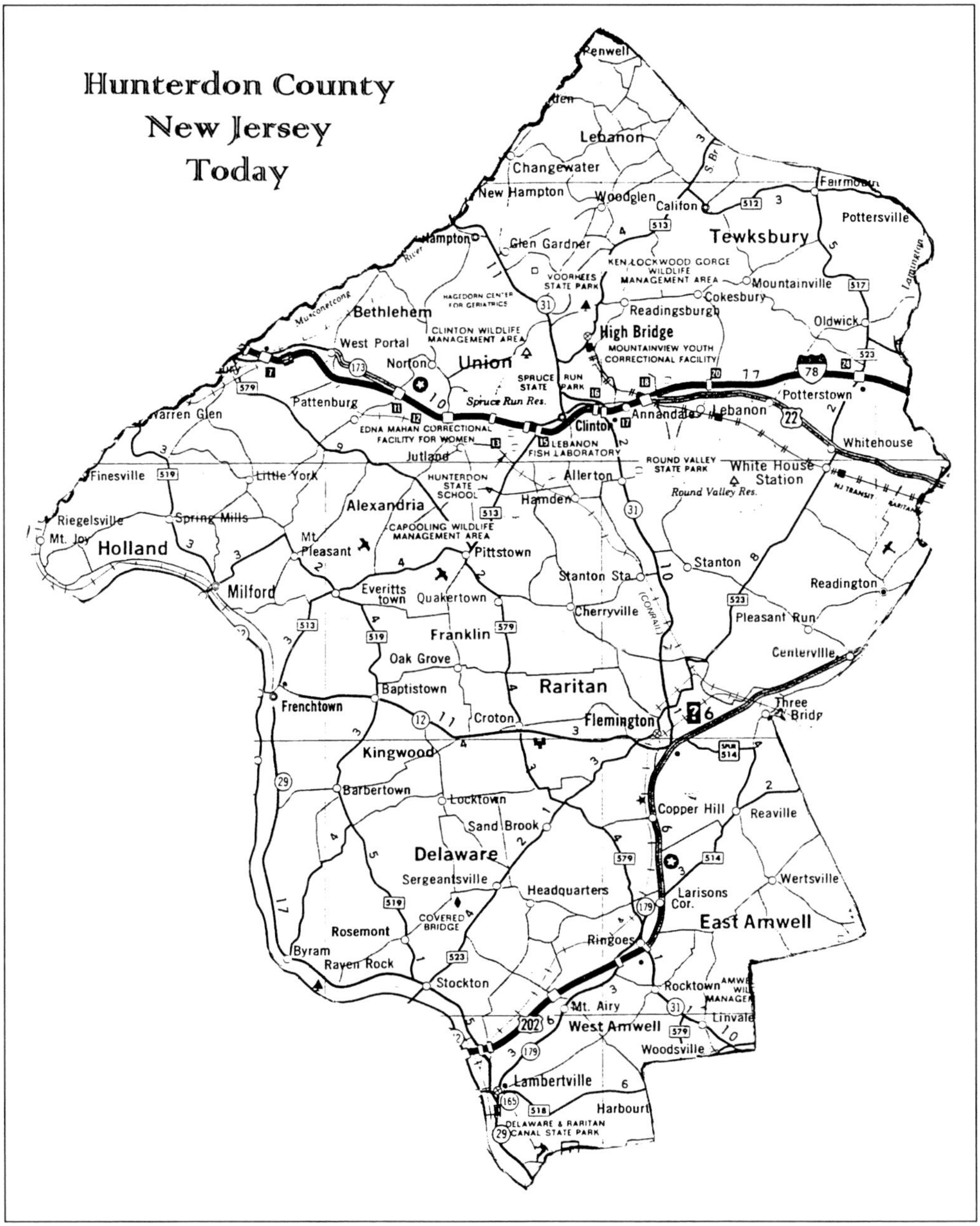
Hunterdon County
New Jersey
Today
Lebanon
Changewater
New Hampton
Woodglen
Califon
Fairmount
Pottersville
Tewksbury
Hampton
Glen Gardner
KEN LOCKWOOD GORGE WILDLIFE MANAGEMENT AREA
Mountainville
VOORHEES STATE PARK
HAGEDORN CENTER FOR GERIATRICS
Cokesbury
Bethlehem
Readingsburgh
Oldwick
CLINTON WILDLIFE MANAGEMENT AREA
High Bridge
MOUNTAINVIEW YOUTH CORRECTIONAL FACILITY
West Portal
Norton
Union
SPRUCE RUN STATE PARK
Spruce Run Res.
Pattenburg
Clinton
Annandale
Lebanon
Potterstown
Warren Glen
EDNA MAHAN CORRECTIONAL FACILITY FOR WOMEN
LEBANON FISH LABORATORY
Whitehouse
Jutland
ROUND VALLEY STATE PARK
White House Station
Finesville
Little York
HUNTERDON STATE SCHOOL
Allerton
Round Valley Res.
Alexandria
Hamden
Riegelsville
Spring Mills
Mt. Joy
CAPOOLING WILDLIFE MANAGEMENT AREA
Holland
Mt. Pleasant
Pittstown
Stanton
Milford
Everitts town
Quakertown
Stanton Sta.
Readington
Cherryville
Pleasant Run
Franklin
Oak Grove
Centerville
Raritan
Frenchtown
Baptistown
Three Bridge
Croton
Flemington
Kingwood
Barbertown
Locktown
Copper Hill
Reaville
Sand Brook
Delaware
Sergeantsville
Headquarters
Wertsville
Larisons Cor.
COVERED BRIDGE
East Amwell
Rosemont
Ringoes
Byram
Raven Rock
Stockton
Rocktown
Mt. Airy
West Amwell
Linvale
Woodsville
Lambertville
Harbourt
DELAWARE & RARITAN CANAL STATE PARK

INTRODUCTION

Clinton, Flemington, and Lambertville are communities located in the north, central, and south sections, respectively, of Hunterdon County on the western border of New Jersey. The hill towns of Tewksbury are just east and north of Clinton. The Native Americans who preceded Europeans in the area were the Lenni Lenape, or "Original People," of the Algonquian family of Indian tribes. Early colonists renamed them the Delaware, after the river near which many of them lived. Although most of the Lenape have moved west, area names such as Musconetcong and Cushetunk recall them to New Jersey residents today.

As the Hunterdon County Cultural and Heritage Commission recounts in its valuable booklet, *The First 275 years of Hunterdon County: 1714–1989*, the ownership of the land by the Lenape was recognized by the English: for "trifling amounts," they bought and paid for several tracts in what is now Hunterdon County between 1688 and 1758. However that recognition did not stop them from parceling out the entire area among themselves as though it were not owned.

England's King Charles II had granted his brother, James, Duke of York, all territory between the Delaware and Connecticut Rivers in 1664, and the Duke gave what is now New Jersey to Sir John Berkeley and Sir George Carteret that same year. In 1676 the jointly owned territory was divided vertically into halves called East Jersey and West Jersey. By then, Berkeley's half, West Jersey (where the present Hunterdon County is located), had been sold to John Fenwick as trustee for Edward Byllinge, a Quaker, who promptly turned over its management to William Penn and two other Quakers. The right of the Quakers to govern their colony was granted in 1680. Because of disputes with the colonists of both East and West Jersey, the owners of the territories gave them up in 1702 and England then united the two areas as a single royal colony, New Jersey.

Colonel John Reading, who purchased a plantation near Stockton in 1704, is considered the county's first settler. John Holcombe, who settled in Lambertville in 1705 or shortly thereafter, was another firstcomer. Other English, Scotch/Irish, Dutch, and German settlers followed, moving northward along the Delaware and the South Branch of the Raritan for the most part. Ferries were soon established at Stockton and Lambertville, and by 1714 there were enough settlers in that area (then called Amwell) to form a company of militia.

At first, most of the Hunterdon County area was part of Burlington County. Hunterdon County was formed by 1714, and named in honor of Robert Hunter, the tactful and sincere Royal Governor of New Jersey between 1710 and 1719. At that time the county was nearly all wooded. Pioneer farms were hewn out of the wilderness and the settlers lived almost totally "off the land." Most never fertilized their fields, but just moved on to another farm when cropland was worn out. By the 1790s, however, lime quarries and kilns were established to produce lime for fertilizer. This further depleted the forest, for it required two cords of wood to produce a ton of burnt limestone.

Centers of population often grew up around a ferry, a crossroads, a tavern, a grist or linseed oil mill, and later around a lime quarry and kiln. A general store was another essential, and, in time, a bank. Clinton, Flemington, and Lambertville filled the needs of the agricultural areas surrounding them, and so they grew. Lambertville, in fact, reached the 5,000 population mark that made it a city in 1872; it continues to call itself a city, although the population today is down to around 3,500.

Three of Hunterdon County's ferries were especially useful to George Washington during the American Revolution. Part of the army with which he crept up on Trenton and surprised the Hessian column of the British army on Christmas Day, 1776, was borne across the Delaware on the Lambertville (Coryell's) and Stockton (Howell's) ferries as well as on the one at Washington Crossing (McKonkey's), 7 miles south of Lambertville, where soldiers also rode in thirty-five commandeered boats. Ferries gave way to covered bridges which were important to turnpike stagecoach lines. The wooden bridges' propensity to be washed away in floods, both on the Delaware and the South Branch of the Raritan, eventually led to their replacement by today's steel bridges.

Washington's various stays in the Lambertville area are only one of that city's claims to fame. Another is the birth and youth there of James Wilson Marshall, who on January 18, 1848, discovered the gold at his Coloma, CA sawmill that started the California Gold Rush of 1849. Flemington's moment in the limelight came in January and February of 1935, when Bruno Hauptmann was tried in Hunterdon County Court House for the kidnapping and murder of the twenty-month-old son of Colonel Charles A. Lindbergh, America's aviation hero. And tiny Stockton is still known today for a 1930s Rodgers and Hart song, "There's a Small Hotel."

While Hunterdon County today is home to an increasing number of industries, it continues to have a rural population, including many who operate horse farms. With the development of major highways, it has also become a community for the New York metropolitan area, and housing developments encroach more and more upon farmland. Community zoning boards conduct a running battle to maintain the open character of this beautiful, rolling land.

One

Two Rivers

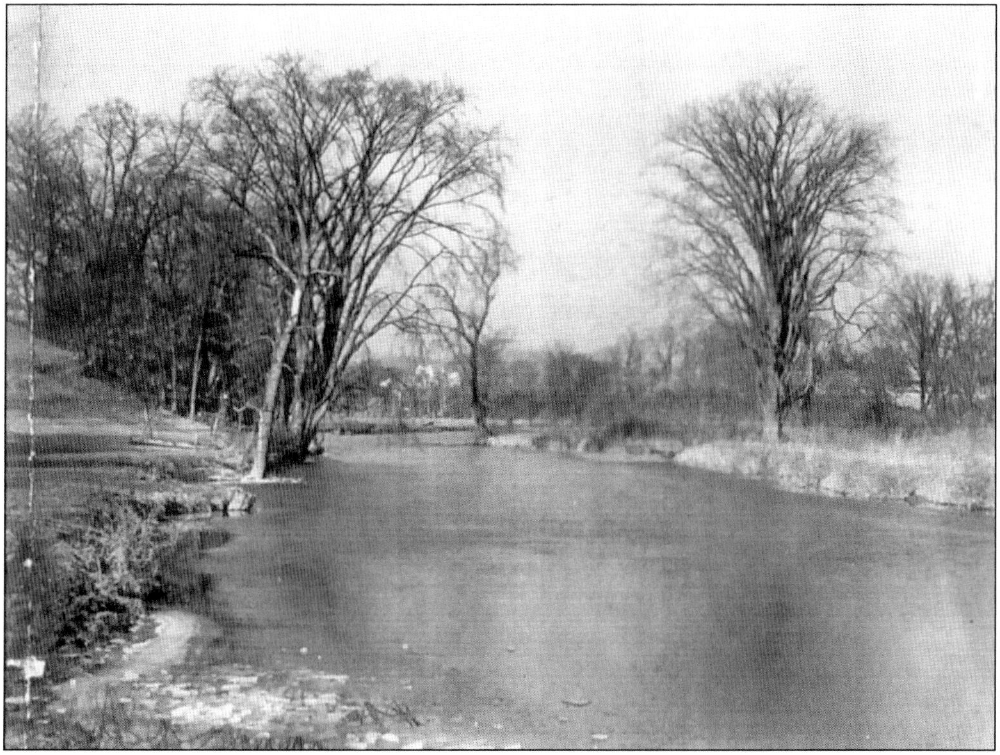

Spruce Run. Several rivers flow among the hills and fields of northwest New Jersey. Two of them are important in Hunterdon County history. The Delaware, a major American waterway, is the border between New Jersey and its neighbor, Pennsylvania, and forms the southwest border of Hunterdon County. The Raritan's South Branch flows from Budd Lake in Morris County down through the center of Hunterdon County and then east to join the North Branch in Somerset County, entering the Atlantic Ocean at Perth Amboy, NJ. At the town of Clinton, the pleasant stream of Spruce Run joins the South Branch. (Clinton Historical Society photo.)

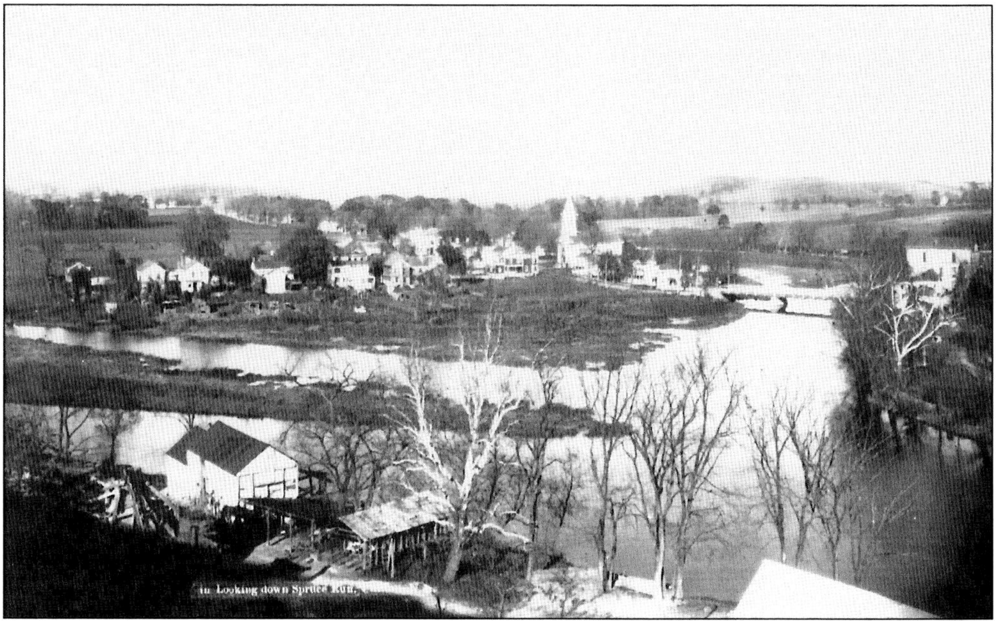

The junction of Spruce Run (left) and the South Branch of the Raritan in Clinton. River ice was stored in the house in the left foreground on the grounds of M.C. Mulligan's limestone quarry. (Clinton Historical Society photo.)

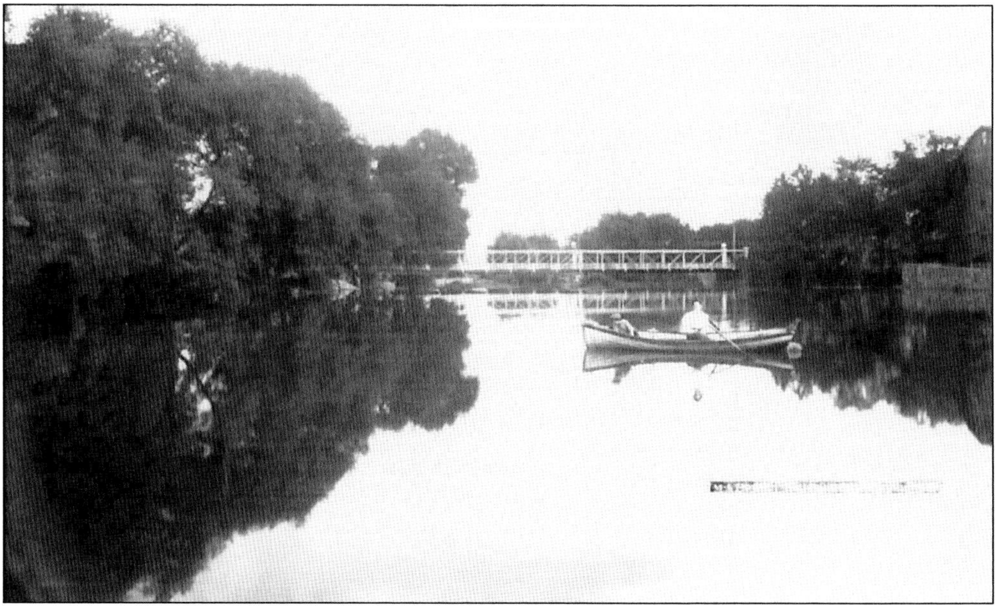

The South Branch. Hidden by trees, Clinton's two mills flank the iron bridge on Main Street. Victorian boaters pose casually, apparently unconcerned about the mills' dam just beyond them. (Clinton Historical Society photo.)

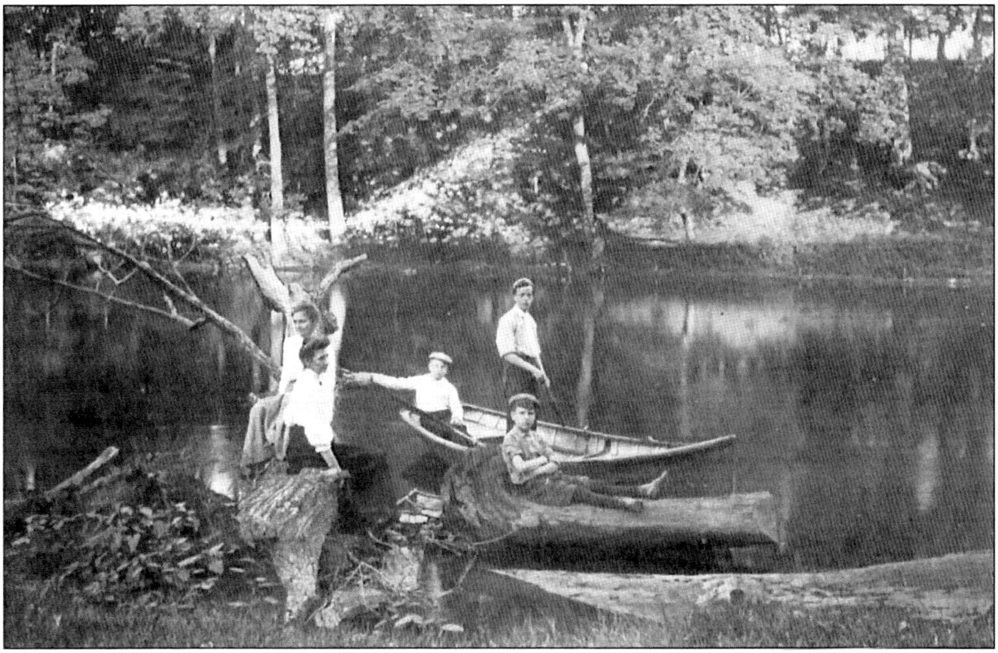

Boating was a favorite form of recreation in Clinton in the Victorian era. Note the women's long skirts, which must have been hard to keep out of the water in the bottom of a rowboat. (Clinton Historical Society photo.)

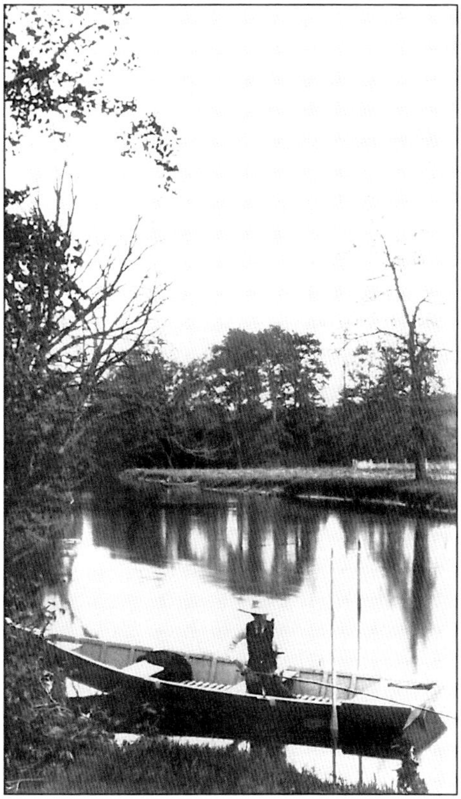

Walter S. Leigh, Clinton's band director and jeweler, fishes in the South Branch wearing an often-seen Panama straw hat—along with stiff collar, tie, and vest. (Clinton Historical Society photo.)

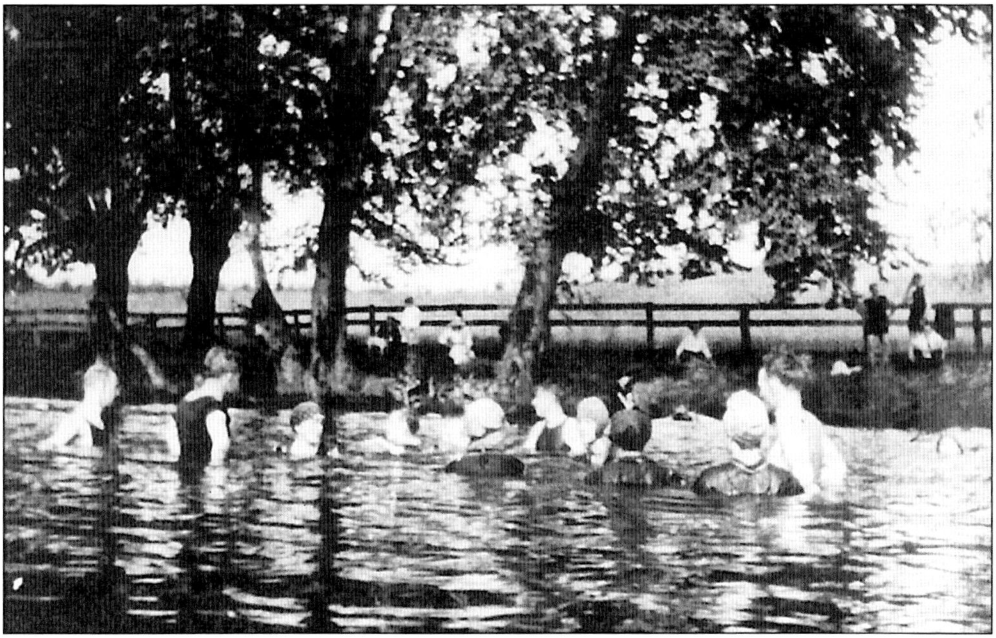

Taking a dip in a "swimming hole"—a calm spot off to the side of the main flow of the river—was another enjoyable pastime on warm summer days in Clinton along the South Branch of the Raritan. (Clinton Historical Society photo.)

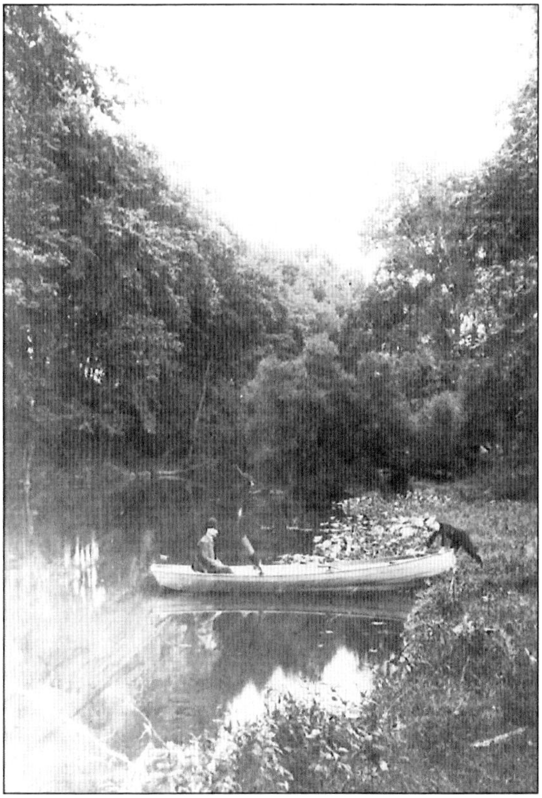

A trip in a rowboat on the South Branch offered a sense of adventure as friends went exploring along the wooded river banks. (Clinton Historical Society photo.)

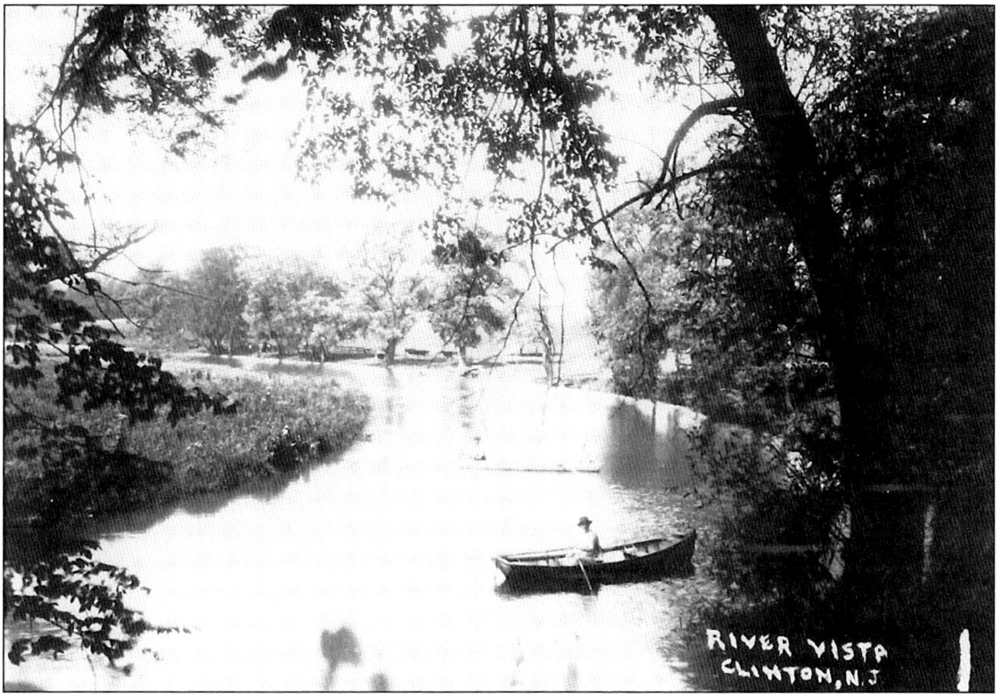

Peace and serenity are projected in this turn-of-the-century postcard scene of two parties of boaters on the South Branch of the Raritan at Clinton. (Clinton Historical Society photo.)

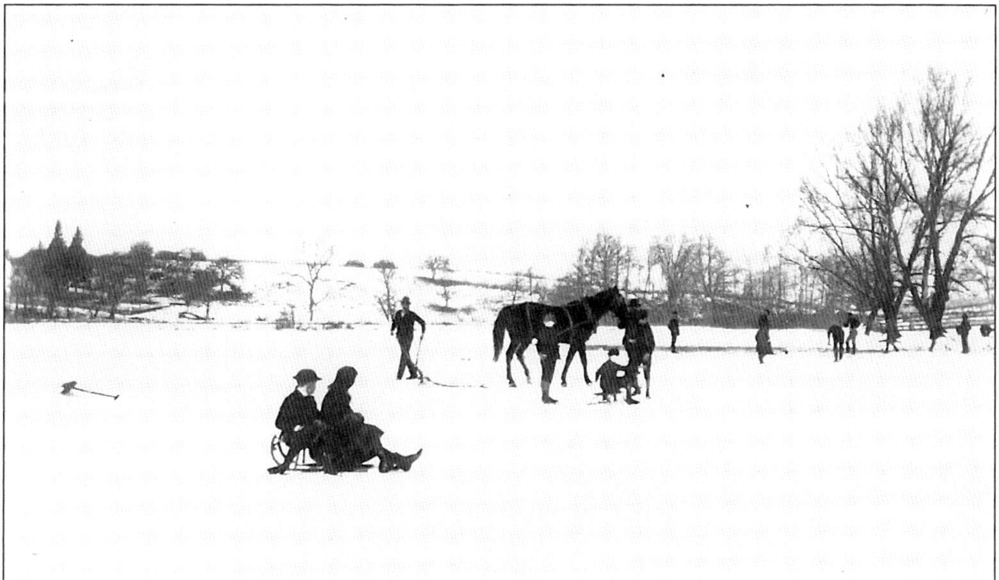

The South Branch in winter. The river froze hard enough to bear the weight of horses used to pull ice plows or saws and then to haul ice blocks back to the quarry. Sledders enjoyed watching the process. (Clinton Historical Society photo.)

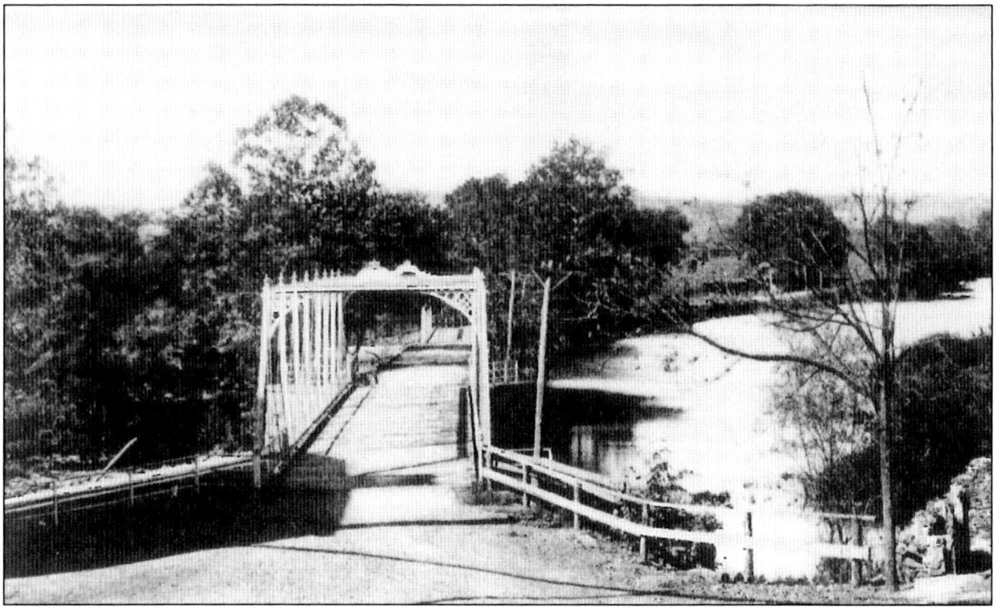

The South Branch of the Raritan at Dart's Mill. The river turned east just north of Flemington at Dart's Mill. A bridge allowed the road to continue along the north bank of the river.

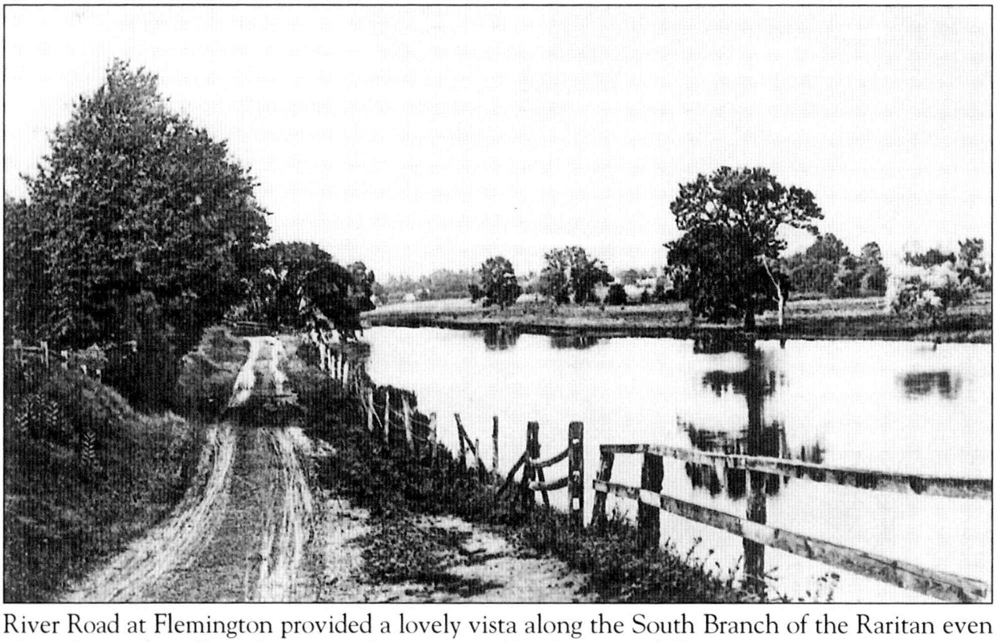

River Road at Flemington provided a lovely vista along the South Branch of the Raritan even when the road itself was bumpy with ruts or muddy after a rainfall.

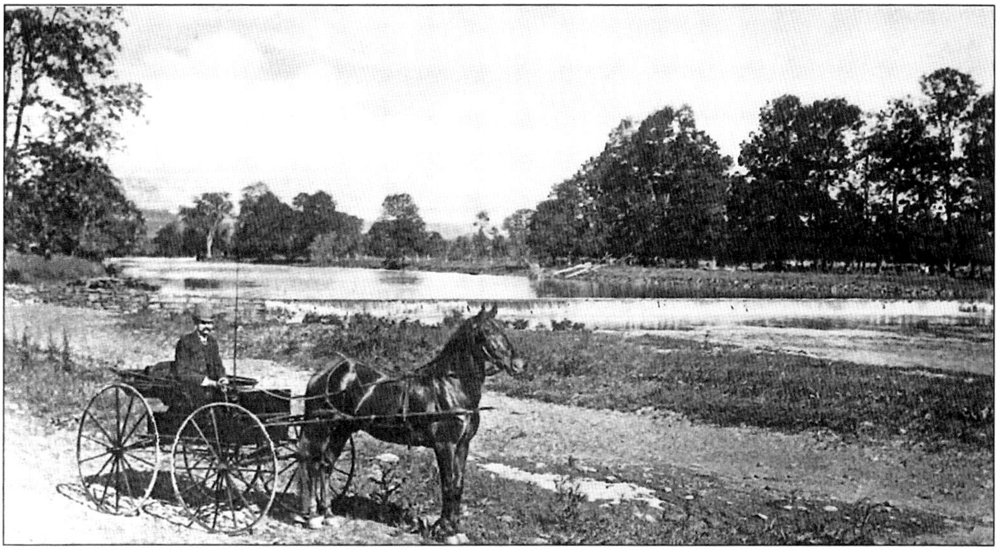

Horse and buggy postcard. M.V. Warren used this postcard scene of a horse and buggy beside Rockefeller's Dam, near Flemington, to send a message to a friend in 1907.

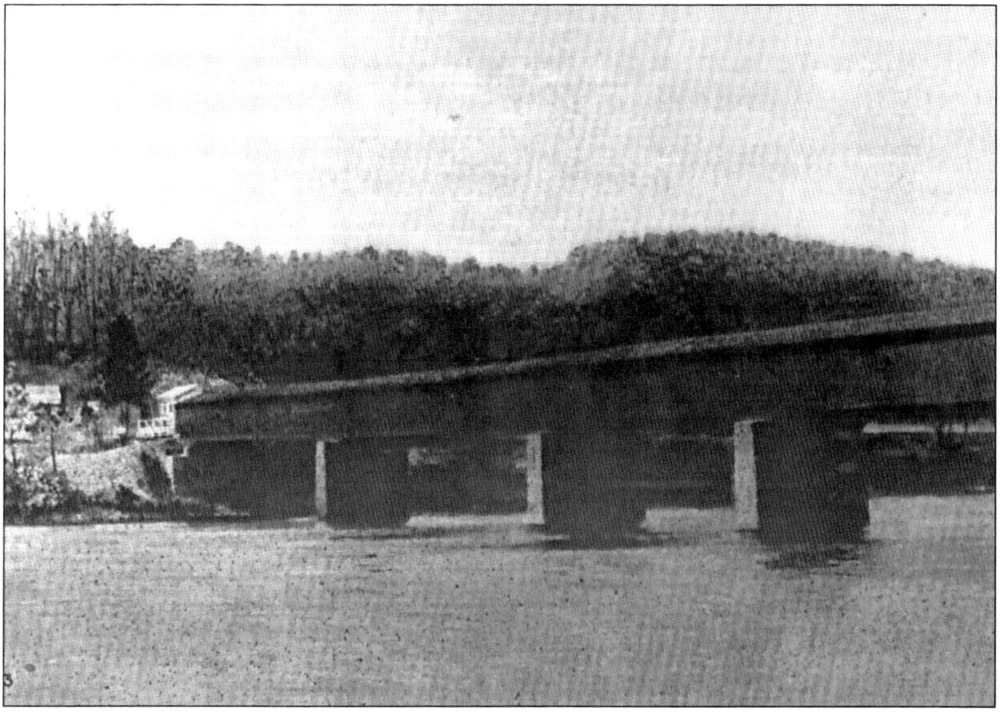

Covered bridge. When folks spoke of "The River" near Lambertville, they meant the Delaware. Several covered bridges crossed it, this one at Stockton, north of Lambertville. The purpose of covering a bridge was to keep it free of snow. (Lambertville Historical Society photo.)

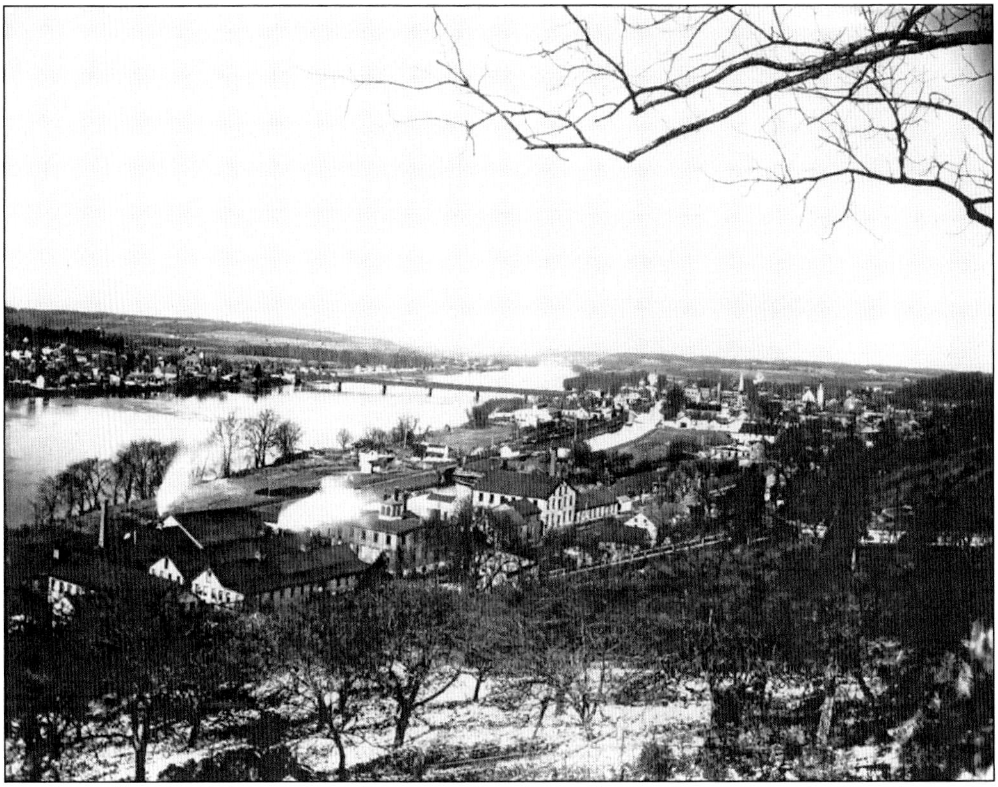

Lambertville. The Delaware River location of Lambertville was important in the Revolution. In the Civil War, the Lambertville Rubber Company (foreground) helped the North's war effort. New Hope, PA is across the river. (Lambertville Historical Society photo.)

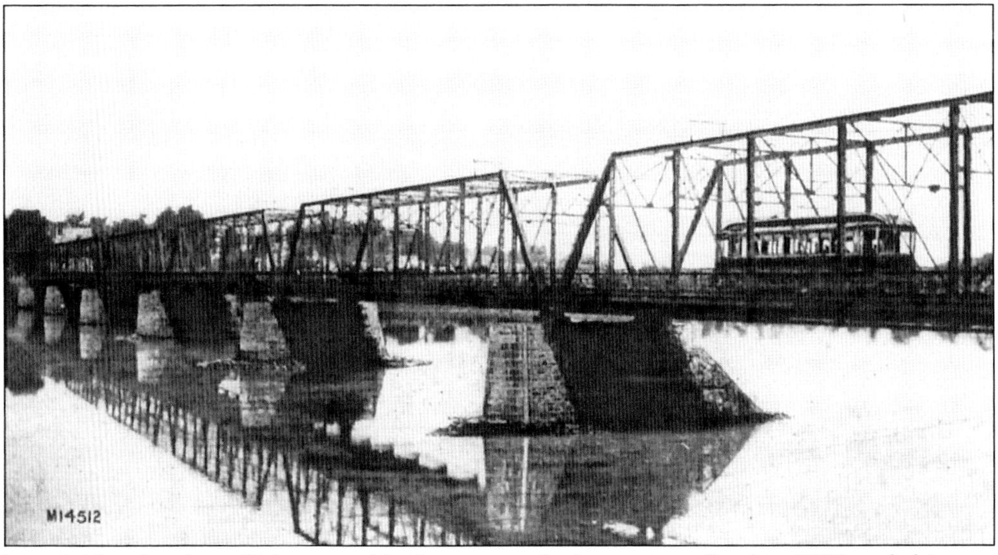

New bridge. Lambertville's covered bridge was washed away in a flood in 1903 and this new Delaware River bridge was built in its place. Note the trolley crossing the bridge. (Lambertville Historical Society photo.)

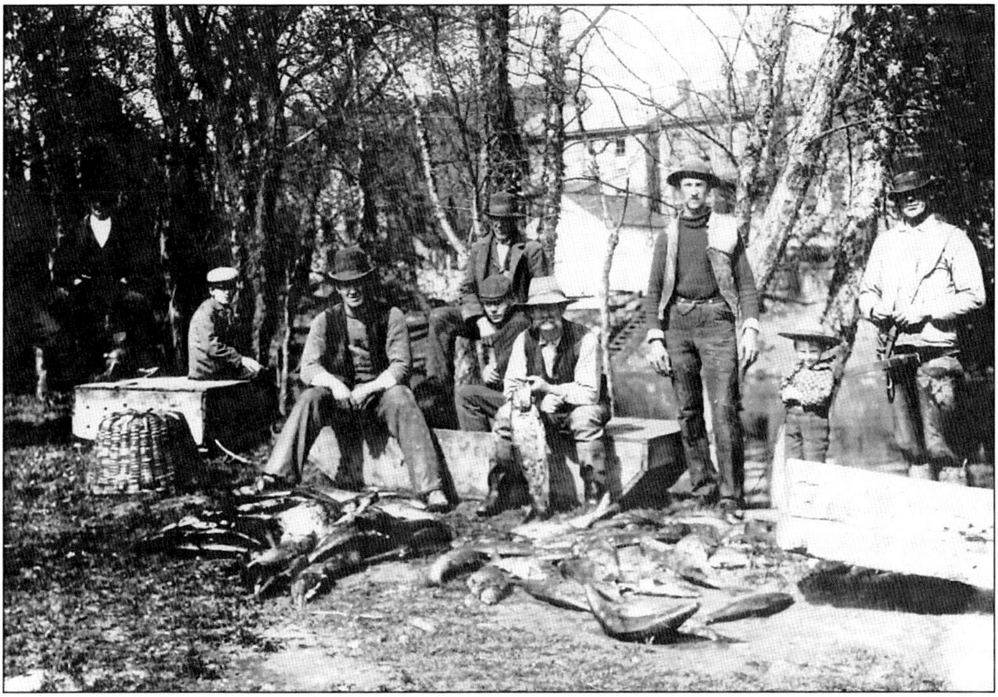

Fishing. The Delaware had other uses for early residents besides transportation. Each spring, shad fishermen would take a large catch off Holcombe Island at Lambertville. (Lambertville Historical Society photo.)

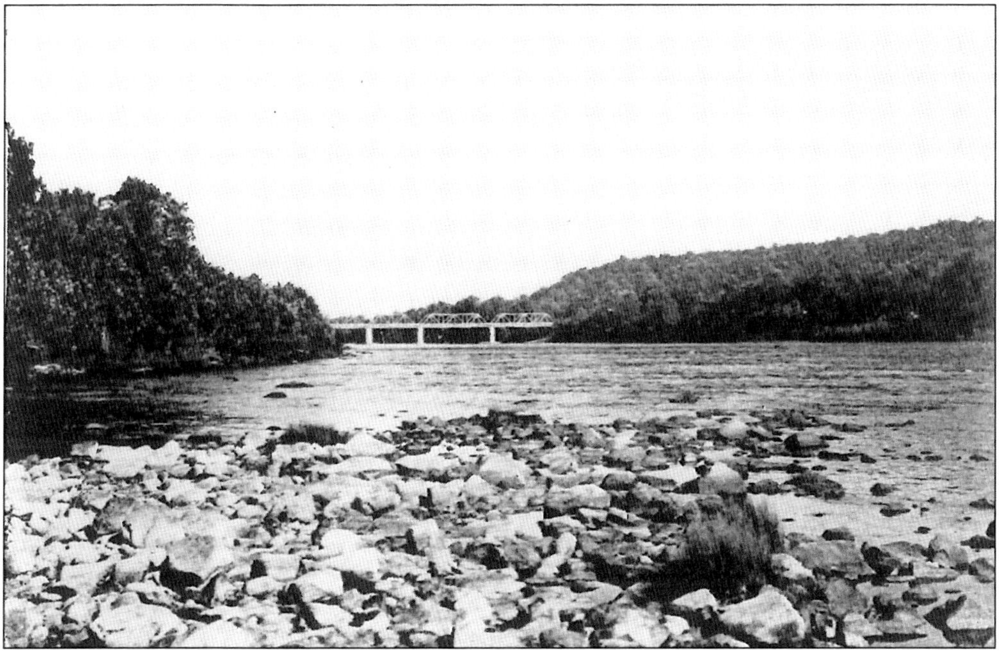

The Delaware at Stockton. Stockton, too, eventually lost its covered bridge in a flood, and the steel bridge in the distance here replaced it. This bridge is still in use today.

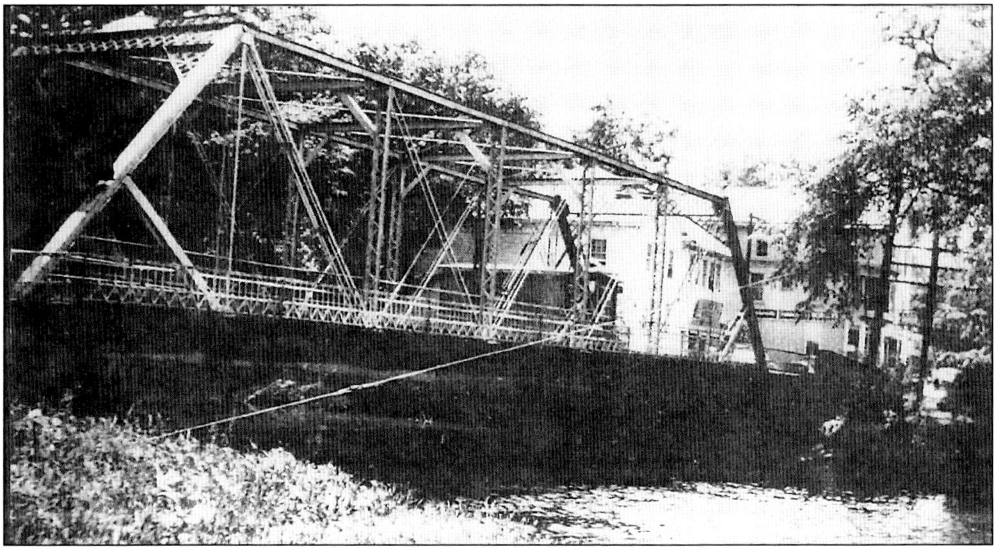

Tiny Califon, at the edge of the Tewksbury Township hills, also has a bridge over the South Branch of the Raritan. It was a single lane bridge until it was widened recently. (Califon Historical Society photo.)

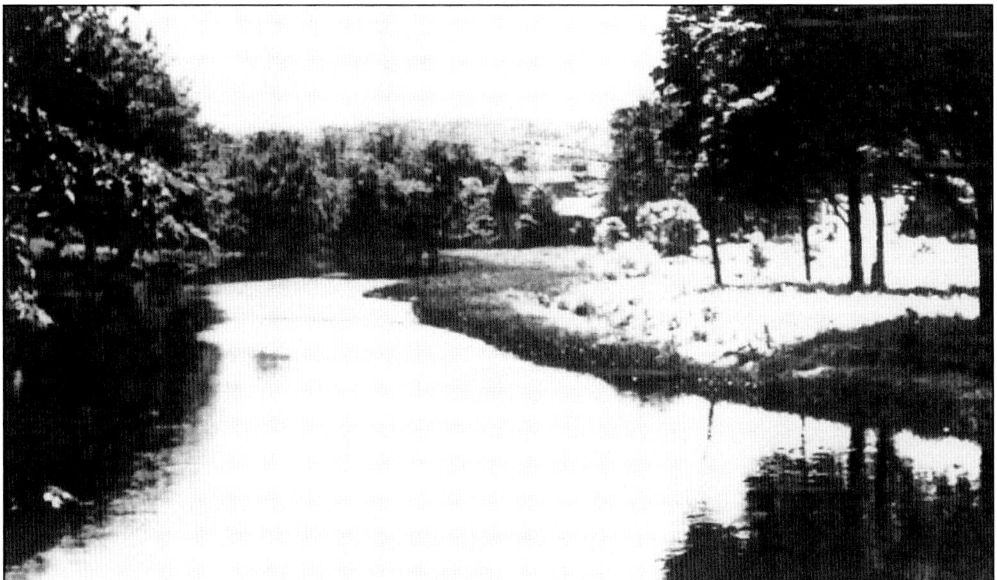

The South Branch at Califon. One of the early structures in Califon was the old mill which can be seen here in the distance. Children have always loved to feed geese—and occasionally a swan—in the peaceful stream below Califon's bridge. (Califon Historical Society photo.)

Two

Clinton and Its Mills

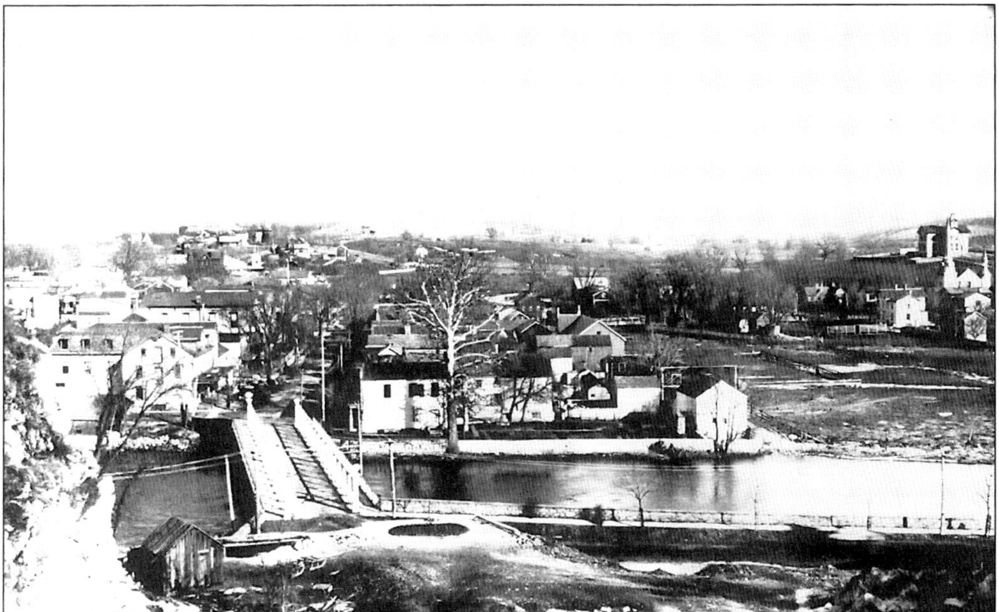

Clinton was named for DeWitt Clinton, a governor of New York. When its plats and streets were laid out in 1828, the present Main Street, across the bridge, was called Bridge Street. The iron bridge was built in 1870 to replace a wooden covered bridge which washed out in 1869. This spot was first a ferry site and then a bridge site on the Easton-Brunswick Turnpike, which turned to the left at the far end of the bridge on what is now Center Street. The black oval in the foreground is the open pit above Michael Charles Mulligan's lime kiln in his quarry. The "Great Fire" destroyed these Main Street buildings in October, 1892. (Clinton Historical Society photo.)

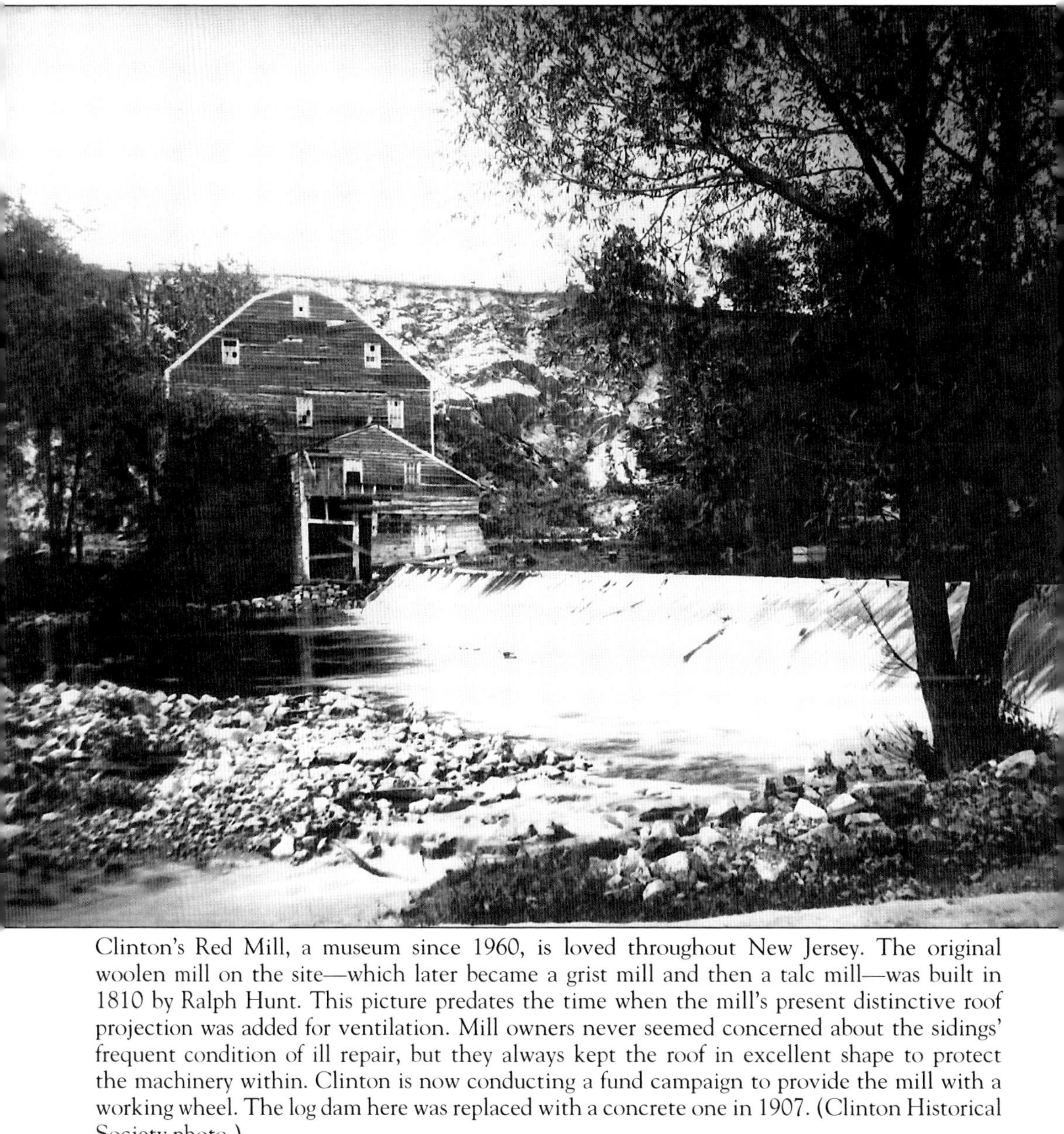

Clinton's Red Mill, a museum since 1960, is loved throughout New Jersey. The original woolen mill on the site—which later became a grist mill and then a talc mill—was built in 1810 by Ralph Hunt. This picture predates the time when the mill's present distinctive roof projection was added for ventilation. Mill owners never seemed concerned about the sidings' frequent condition of ill repair, but they always kept the roof in excellent shape to protect the machinery within. Clinton is now conducting a fund campaign to provide the mill with a working wheel. The log dam here was replaced with a concrete one in 1907. (Clinton Historical Society photo.)

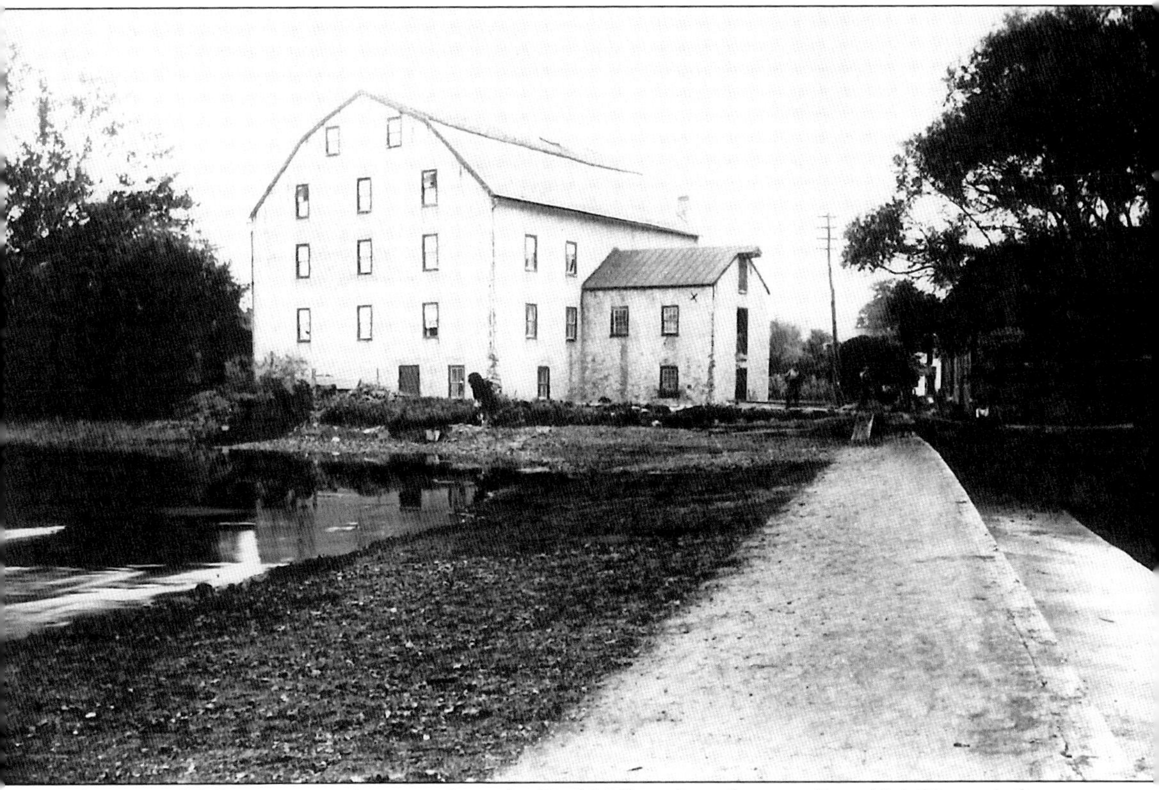

The Stone Mill sits across the river from the Red Mill and predates it. David McKinney's first linseed oil mill, built in 1763, burned in 1834 and the present mill was built by Nehemiah Dunham in 1836. From 1810 to 1828, Ralph Hunt owned the mills on both sides of the river, and the town was called Hunt's Mills. It became Clinton in 1828. After Dunham, Samuel Parry operated the stone building as a flour mill for close to fifty years, and it is listed in the National Register of Historic Places as Dunham-Parry's Mill. It ceased operating as a mill in 1955 and became the home of the Hunterdon Art Center. (Clinton Historical Society photo.)

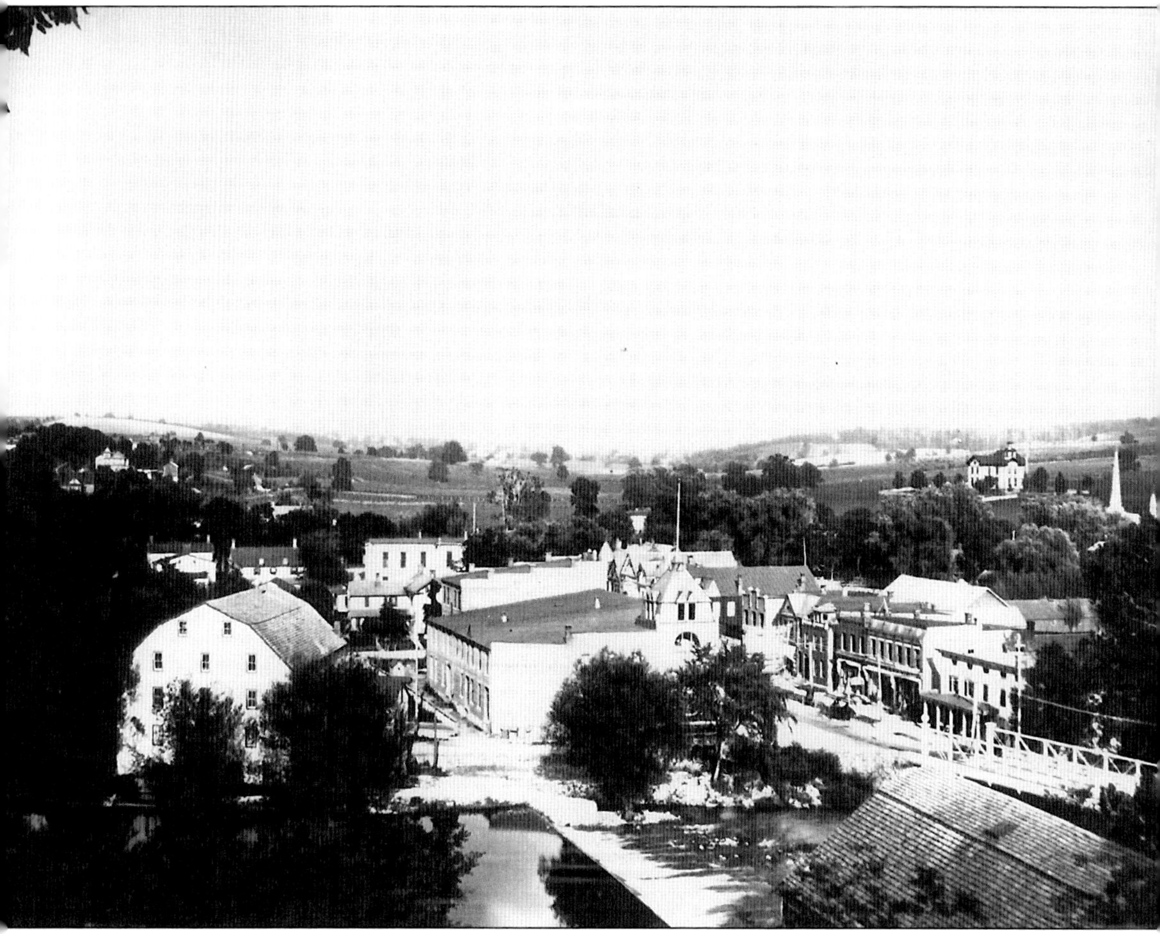

This turn-of-the-century view of Clinton shows the roof of the Red Mill in right foreground and the Dunham-Parry Mill across the river. No more than ten years after the Great Fire of 1892, Main Street has been completely rebuilt. The spires on the right are on the Baptist Church on Leigh Street, built by John T. Leigh after he had an argument with the pastor of the Pattenburg Baptist Church (Union Township), quit, and moved to Clinton. Clinton Public School is on the hill to the left of the spires. It burned in 1922. (Clinton Historical Society photo.)

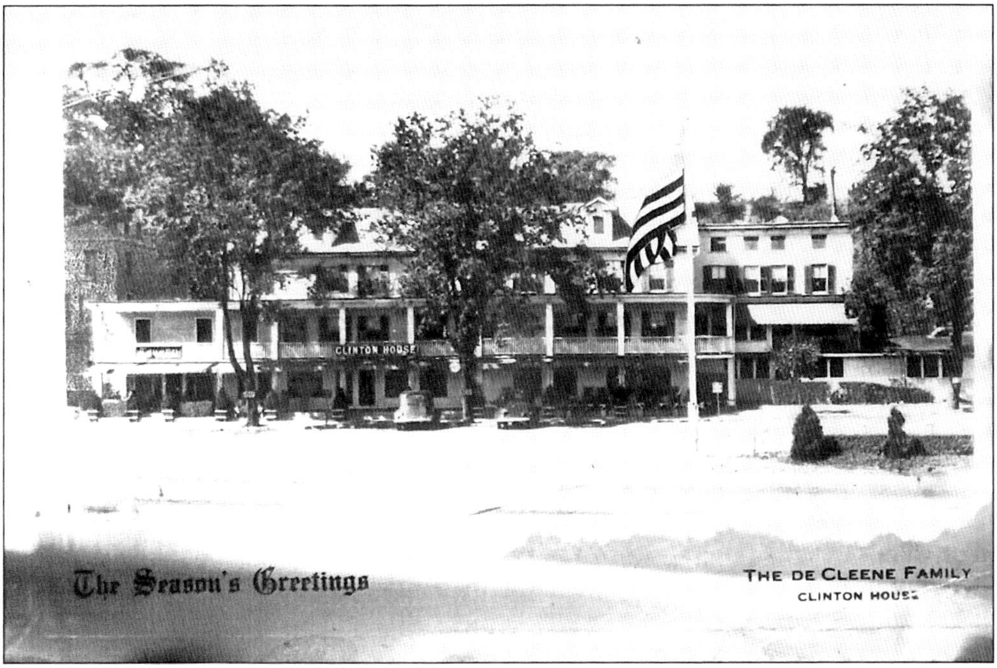

The Clinton House inn on West Main Street was built in 1831 to accommodate coach travelers on the Easton-Brunswick Turnpike. (Clinton Historical Society photo.)

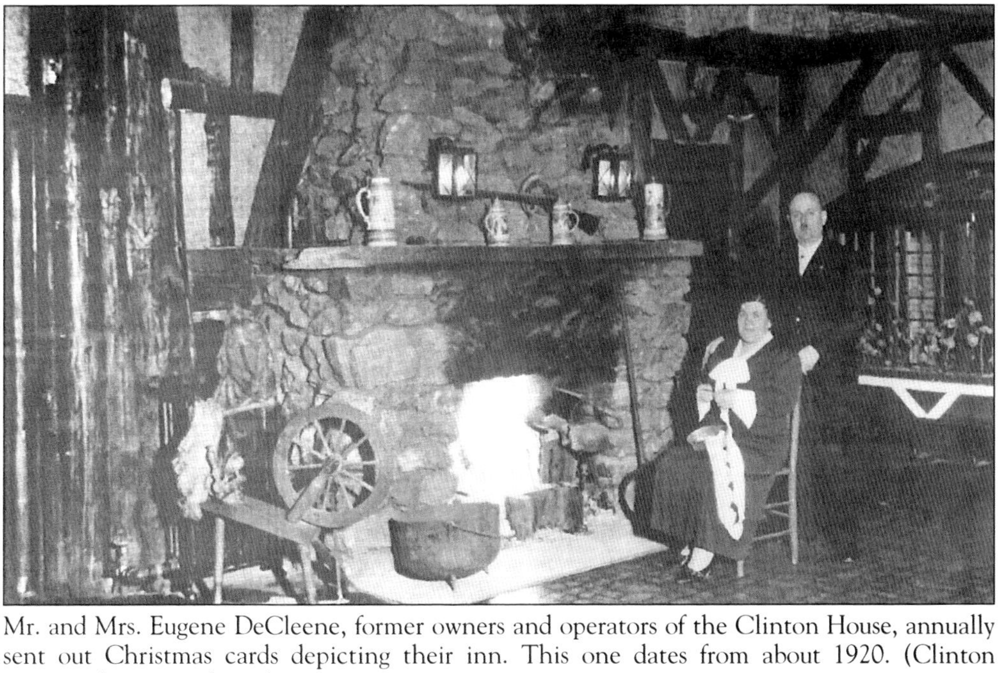

Mr. and Mrs. Eugene DeCleene, former owners and operators of the Clinton House, annually sent out Christmas cards depicting their inn. This one dates from about 1920. (Clinton Historical Society photo.)

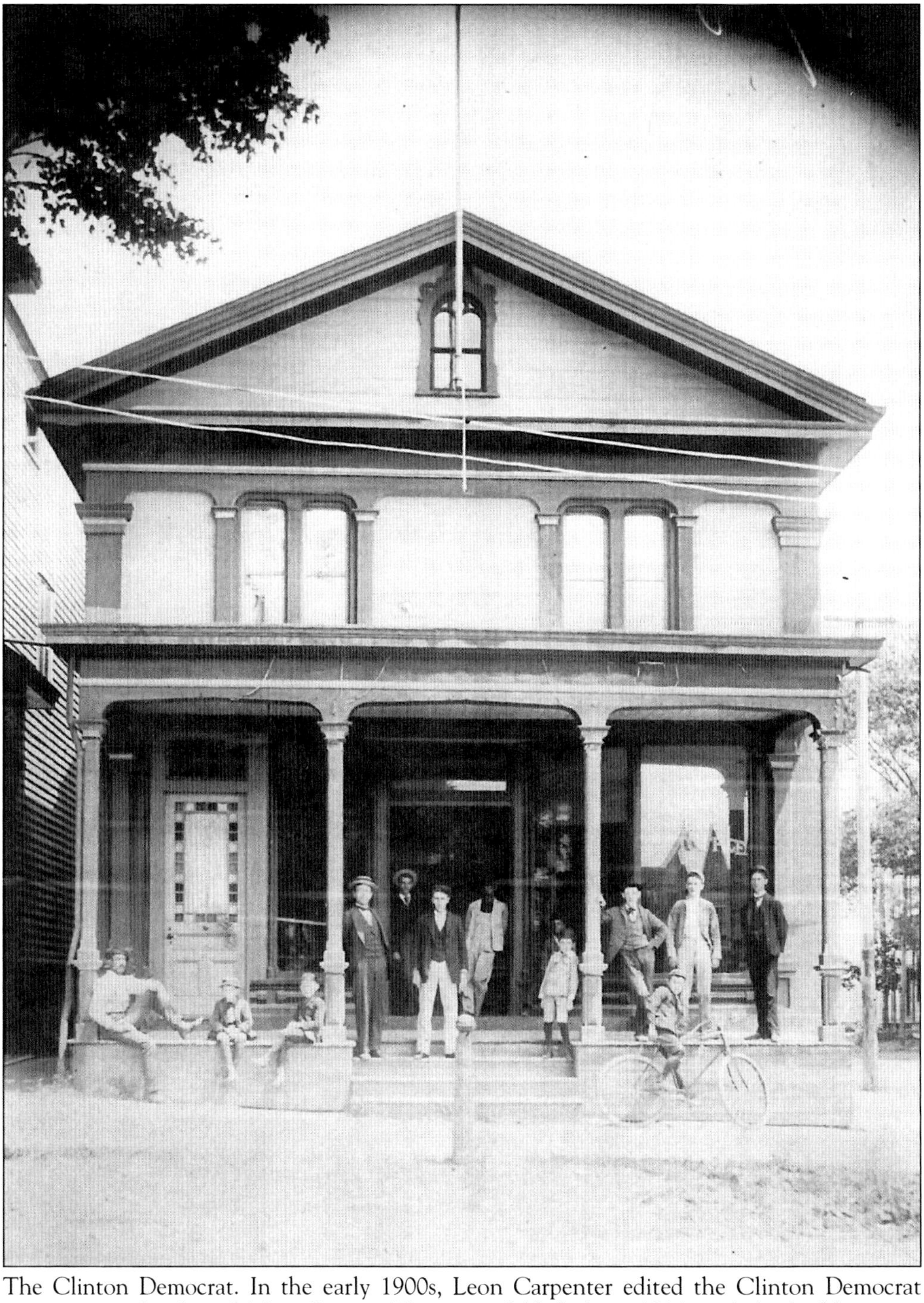

The Clinton Democrat. In the early 1900s, Leon Carpenter edited the Clinton Democrat newspaper at Leigh and Main Streets. The paper folded about 1914, and the building now houses a dress shop. Seated on porch are: (from left) Wes Hoffman, Roy Duckworth, Lew Gulick, John Carpenter, Theo Gulick, George Hall, Dock Buhner, James Rhea, Robert Leigh, Bern Mulligan, Wescot Carpenter, Buddy Rodenbaugh, and (on bicycle) Pat Knight. (Clinton Historical Society photo.)

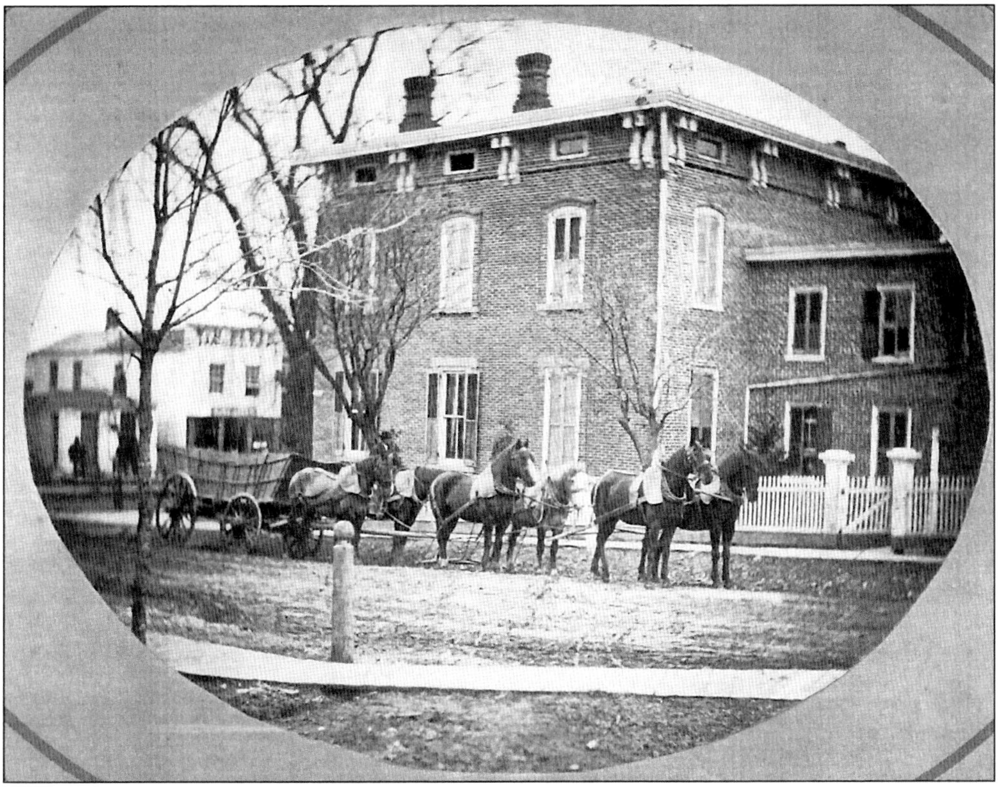

When he moved to Clinton from Pattenburg, John T. Leigh built the Clinton National Bank on Main Street and became its president. The farm wagon attests to the importance of agriculture to the town. (Clinton Historical Society photo.)

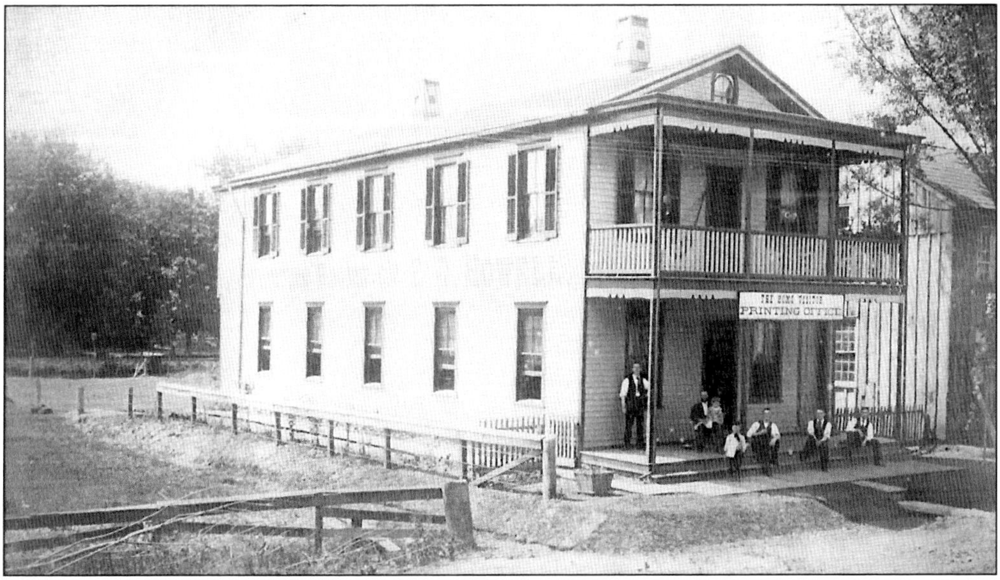

E.O. Howell's Printing Rooms, another Main Street business, printed "Picturesque Clinton" in 1898. It ws a promotional tract for the Clinton Board of Trade following the Great Fire and the rebuilding process. (Clinton Historical Society photo.)

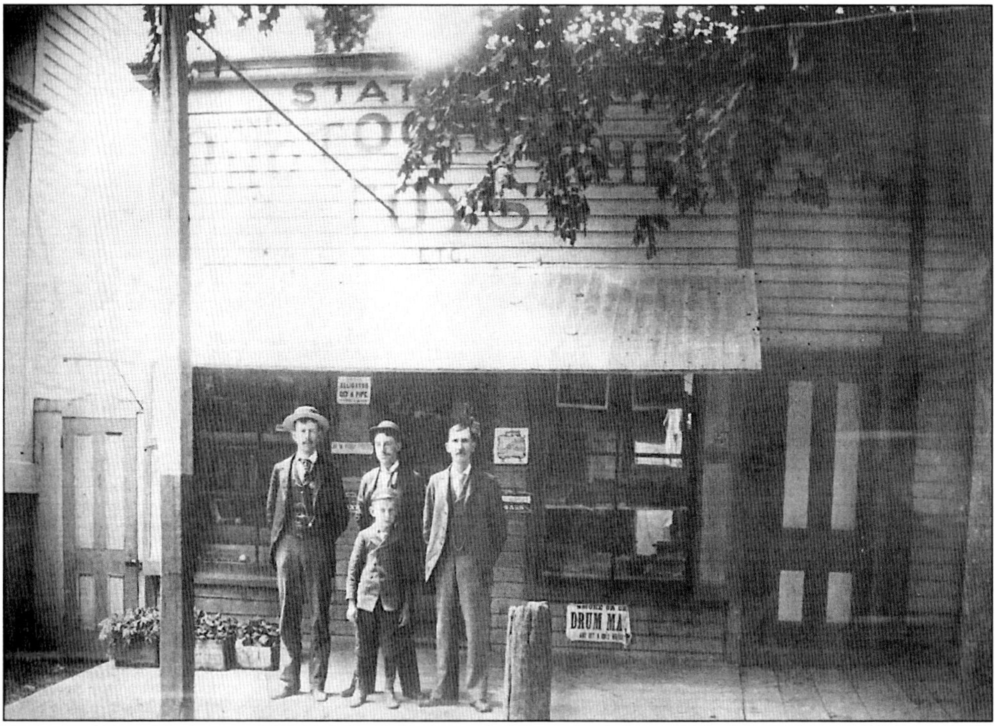

This Stationery and Photo Studio on Leigh Street is the Clinton Bakery today. This group may include the owner G.C. Angle who was one of Clinton's two professional photographers at the time. (Clinton Historical Society photo.)

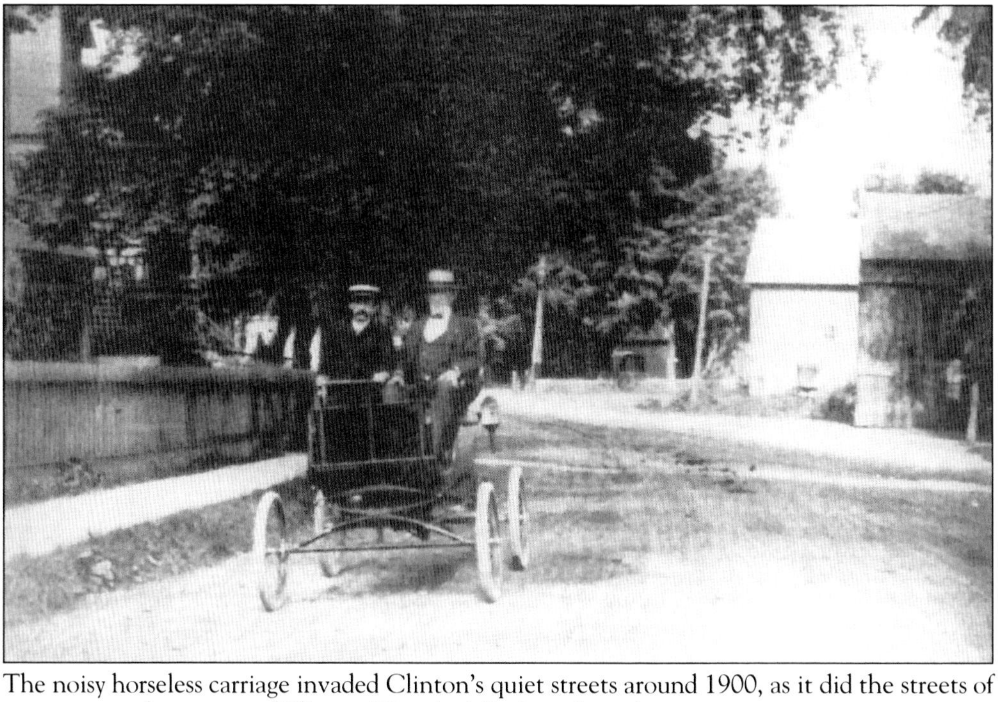

The noisy horseless carriage invaded Clinton's quiet streets around 1900, as it did the streets of towns across the country. (Clinton Historical Society photo.)

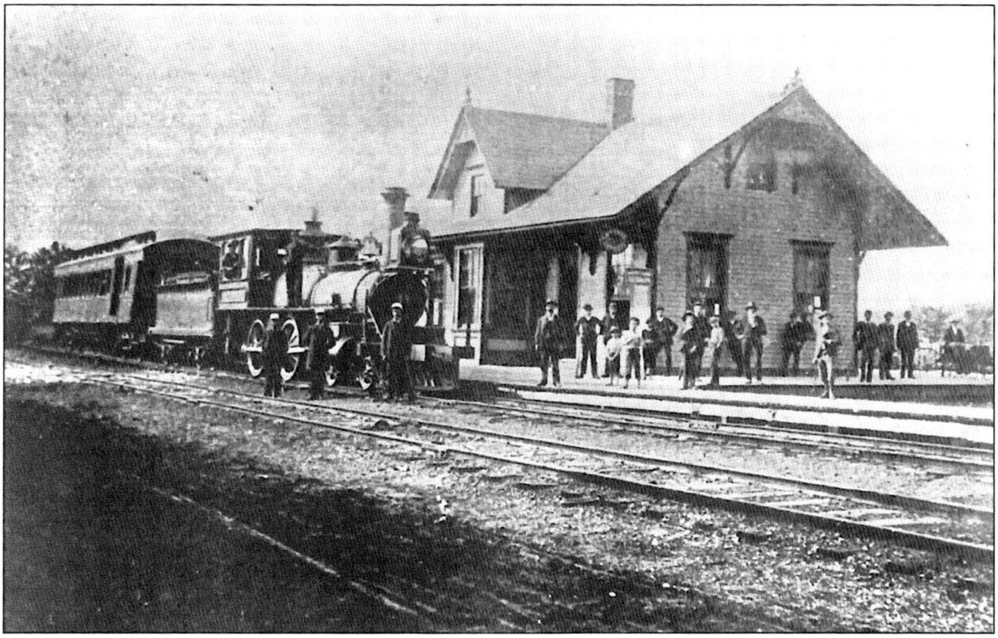

A spur of the Lehigh Valley Railroad arrived in Clinton in November, 1875, to residents' delight. Cyrus Fox Lumber company occupies the station's site today. (Clinton Historical Society photo.)

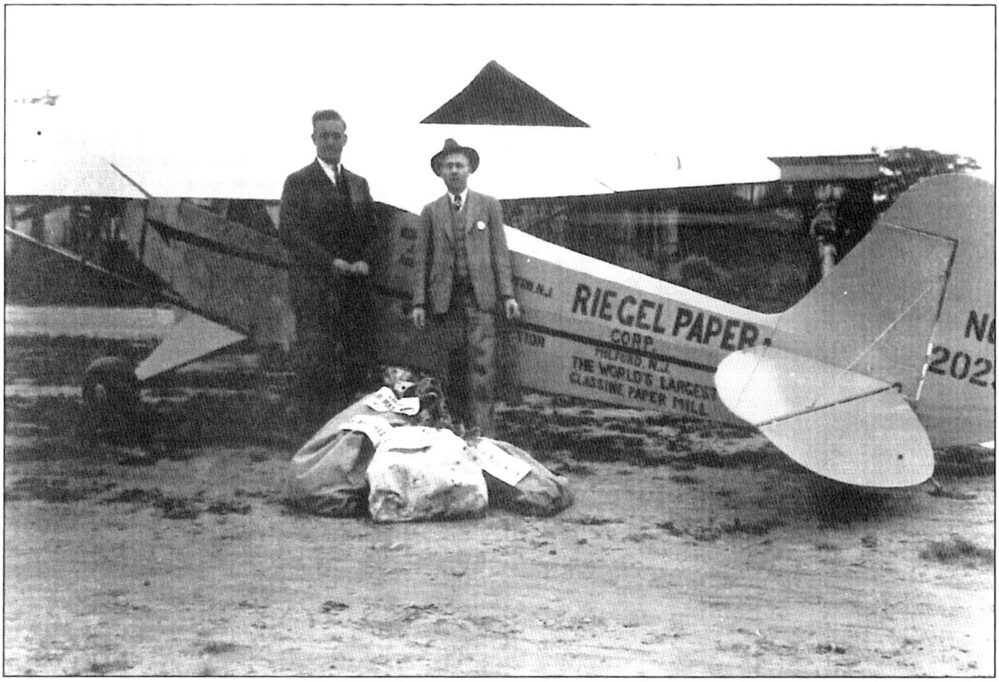

The start of air mail delivery on May 19, 1938, was another event to be celebrated in Clinton. The town's postmaster, Nelson Pickel, welcomes Pilot Marvin Everett here. (Clinton Historical Society photo.)

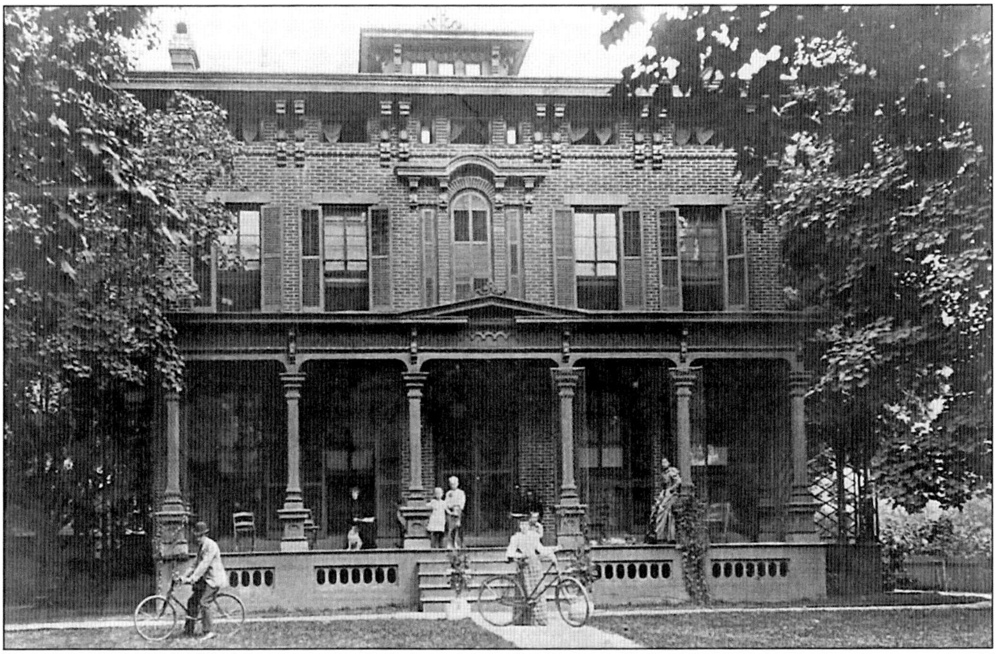

John T. Leigh's mansion was built for his second wife, Mary Van Syckel, aged eighteen, and his ten children; the couple then had seven more. Besides his bank, Leigh owned a brickyard for which this house was a kind of advertisement, but Clinton still has only three brick homes. (Clinton Historical Society photo.)

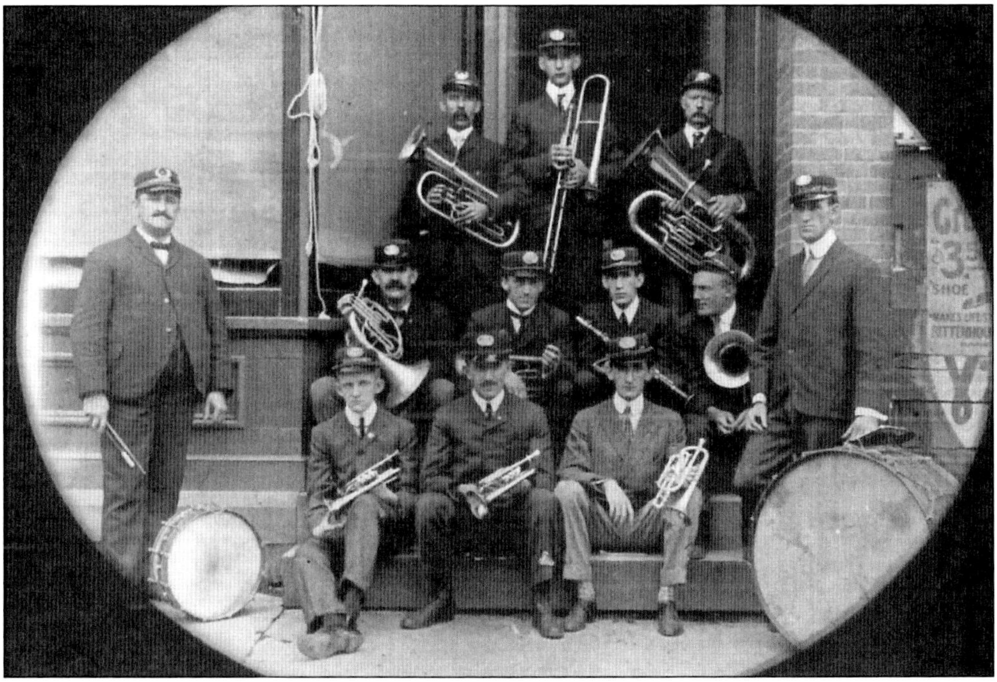

The town band was led by Walter Leigh in 1903. He is in the center of the first row, between his brothers, Mose (left) and Bob. The group is in front of Walter's jewelry store. (Clinton Historical Society photo.)

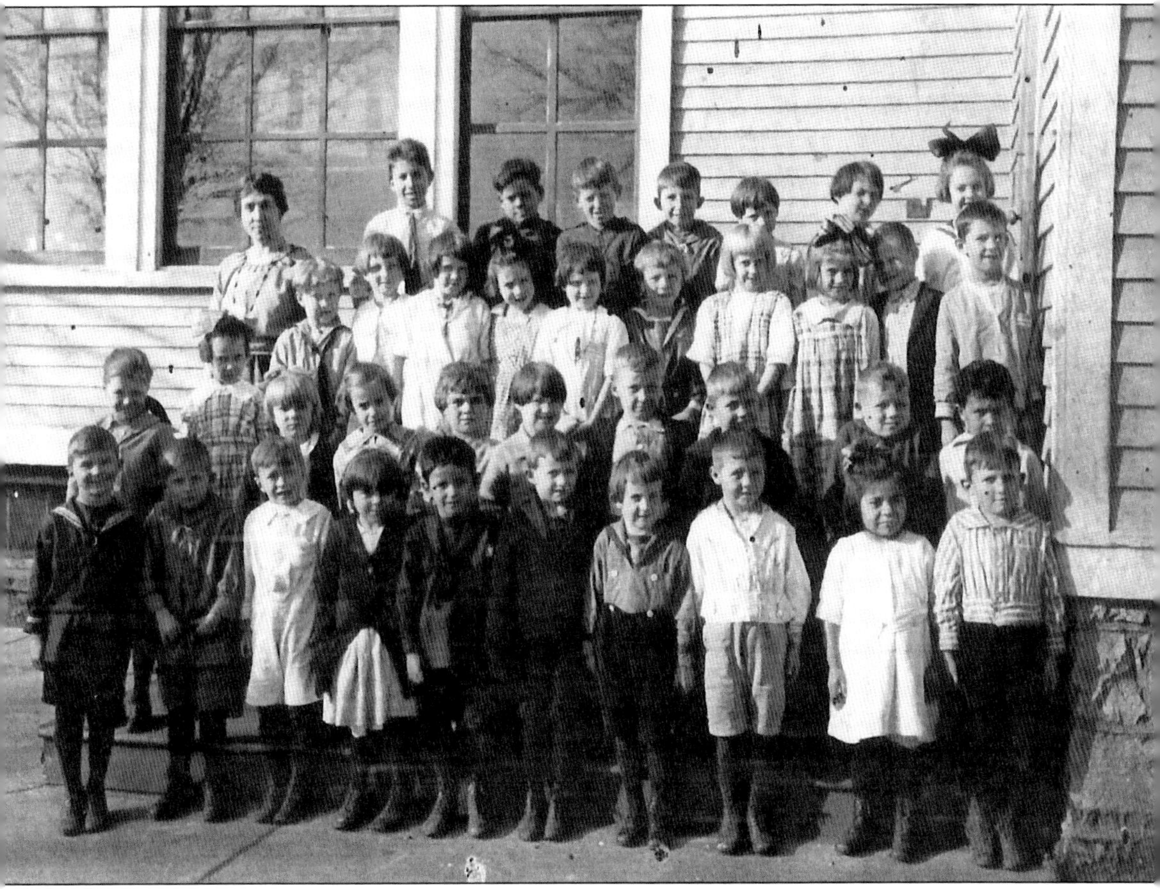

Clinton first and second graders posed with their teacher, Ella Schomp Daggett (upper left), outside their school before it burned in 1922. They included: (back row, from left) Leroy Lisk, unknown, Charlie Studer, Frank Deiter, unknown, unknown, Louise Smith; (second row) Bill Sharp, Francis Hall, Glenda Stockton, Helen Hall, Janet Exton, unknown, Mary Haver, Mary Seals, George Kramer, Eugene Hankin; (third row) Beatrice Hunt, Nora Sine (who identified her schoolmates in 1989), Nellie Wach, Ruth Weider, Rose Hodulick, Helen Kramer, Abbott Carpenter, unknown, William Smith, Cameron Lanni; (front row) Anthony Colognato, Howard Dieter, Carl Bergner, Steffi Wach, Joe Dughi, Harold Van Natta, Robbin Duckworth, Herbert Apgar, Rosie Tarantola, and Harry Mitchell.

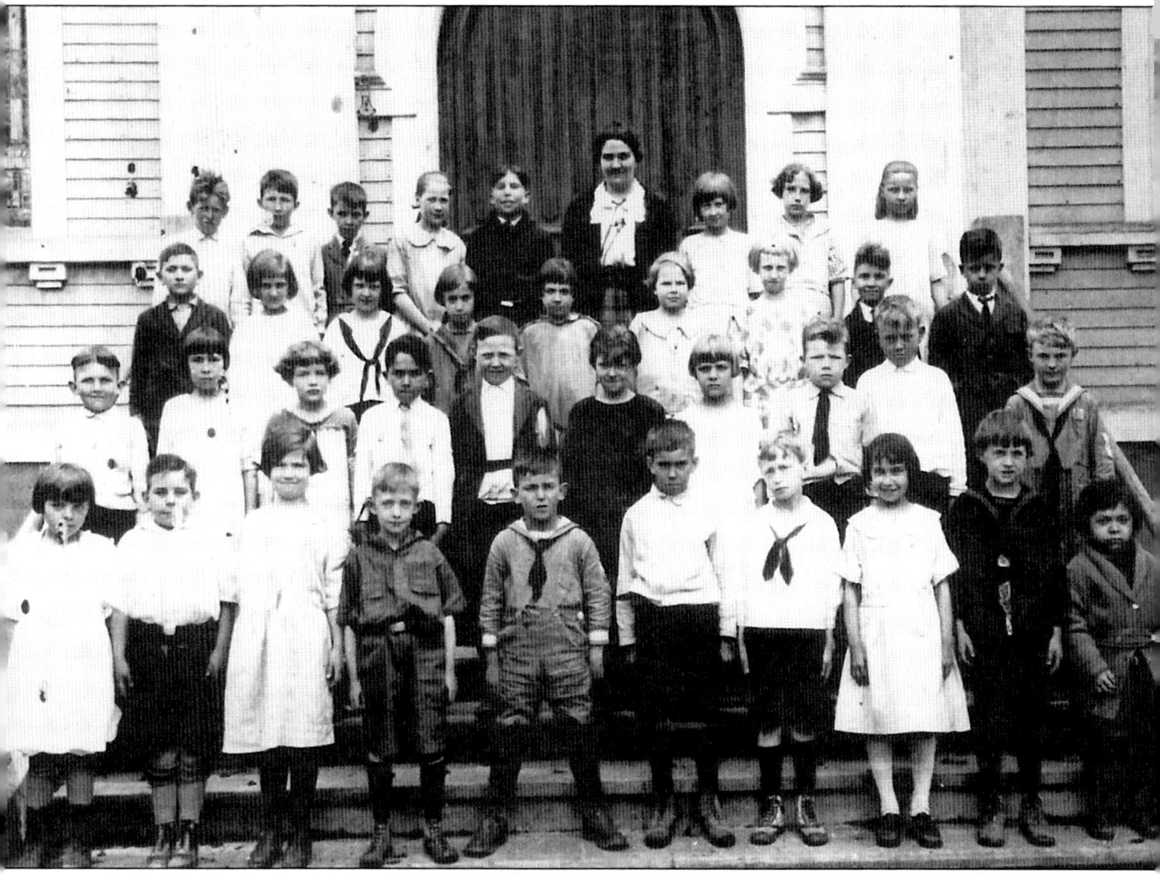

Nora Sine's third and fourth grade class met in Clinton Methodist Church during 1923 and 1924 while their school was being rebuilt. They include: (back row, from left) Charlie Studer, Frank Dieter, Eugene Hankin, Gladys Elgard, Leroy Lisk, Mrs. Hazel Knox (teacher), Florence Fransson, Lana Dalrymple, Floretta Rupell; (second row) Roy Dennis, Mary Seals, Janet Exton, Ruth Knox, Jean DeCleene, Ella Eick, Mary Haver, Anthony Colognato, Tenif Compton; (third row) Harry Mitchell, Helen Hall, Louise Hodgson, Donald Carey, George Kramer, Beatrice Hunt, Nellie Wach, William Smith, Marvin Everitt, Billy Sharp; (front row) Steffie Wach, Jack Knox, Helen Kramer, Robbin Duckworth, Joe Dughi, Donald Carey, Carl Bergner, Nora Sine, Harold August Van Natta, and Rosie Tarantola.

Three

FLEMINGTON: COUNTY SEAT

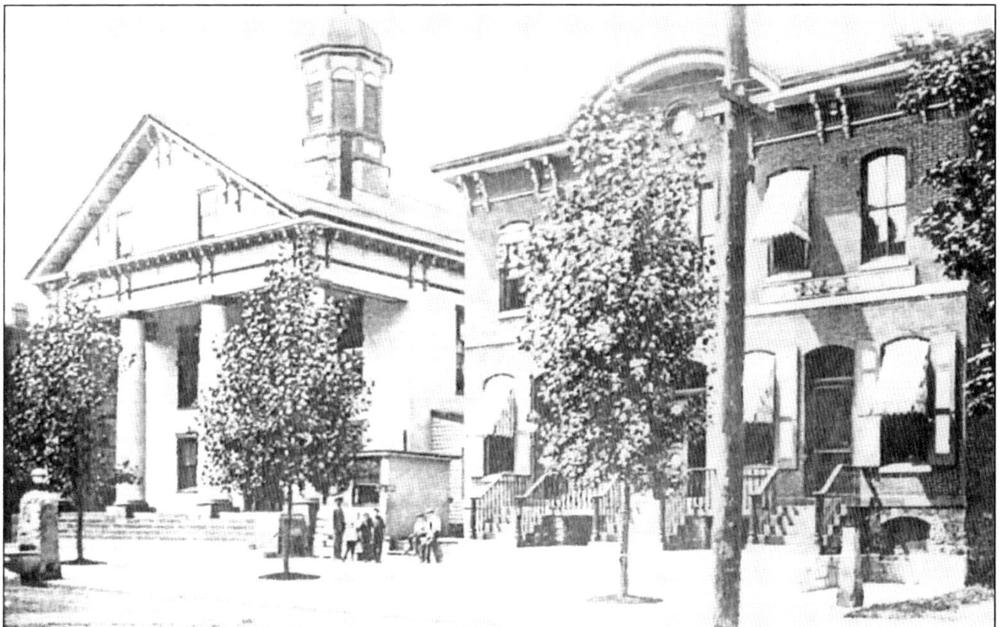

Hunterdon County Court House was built in Flemington in 1828 to replace a previous one which was destroyed by fire. Flemington was located not only in the center of the county but also at the junction of two important early roads, one joining the South Branch of the Raritan to the Delaware River and the other joining New York City to Philadelphia, so it was a good choice for a county seat in 1791. The court house became world famous during the trial of Bruno Hauptmann in 1935 for the kidnapping-murder of Col. Charles Lindbergh's twenty-month-old son (see Section Ten). The Hall of Records next door was built in 1870.

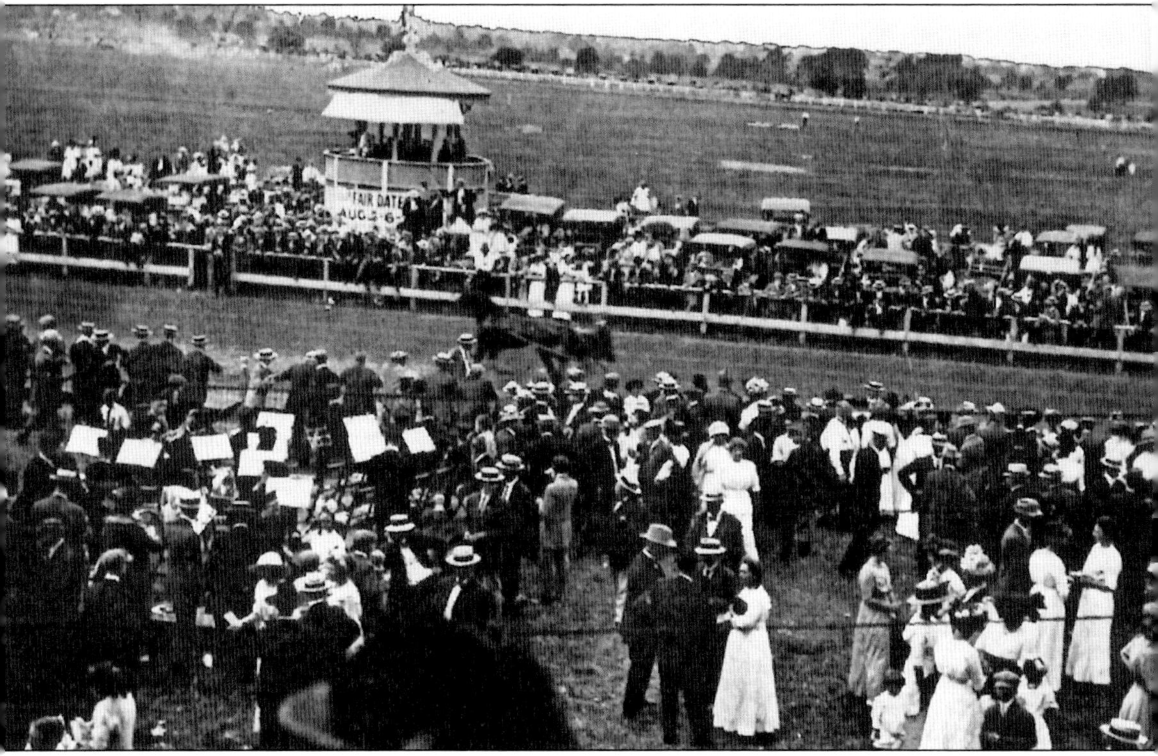

The Flemington Fair is a treasured institution in Hunterdon County. The first was sponsored in 1840 by the Hunterdon County Agricultural Society to give recognition to farmers and encourage their rivalry as well as to promote the area's agricultural interests. Maj. Edward B. Allen managed it for the Flemington Fair and Carnival Association from 1910 until his death at age eighty-five in 1947. The fair was interrupted by wars, including the Civil War, when the fair grounds were used as a rendezvous area for the training of soldiers. Horse racing was a part of the fair until 1970.

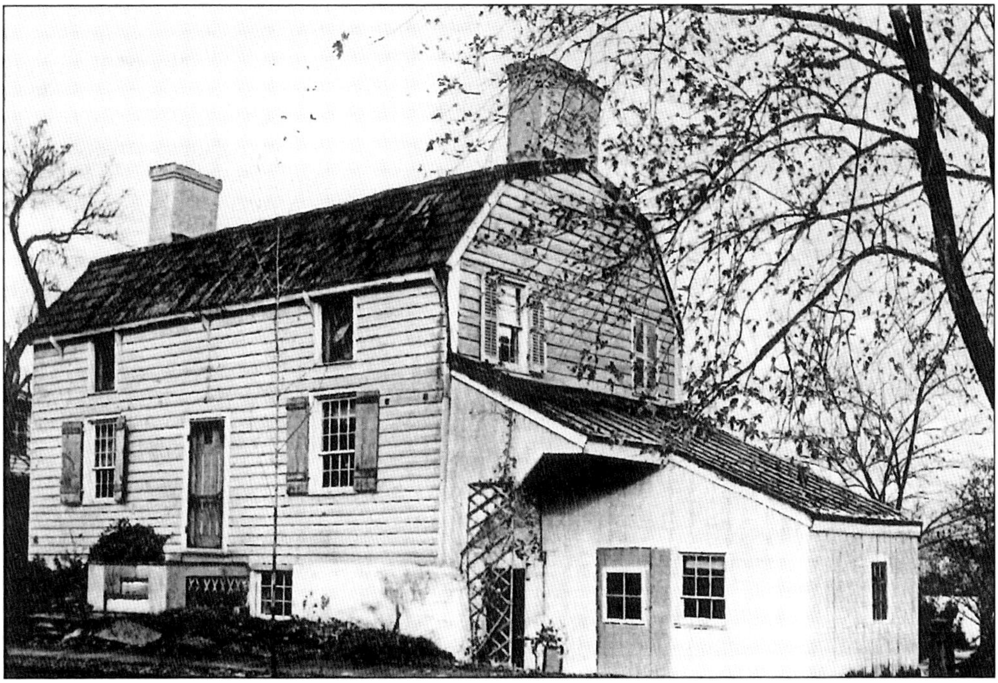

Fleming Castle, built as a tavern and home by Samuel Fleming in 1756, still stands at 5 Bonnell Street, Flemington. After many private ownerships, it was given to the local Daughters of the American Revolution chapter in 1928.

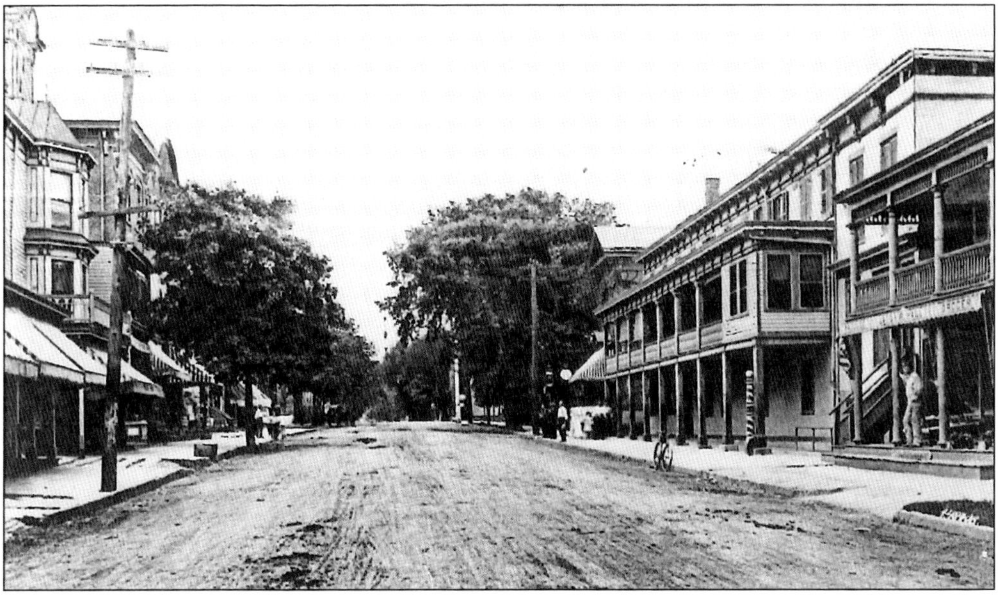

Flemington's Main Street was yet to be paved when this photograph was taken of the County House hotel, right, one of three hotels in town at the time. A sign on the sidewalk at 65 Main Street marks the site of the County House today.

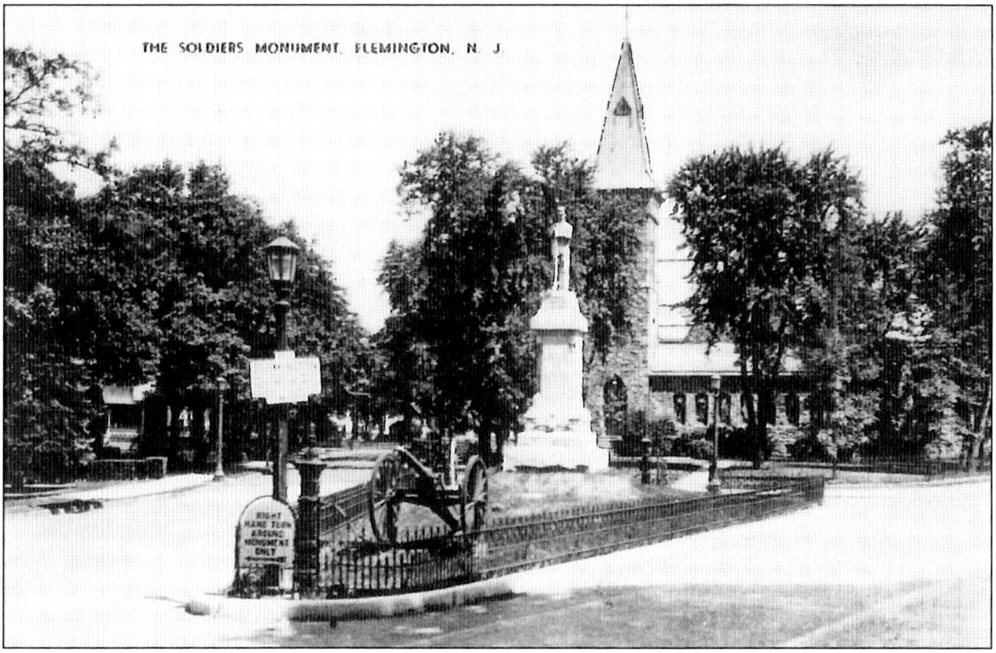

The Civil War Soldiers' Monument in Flemington is at the convergence of North Main and East Main Streets. Beyond it is the Flemington Presbyterian Church, built in 1883 of materials including stone and timbers from two earlier Presbyterian churches on the site.

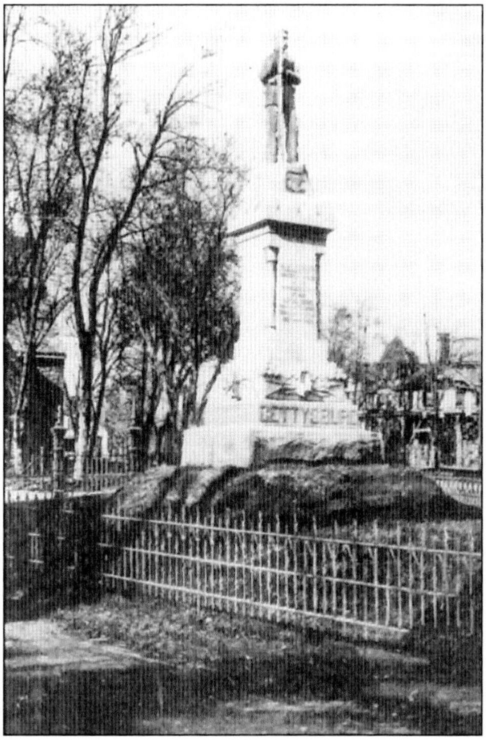

The dedication of the Civil War Soldiers' Monument was held on Memorial Day, 1892. The monument was given to the town by the Lambert Boeing Post Number 48, Grand Army of the Republic.

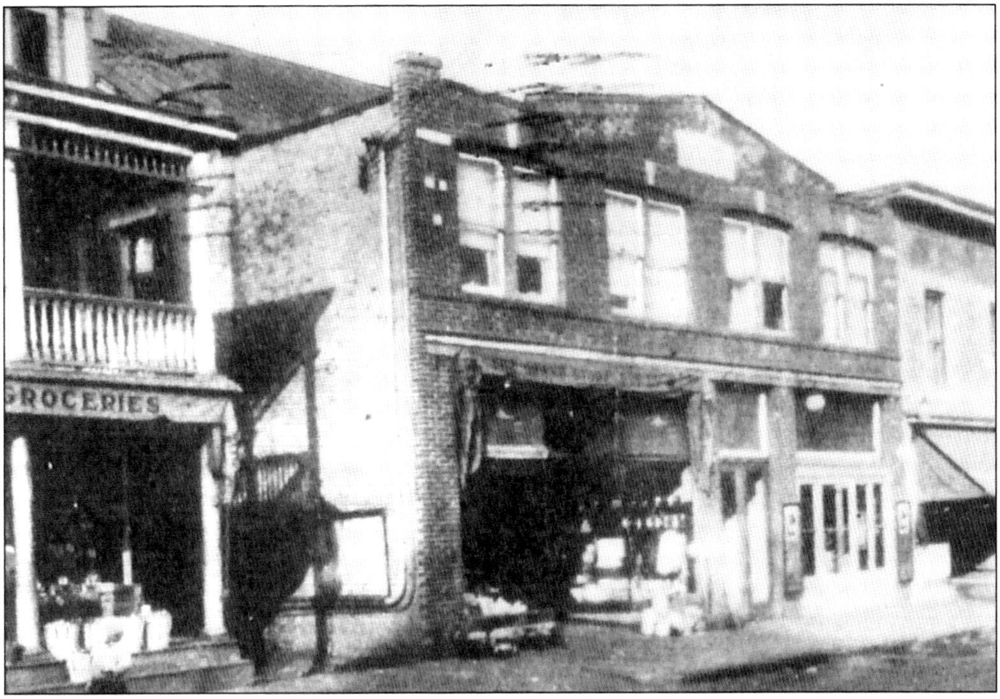

The Palace Theater on Main Street in Flemington. Like theaters across the land in the early years of this century, the Palace showed silent movies accompanied by piano players who matched the pace of their music to the action on the screen.

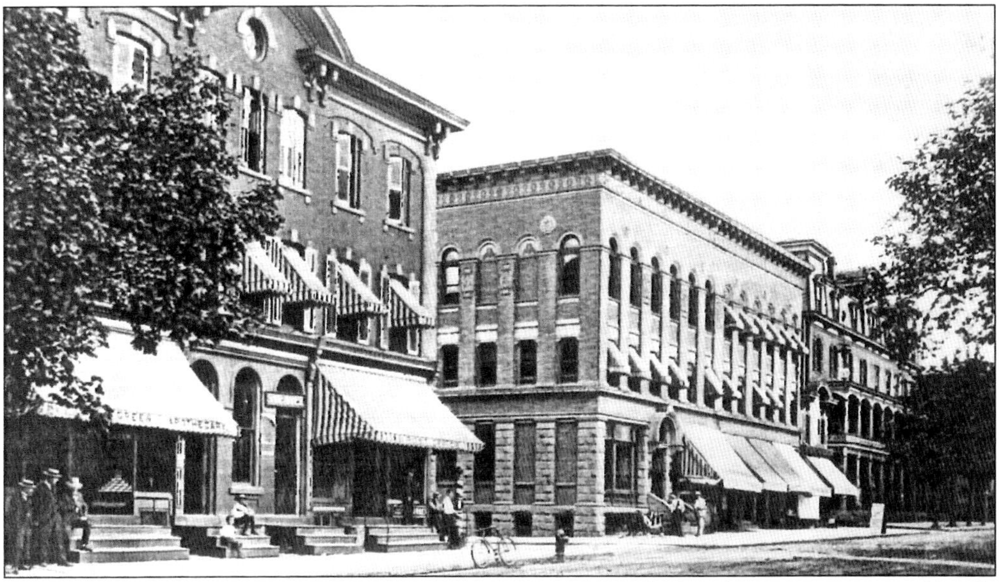

The old Flemington Post Office was on Main Street along with the Flemington National Bank, built in 1897, and the Union Hotel. The hotel was built of brick in 1877 on the site of two previous wooden ones, the first of them dating from 1814.

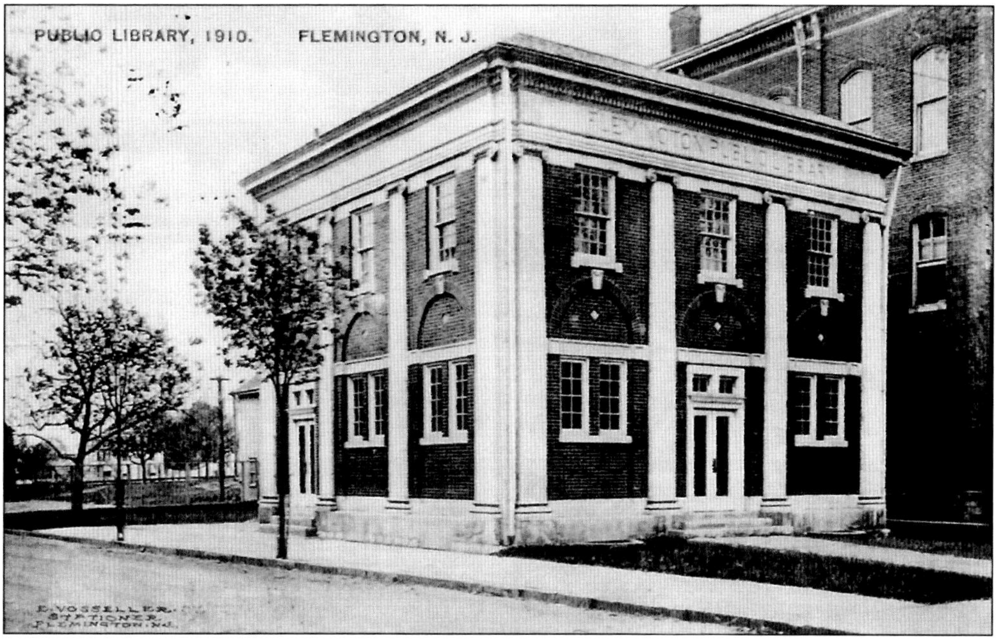

The Flemington Woman's Club helped establish the borough's library. The building was built in 1910 on Main Street in the Renaissance Revival style and has a pleasant fireplace inside.

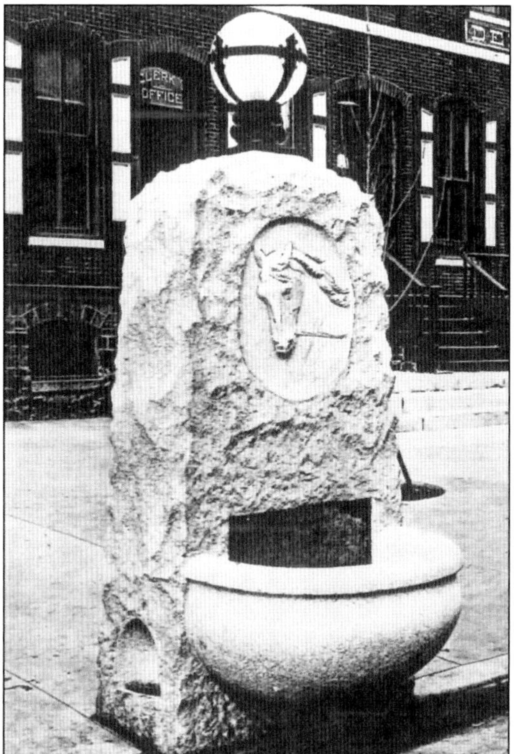

This water trough for horses, people, and pets in front of the County Court House was also provided by the Flemington Woman's Club.

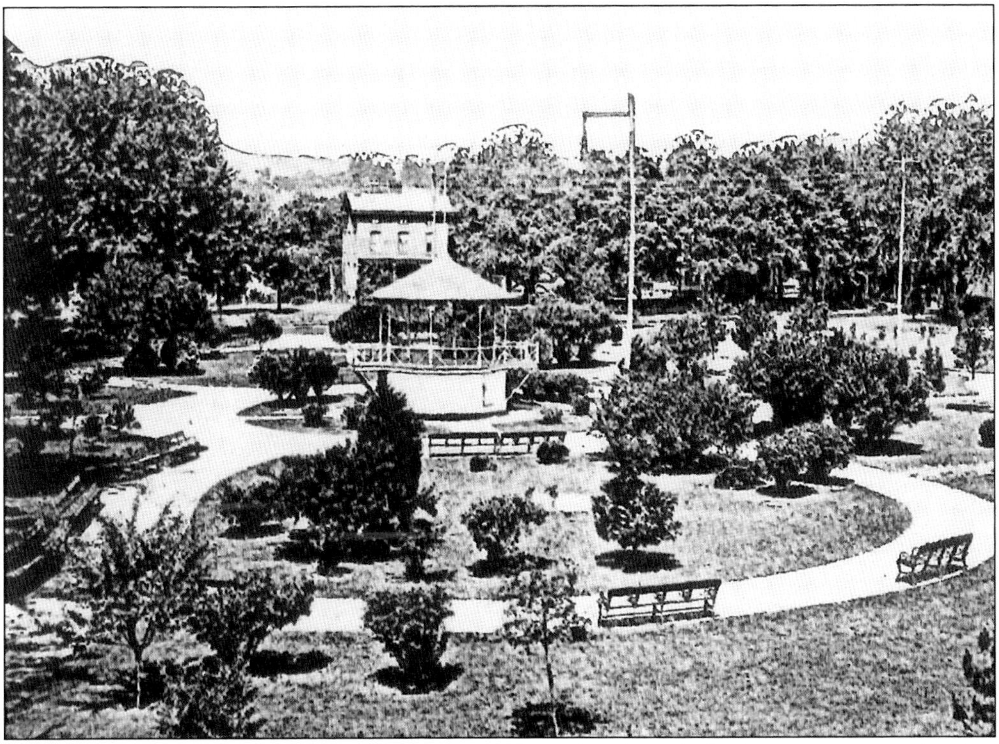

Borough Park, at Park Avenue and Court Street, has a bandstand which was once a gazebo that stood in a private garden where the library is now located.

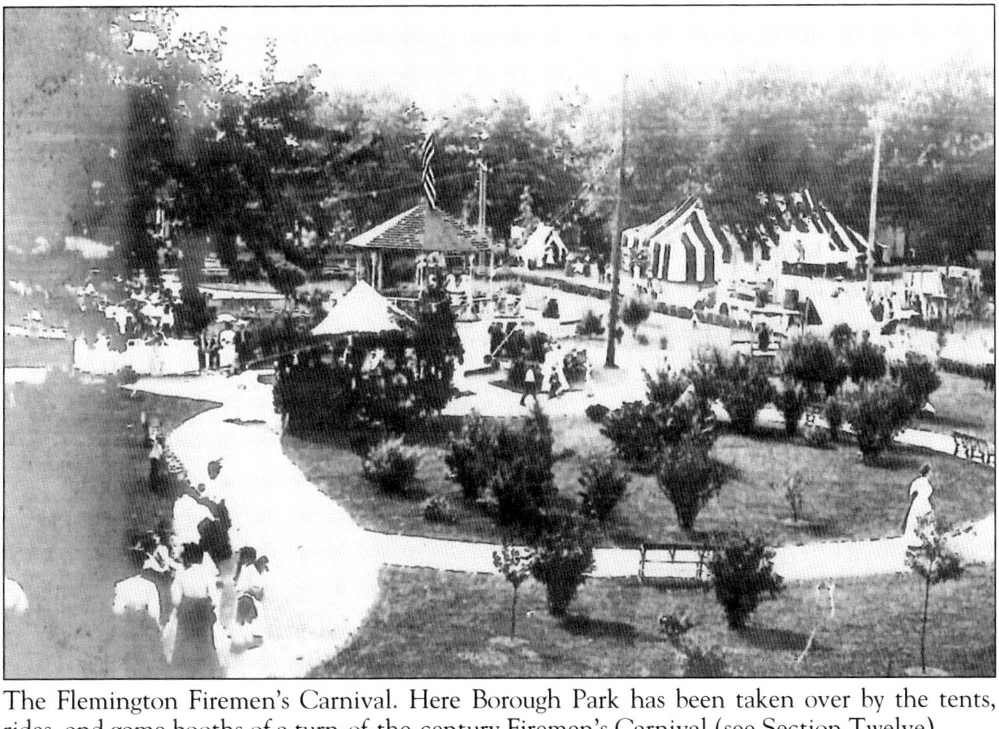

The Flemington Firemen's Carnival. Here Borough Park has been taken over by the tents, rides, and game booths of a turn-of-the-century Firemen's Carnival (see Section Twelve).

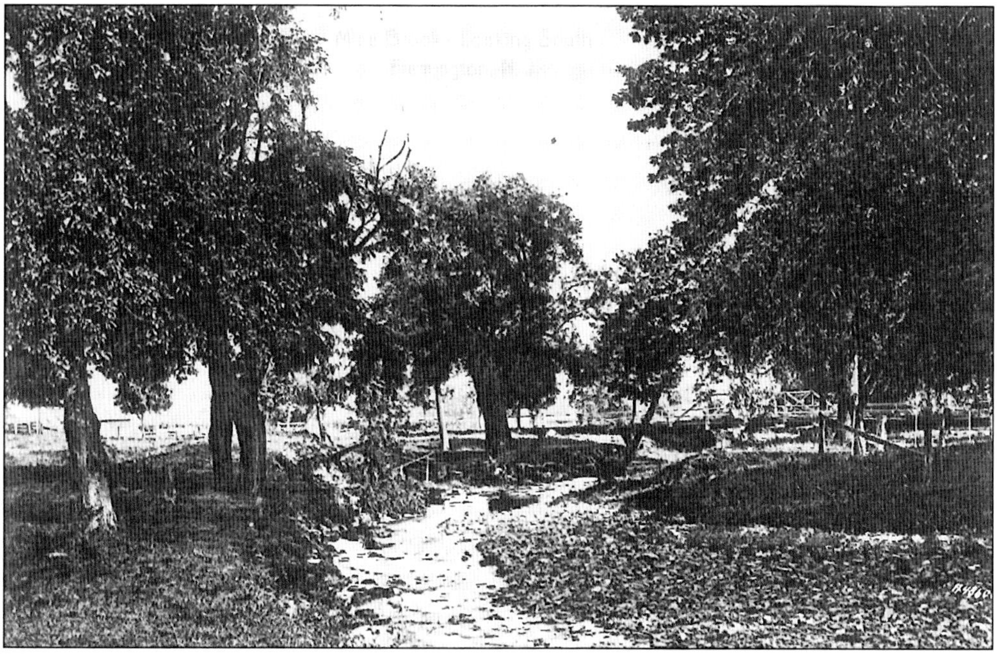

Mine Brook, now part of a park in this area, was called Tuccaminjah Creek when German settler John Philip Kase bought land along it from William Penn's sons in 1738.

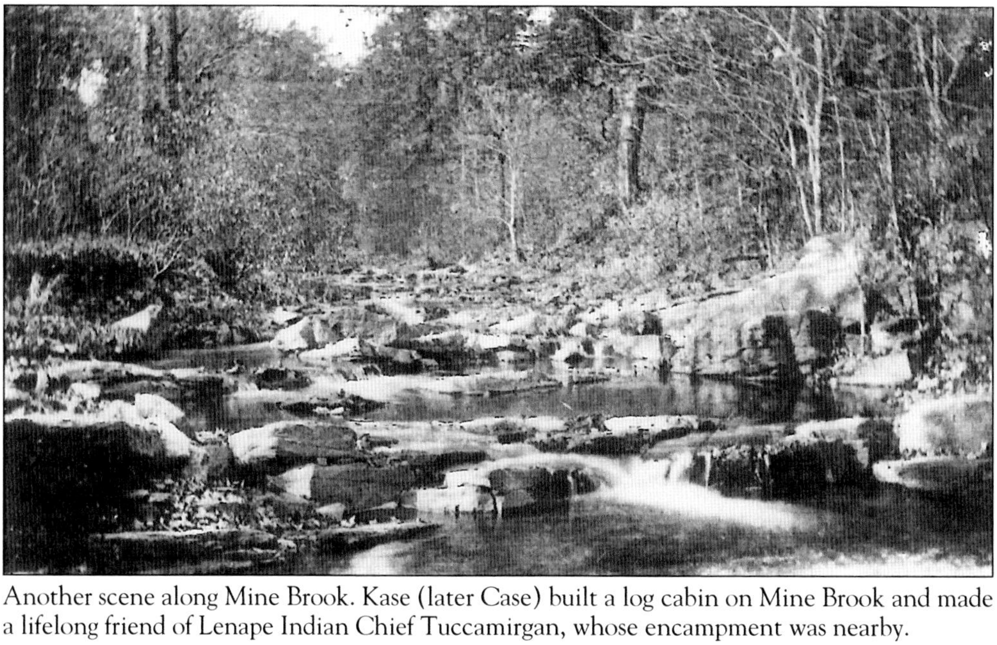

Another scene along Mine Brook. Kase (later Case) built a log cabin on Mine Brook and made a lifelong friend of Lenape Indian Chief Tuccamirgan, whose encampment was nearby.

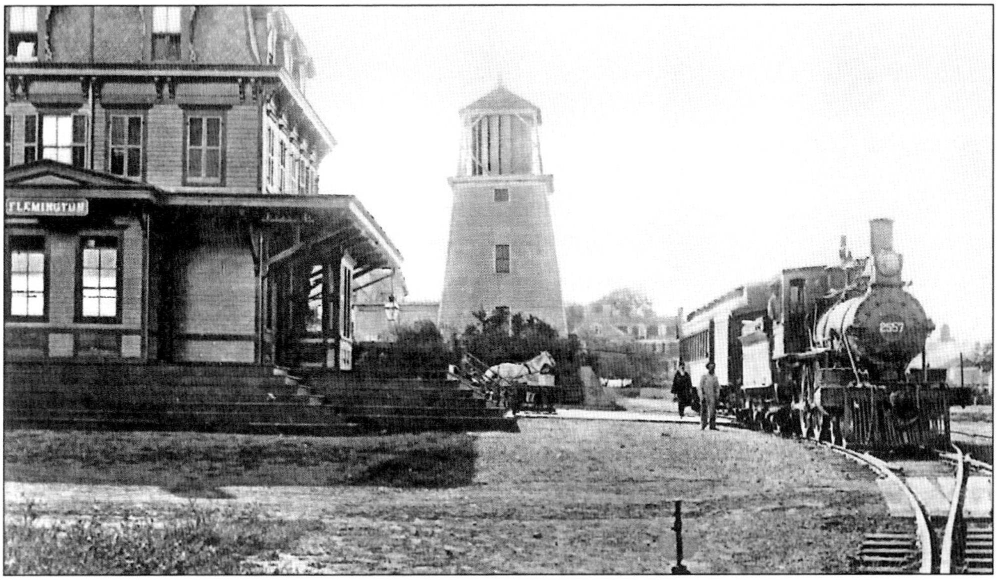

Lehigh Valley Branch Railroad Station, built in 1886 where Agway's now stands, served passengers with a shuttle train connecting Flemington with the railroad's main line (the Eastern and Amboy Railroad), at Flemington Junction.

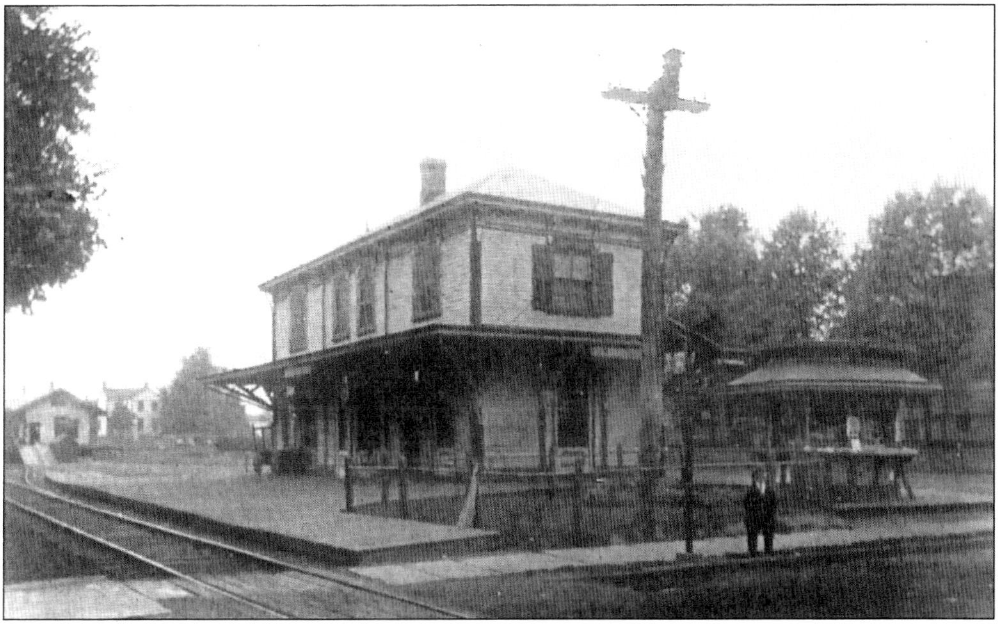

Central Railroad Station. In 1870, the Central Railroad of New Jersey ran a branch line from Flemington to Somerville to connect with its main line running from Easton, PA, to Jersey City.

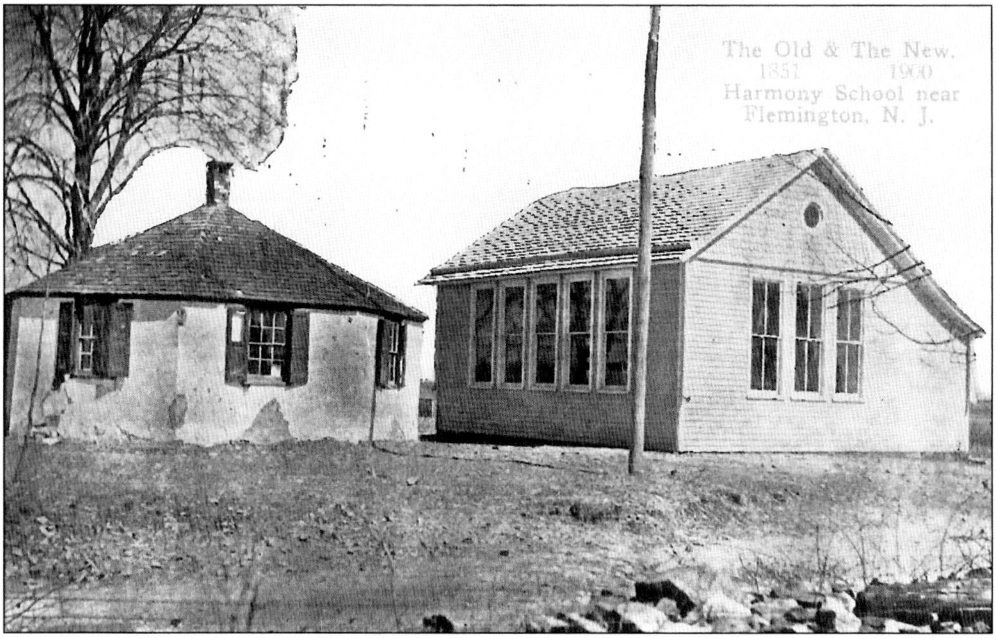

Children in the rural area around Flemington attended tiny one room schools like the Harmony School, here shown as the old (1851) and the new (1900).

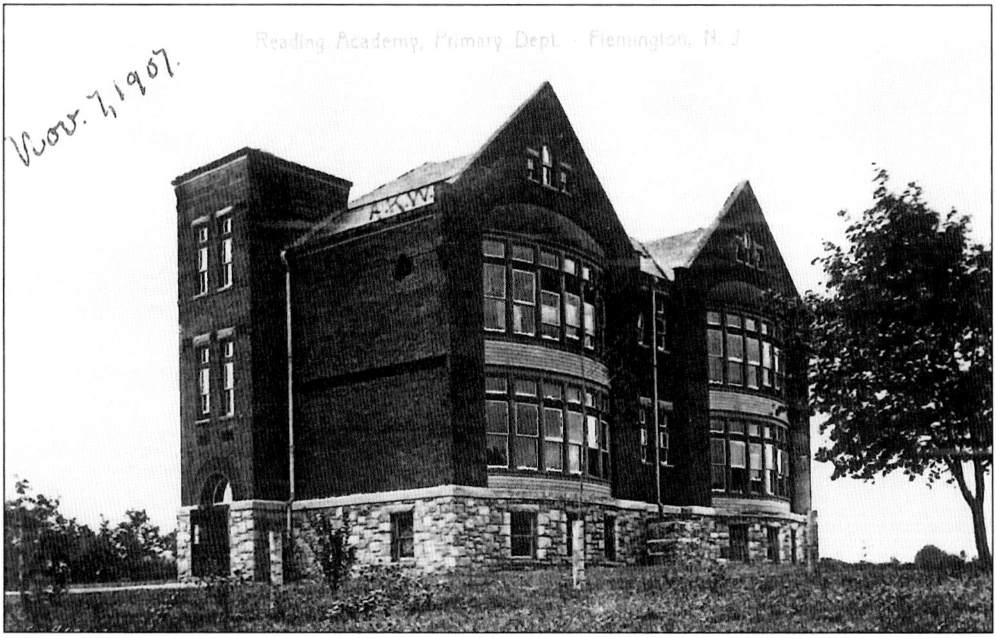

The Reading Academy was the only public school in Flemington when it was established in 1862. A private classical school called the Flemington Academy preceded it.

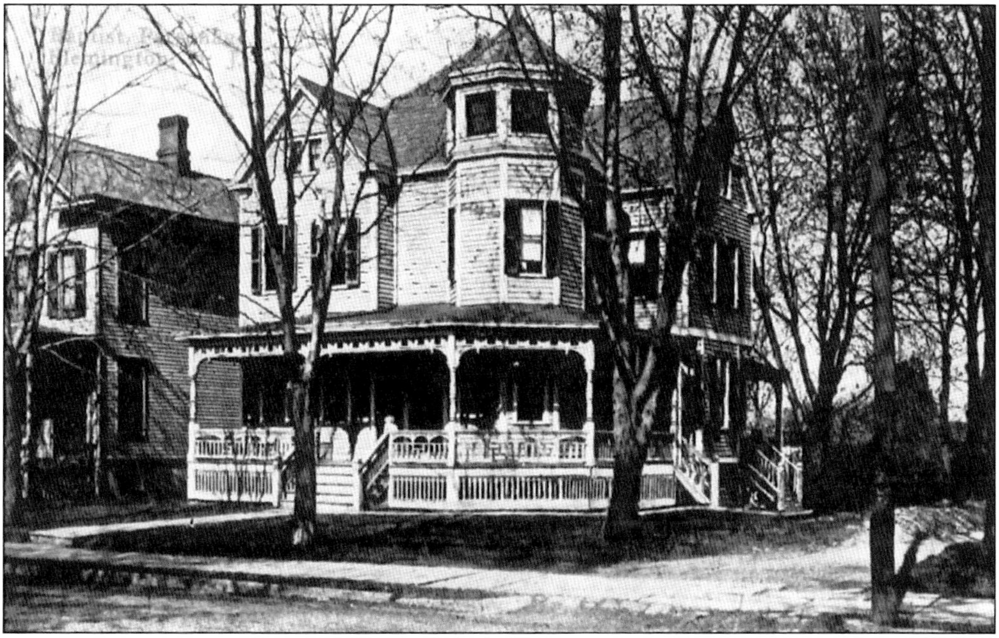

The Baptist Parsonage. Flemington is known for its beautiful Victorian homes. This one, with its wrap-around porch, served as parsonage for the Flemington Baptist Church.

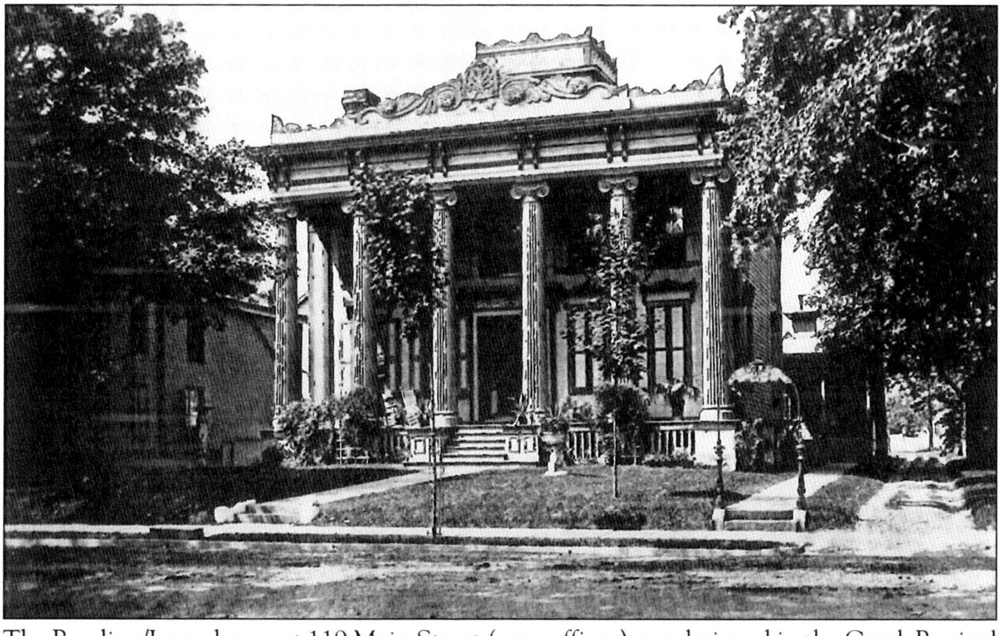

The Reading/Large house at 119 Main Street (now offices) was designed in the Greek Revival style by Mahlon Fisher in 1847 for James N. Reading. George H. Large owned it from 1900 to 1937.

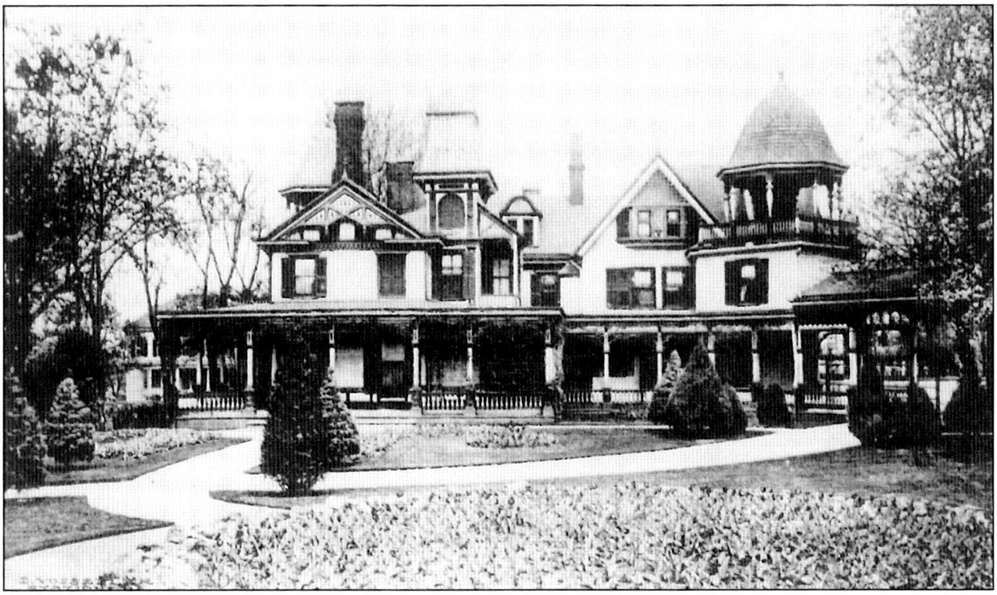

Roselawn, also called Rose Lodge, at 3 East Main Street, was the home of William E. Emery, a successful merchant in New York City and Kansas City who returned to his native Flemington to retire. He died in 1912.

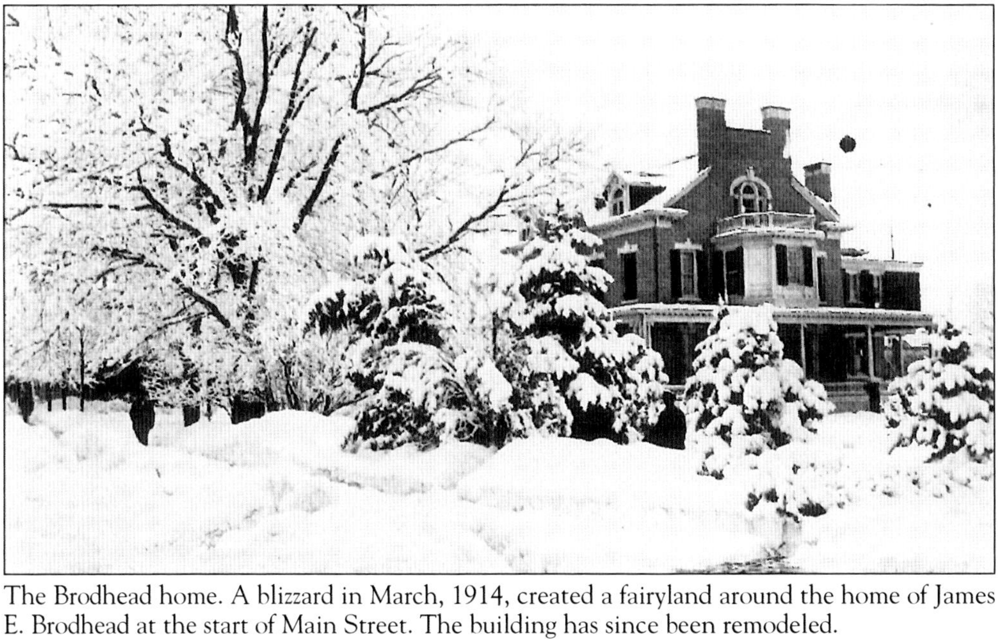

The Brodhead home. A blizzard in March, 1914, created a fairyland around the home of James E. Brodhead at the start of Main Street. The building has since been remodeled.

Four

Lambertville and Its Canal

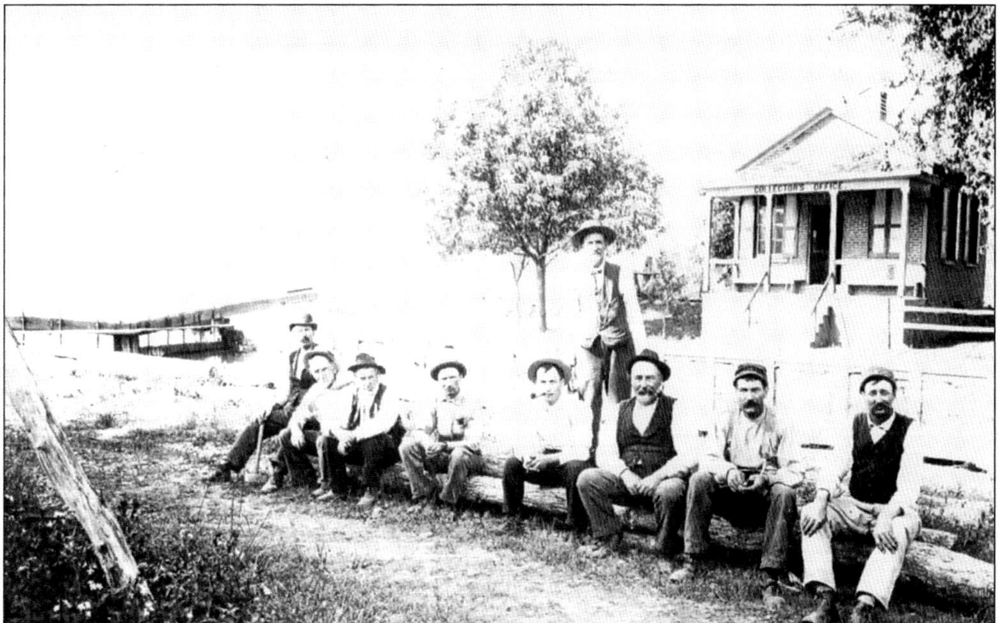

The crew of the Lambertville lock of the 22-mile Delaware and Raritan Feeder Canal rests from its labors in front of the toll collector's office. The canal began operations in 1834 as a connector for the freight of the Lehigh and Delaware Canal—mostly anthracite coal from the Lehigh Valley—to the Delaware and Raritan Canal, which extended 44 miles from Bordentown on the Delaware to New Brunswick on the Raritan. The feeder joined the canal's main channel at Trenton. It was built by Ashbel Welch, civil engineer, who later helped design the Panama Canal. (Lambertville Historical Society photo.)

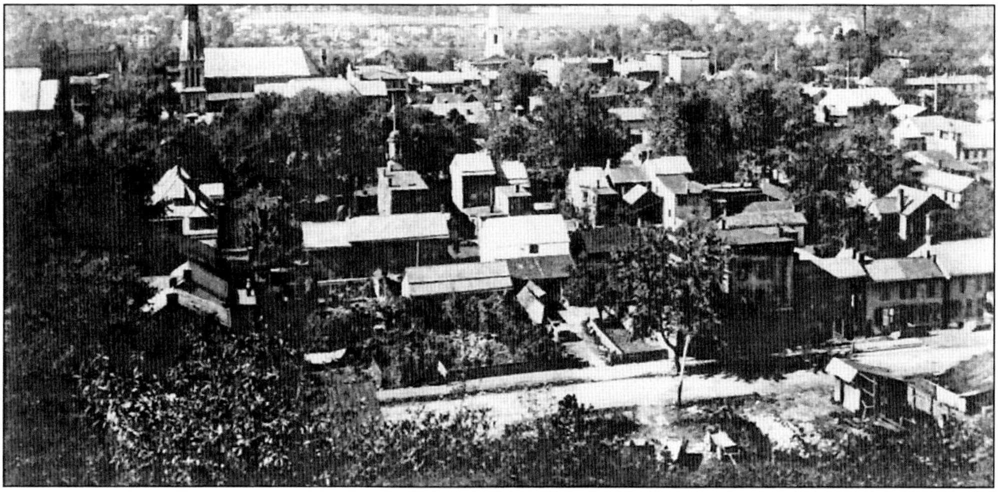

Lambertville essentially began in 1733 when Emanuel Coryell, a French Huguenot, took out a patent to operate a ferry across the Delaware River. This view of Lambertville was taken from High School Hill. (Lambertville Historical Society photo.)

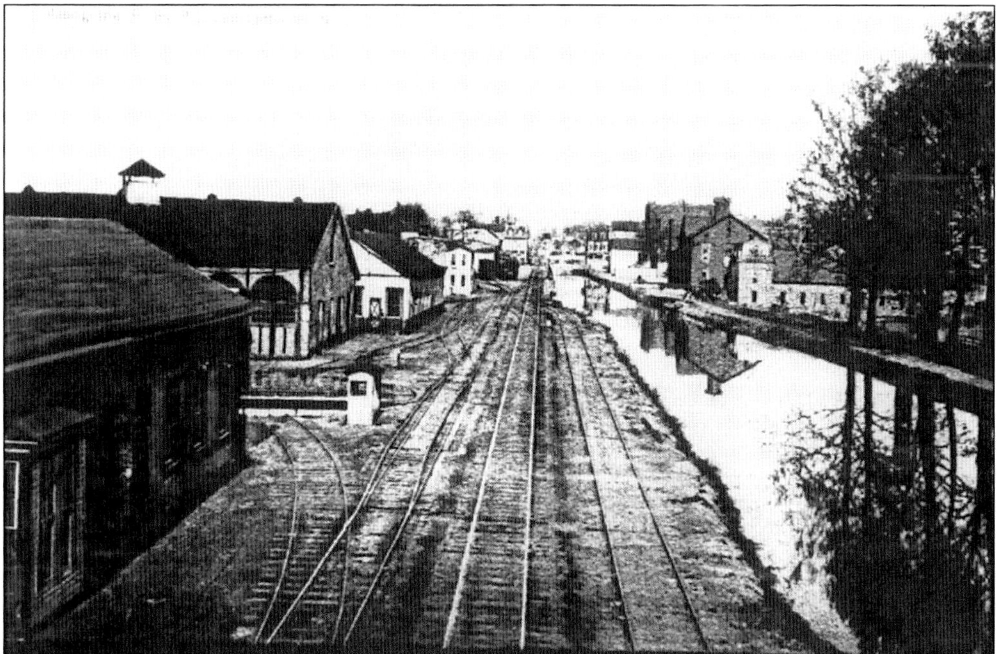

The Belvidere-Delaware Railroad tracks. The rail line, completed in 1851, helped the canal with freight movement, especially in freezing weather. It connected with the Camden and Amboy Railroad in Trenton. (Lambertville Historical Society photo.)

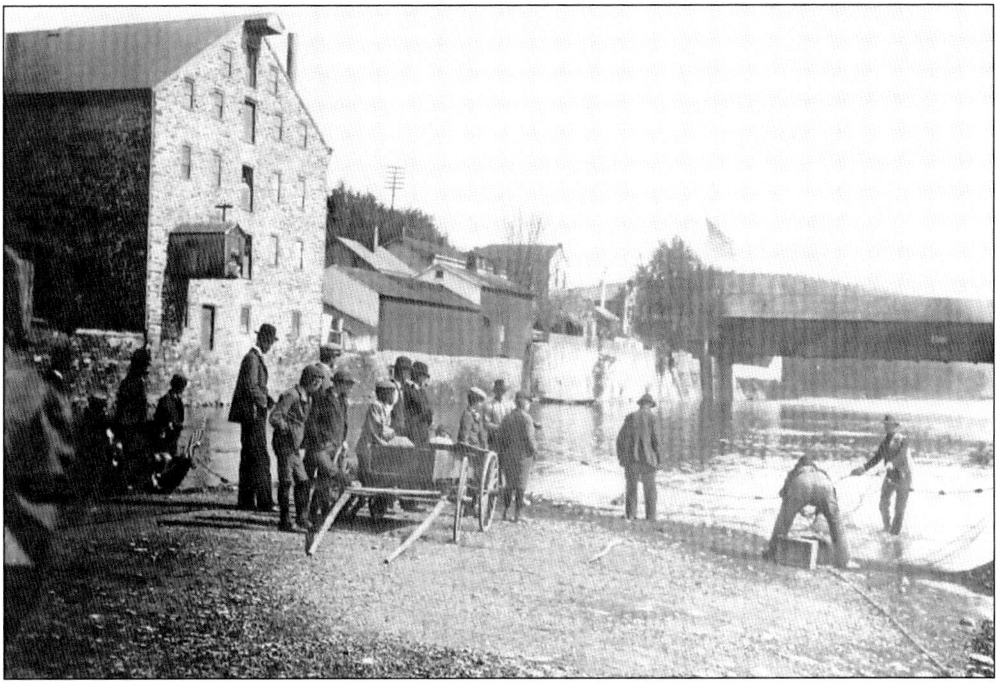

The Liberty Fishery on Holcombe Island was one of five fisheries in the Lambertville area. Today shad fishing has only hobby status, but each April Lambertville still celebrates the shad's return to spawn. (Lambertville Historical Society photo.)

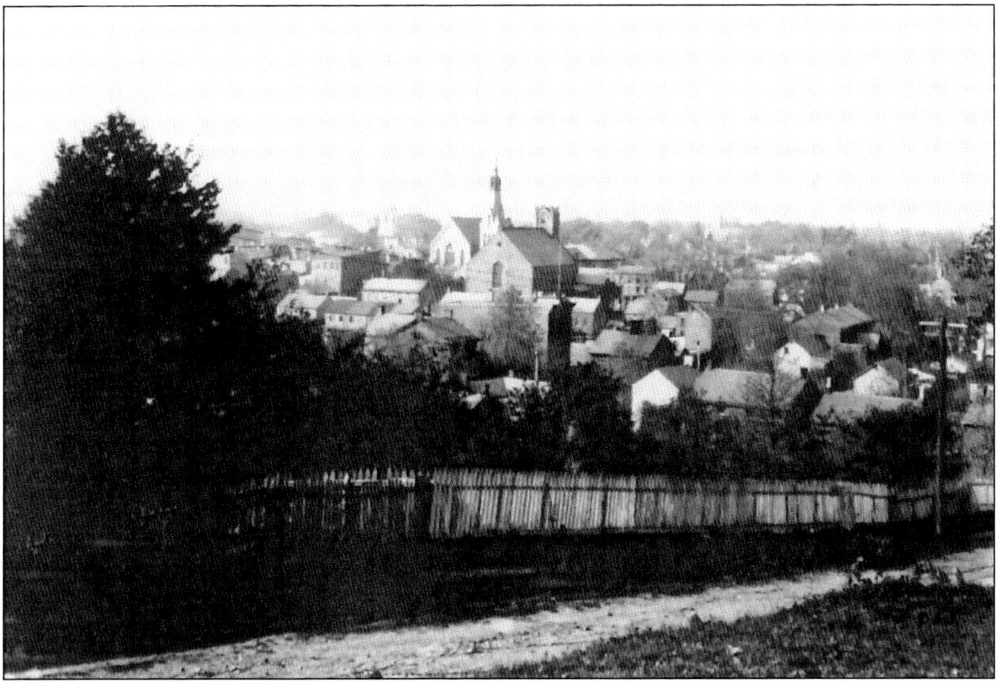

View of Lambertville from Mount Hope Cemetery, c.1890. By 1872 the population had reached 5,000, enough for it to be designated a city by the state. It is still the only city in Hunterdon County. (Lambertville Historical Society photo.)

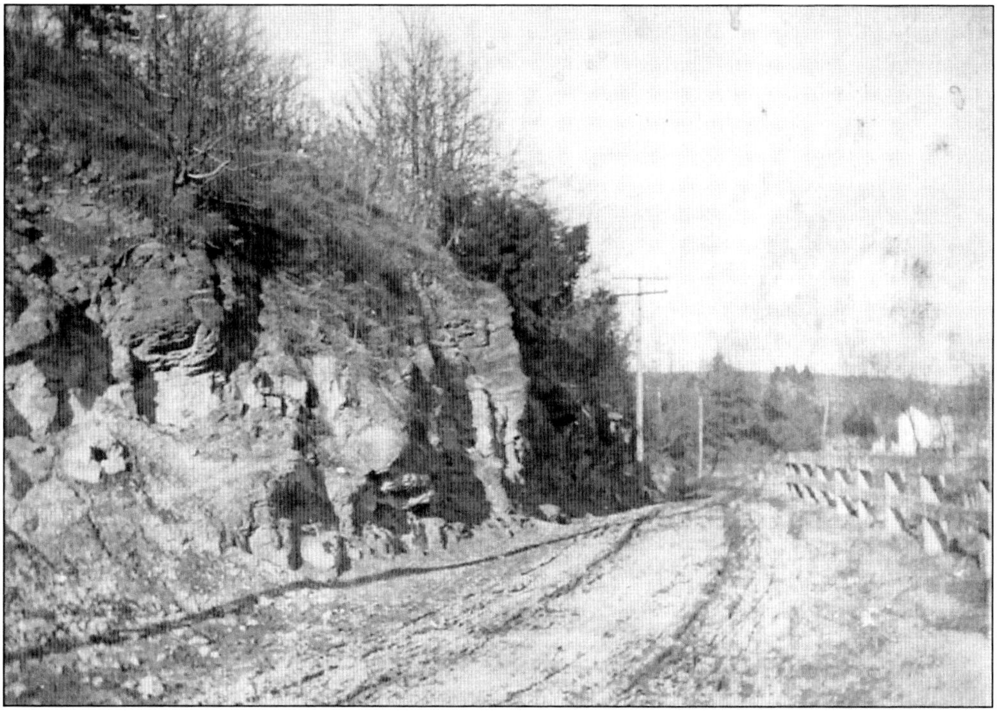

Old York Road. Farmers originally maintained this curve called "The Hook" outside Lambertville and other sections of the Old York Road which ran between Philadelphia and Elizabeth, NJ. (Lambertville Historical Society photo.)

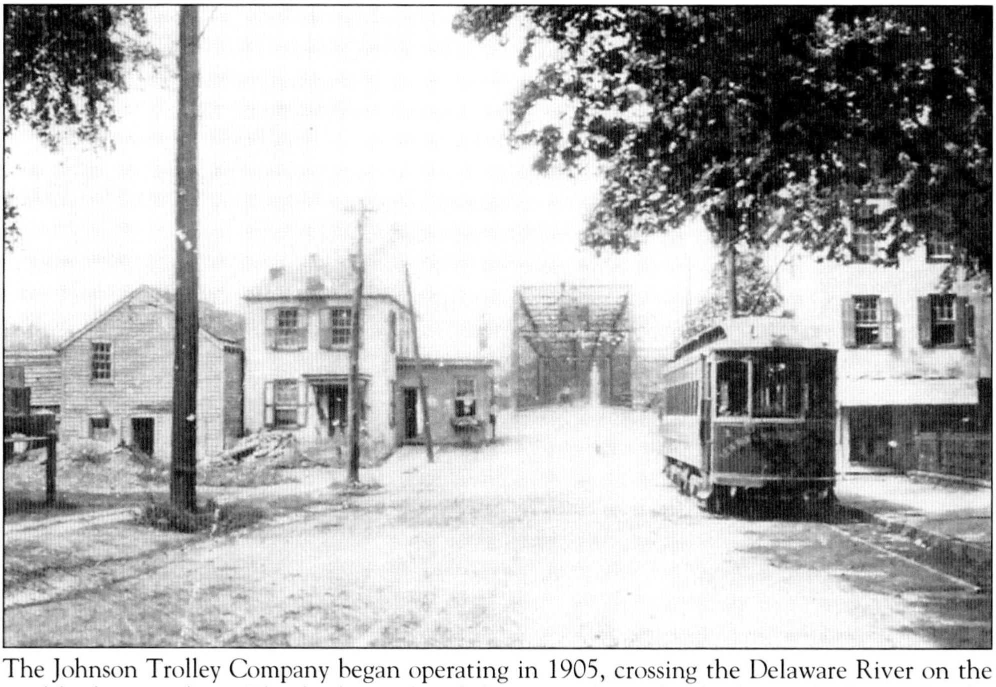

The Johnson Trolley Company began operating in 1905, crossing the Delaware River on the steel bridge seen here. This bridge replaced the covered wooden bridge washed away by the flood of October 9, 1903. (Lambertville Historical Society photo.)

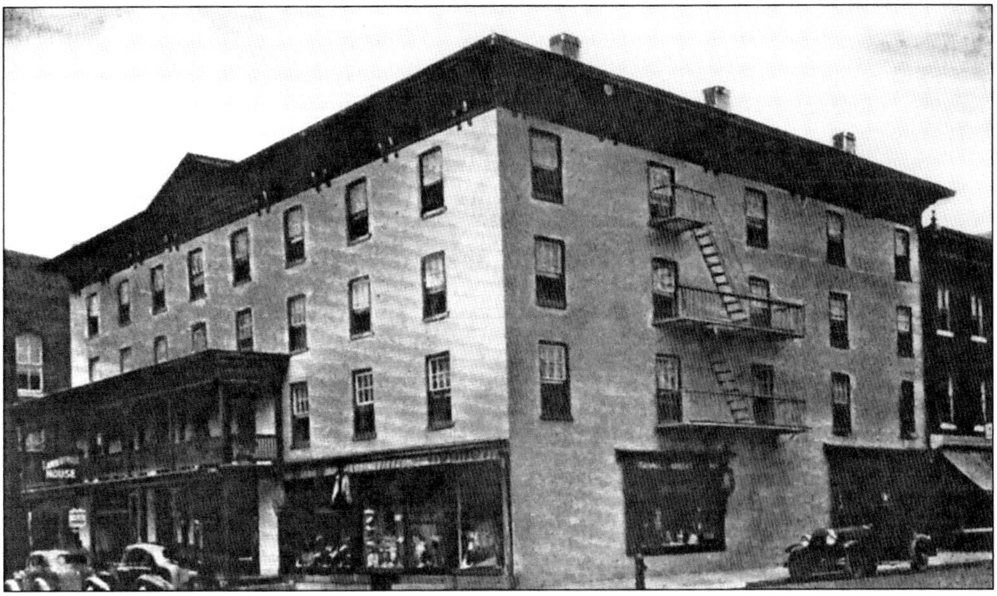

The Lambertville House on Bridge Street opened for business in 1814 to accommodate stageline travelers on the Old York Road. It was enlarged in 1851 and again in 1888. (Lambertville Historical Society photo.)

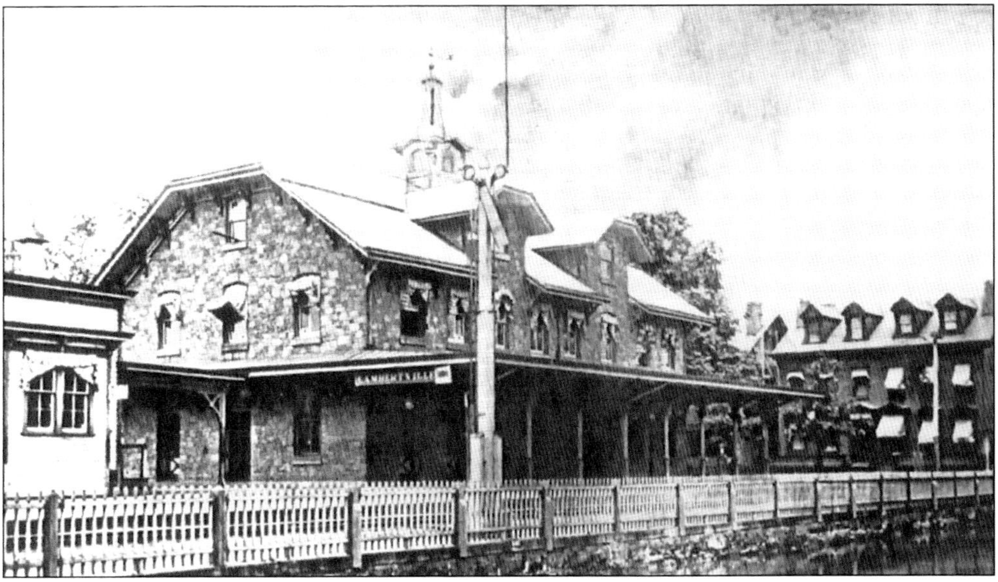

Lambertville's Pennsylvania Railroad Station is now occupied by a restaurant. The Pennsylvania Railroad took over the Belvidere-Delaware system in 1871. The railroads stimulated manufacturing in Lambertville. (Lambertville Historical Society photo.)

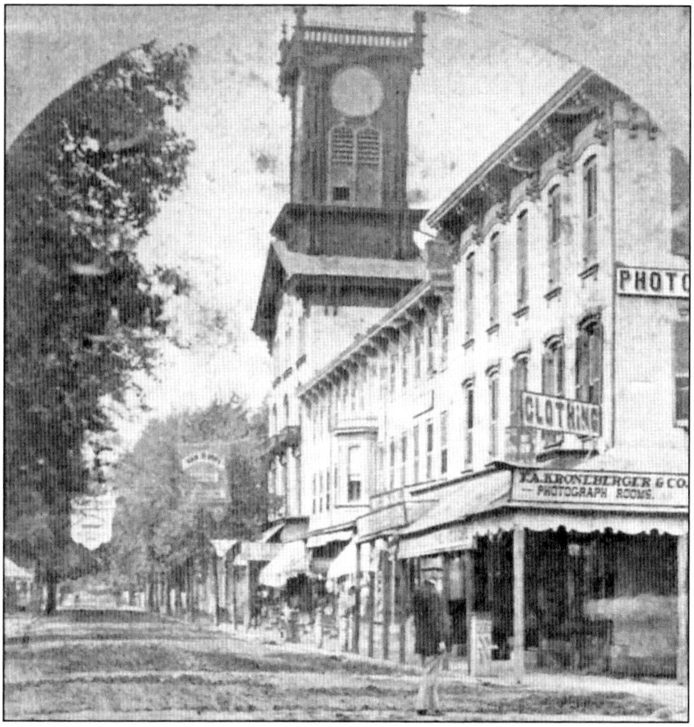

Stereoscopic slides were often made of street scenes like this in the early 1900s. The tower of the Hooker Building on North Union Street was destroyed by fire on December 26, 1903. (Lambertville Historical Society photo.)

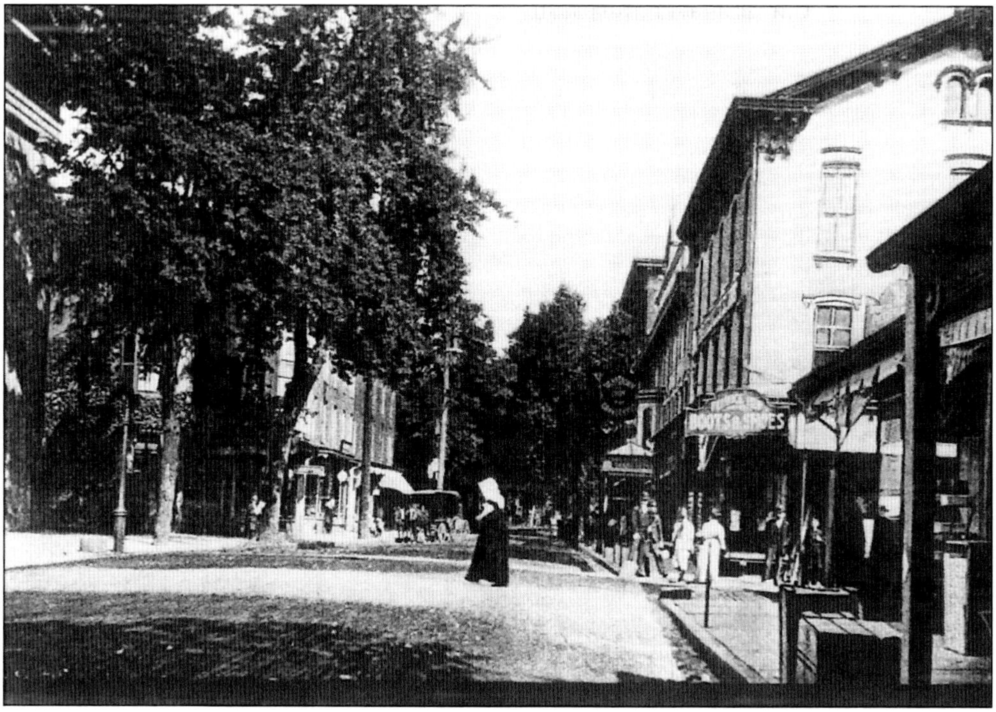

Commercial Row. Another view of North Union Street near Church Street. The area between Church and Coryell Streets was called "Commercial Row" in the 1860s. Note the buggy in the distance. (Lambertville Historical Society photo.)

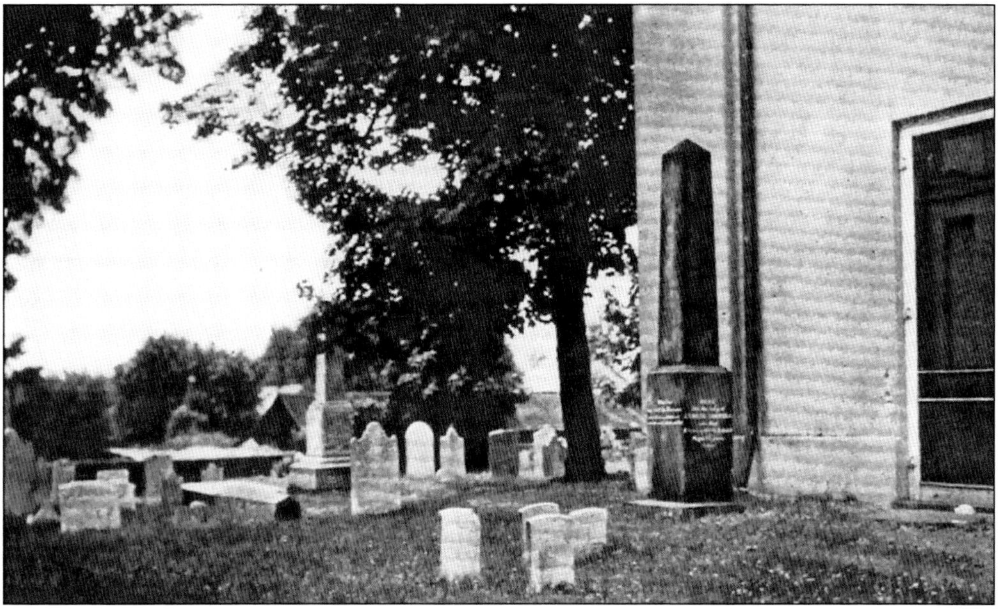

Coryell Monument. The tall black monument on the right in the First Presbyterian Churchyard marks the grave of George Coryell, a grandson of Emanuel Coryell, the early ferryman. George was one of Washington's pallbearers. (Lambertville Historical Society photo.)

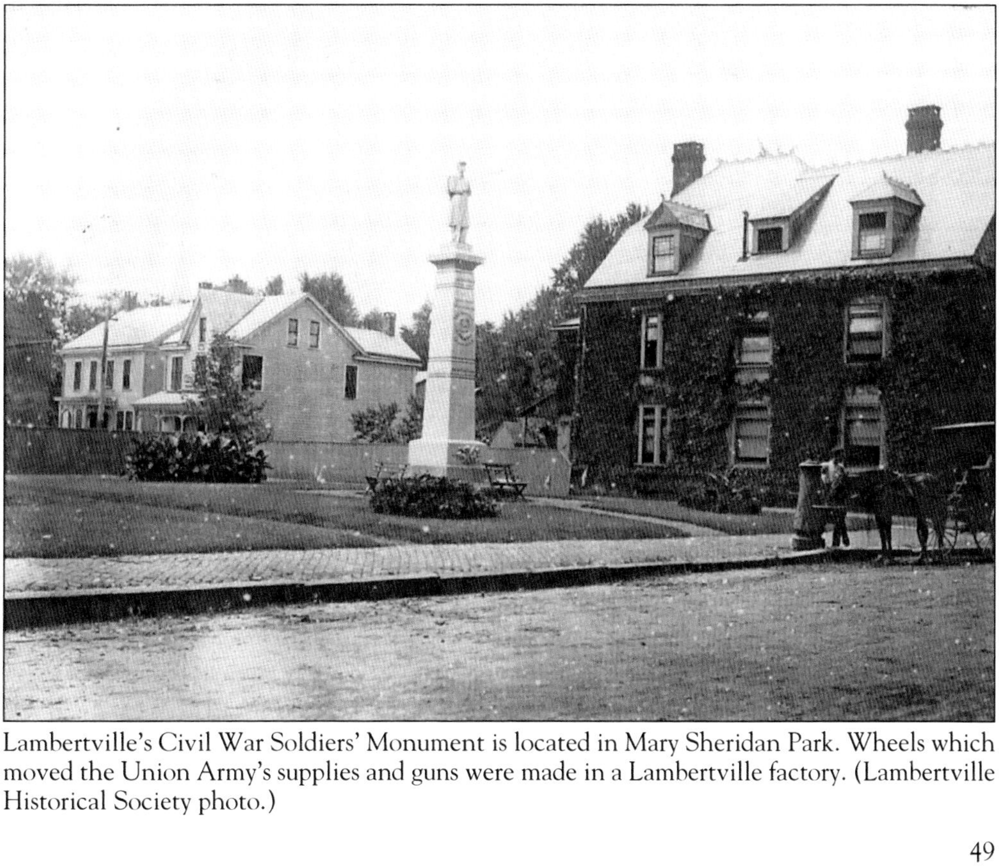

Lambertville's Civil War Soldiers' Monument is located in Mary Sheridan Park. Wheels which moved the Union Army's supplies and guns were made in a Lambertville factory. (Lambertville Historical Society photo.)

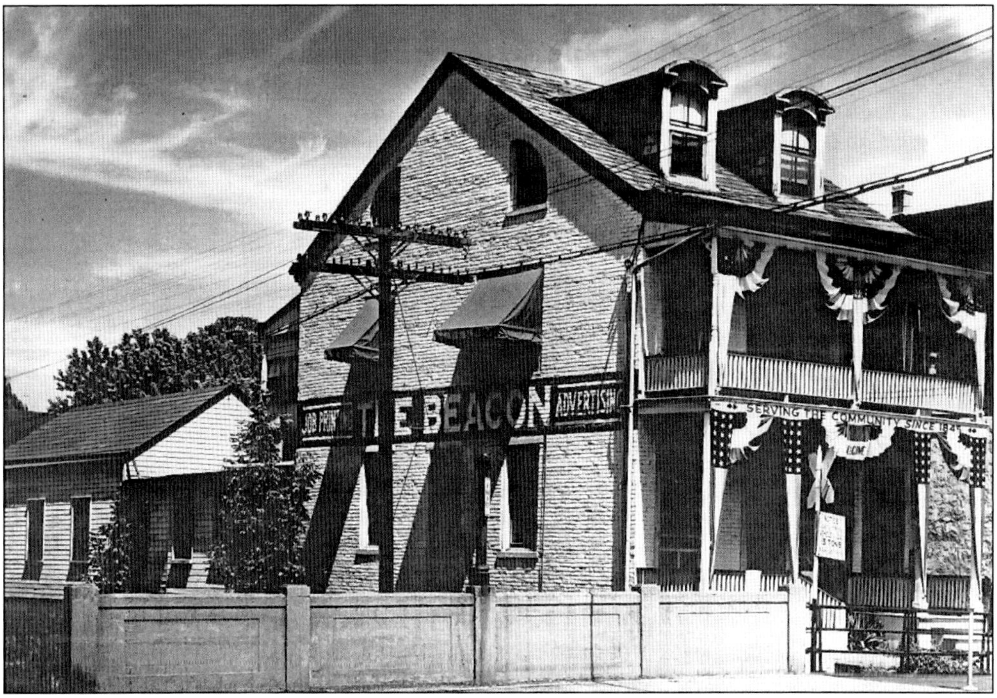

The Beacon newspaper building at 14 Bridge Street is one of several locations which have been used for the paper since its start in 1845. It was first owned by Phineus Hazen. (Lambertville Historical Society photo.)

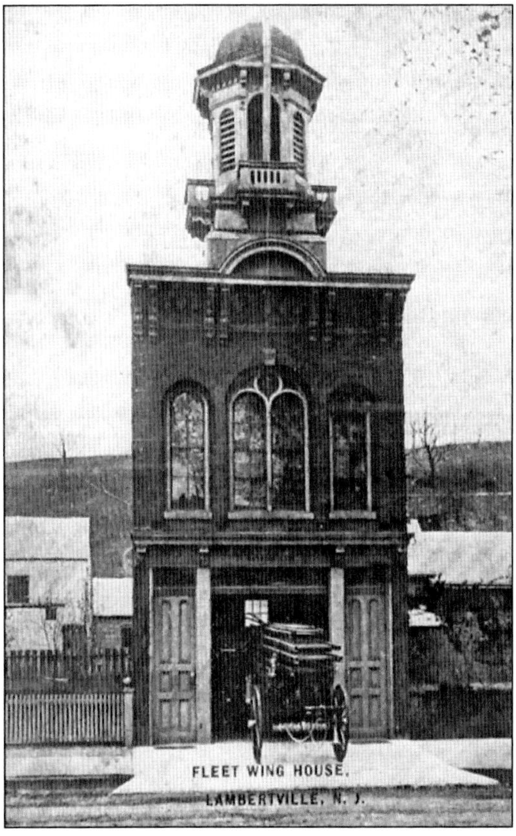

Fleet Wing Fire Company was organized in 1864 and built this firehouse three years later on North Main Street. (Lambertville Historical Society photo.)

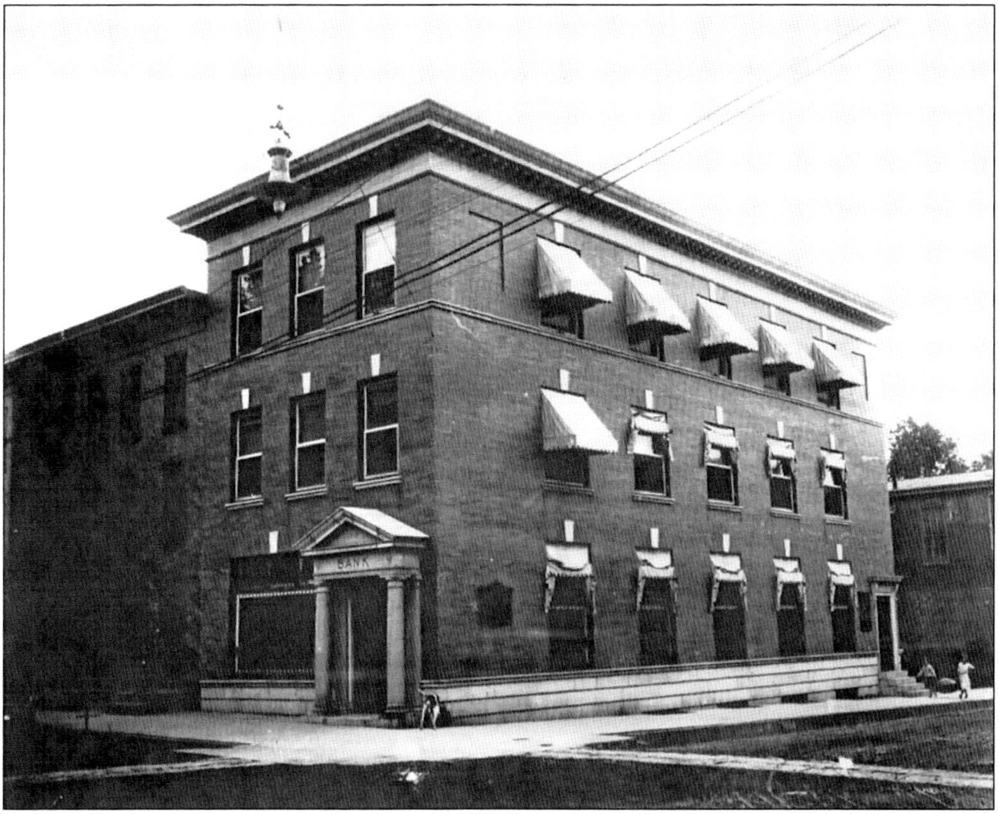

New Jersey National Bank, at the corner of Bridge and Union Streets, shaded its windows with awnings in 1906. The Lambertville Chamber of Commerce now has offices above the bank. (Lambertville Historical Society photo.)

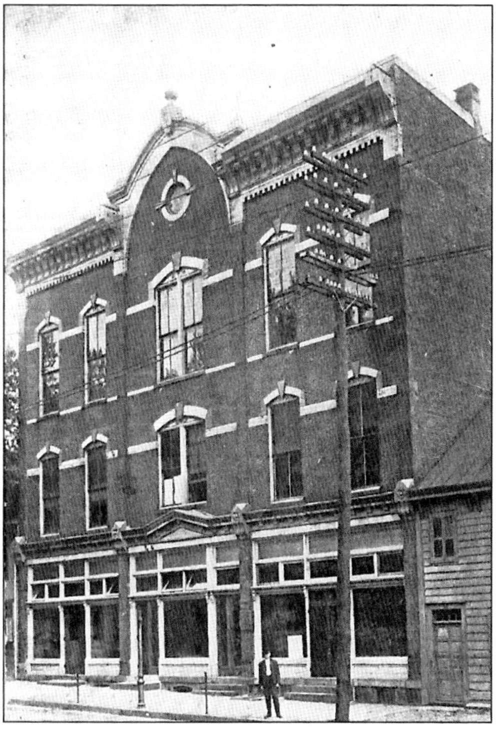

Lambertville Masonic Temple on Bridge Street was built in 1877. It was because he was a Mason that George Coryell happened to serve as a pall bearer for George Washington. (Lambertville Historical Society photo.)

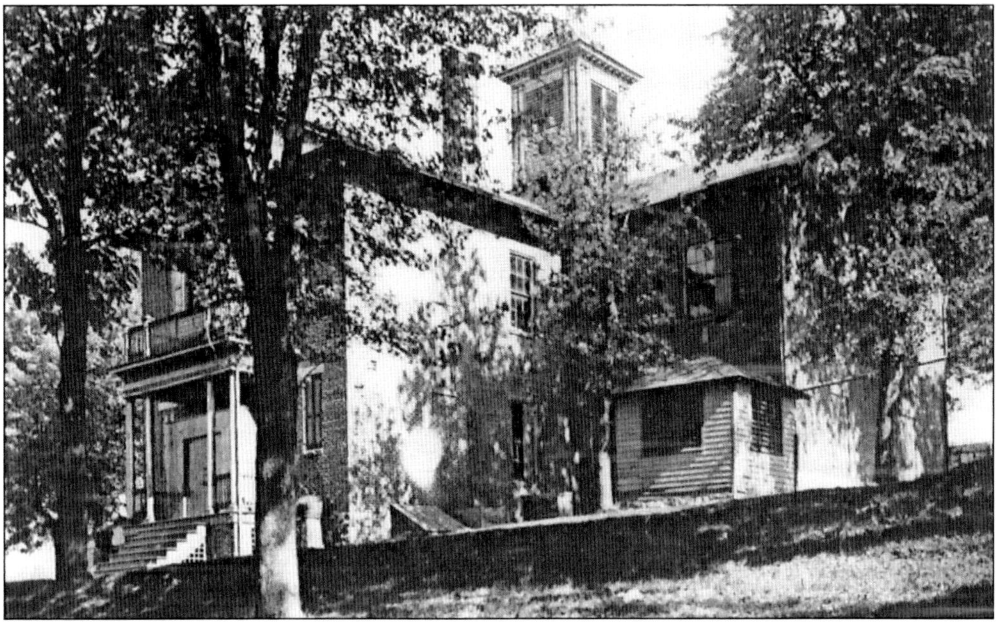

Lambertville High School. When the high school was built in 1854 on Coryell's Hill the name of the hill changed through usage to High School Hill. The building was given an addition in a 1925 expansion program. (Lambertville Historical Society photo.)

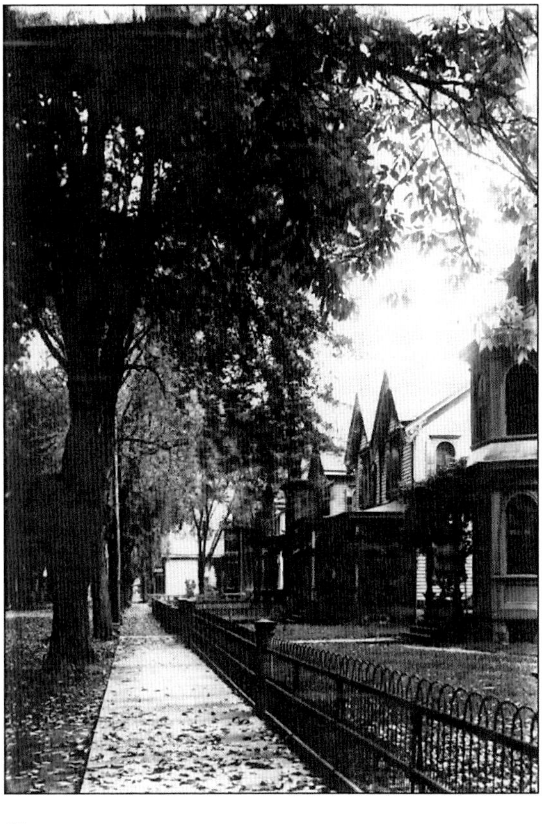

North Union Street. The quiet charm of a small town is evident in this view of North Union Street, c.1890. Lambertville's population today is around 3,500, but it still clings to its "city" designation, earned when it totaled 5,000. (Lambertville Historical Society photo.)

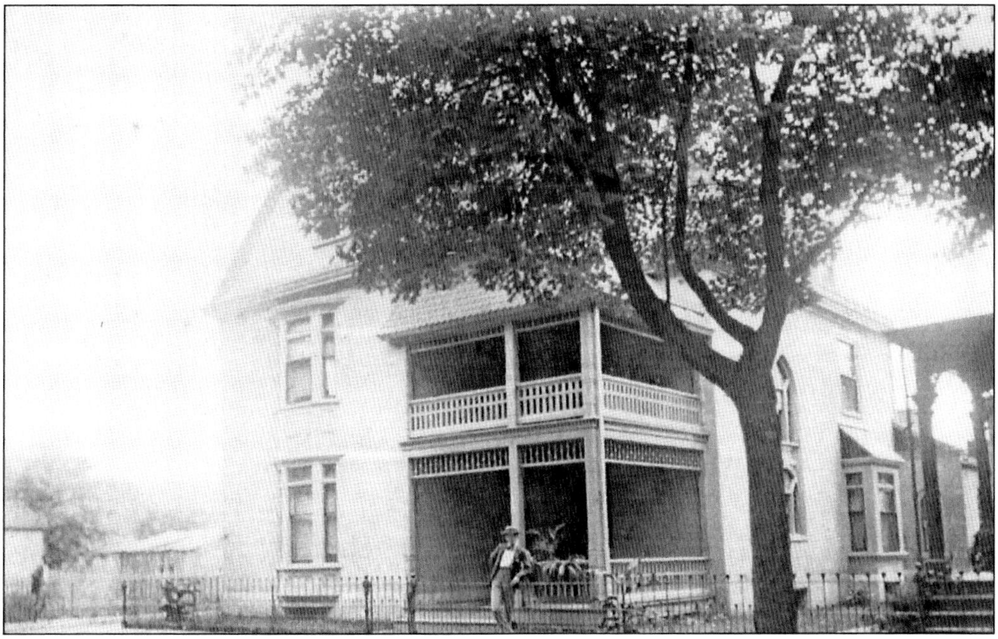

St. Andrew's Episcopal Church on York Street burned in 1891, and was then rebuilt as a residence. Some of the church's Gothic window frames were incorporated into the residence; note the window behind the tree. (Lambertville Historical Society photo.)

The largest building built in Lambertville in the nineteenth century was St. John The Evangelist Church on Bridge Street, which dates from 1893. (Lambertville Historical Society photo.)

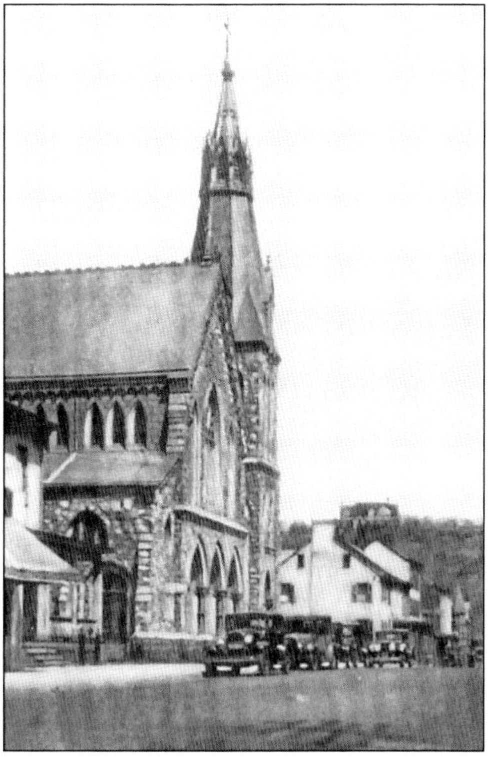

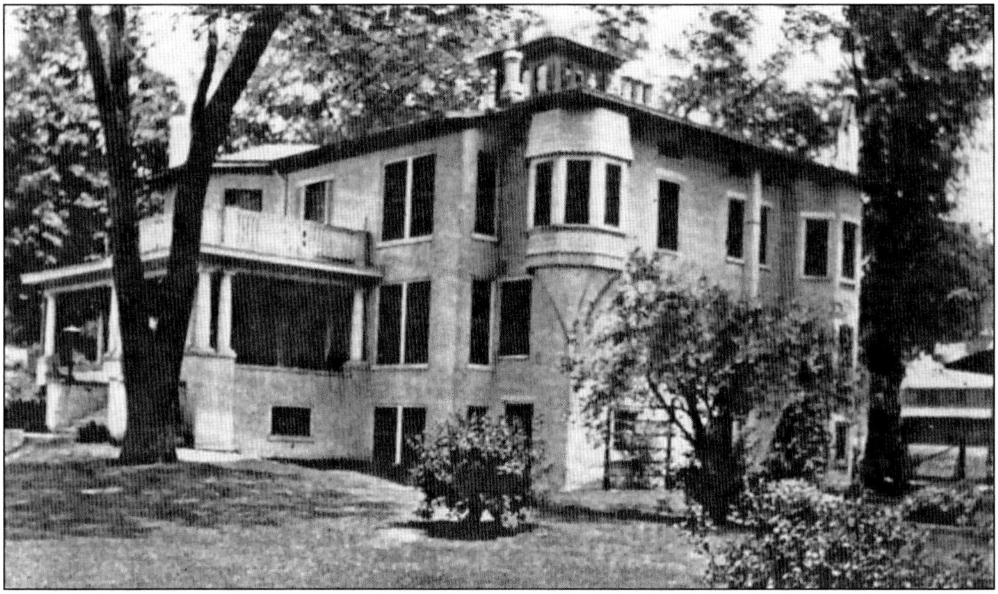

Dr. John Lilly's mansion at Main and Lilly Streets was built in three sections between 1812 and 1830. It served as the Moose Hall during the 1940s. In 1993 it became the city library. (Lambertville Historical Society photo.)

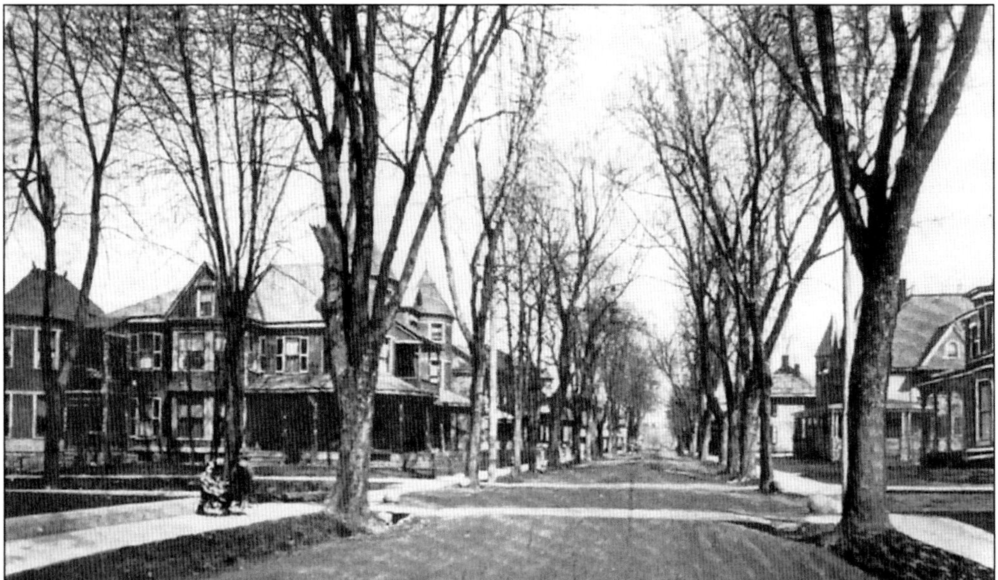

Another view of North Union Street. Formerly called Amwell, the town was given the name Lambertsville in 1822 by John Lambert, postmaster, for the use of the U.S. Post Office. This upset people at the time, but they came to accept it. (Lambertville Historical Society photo.)

Five

The Hill Towns of Tewksbury

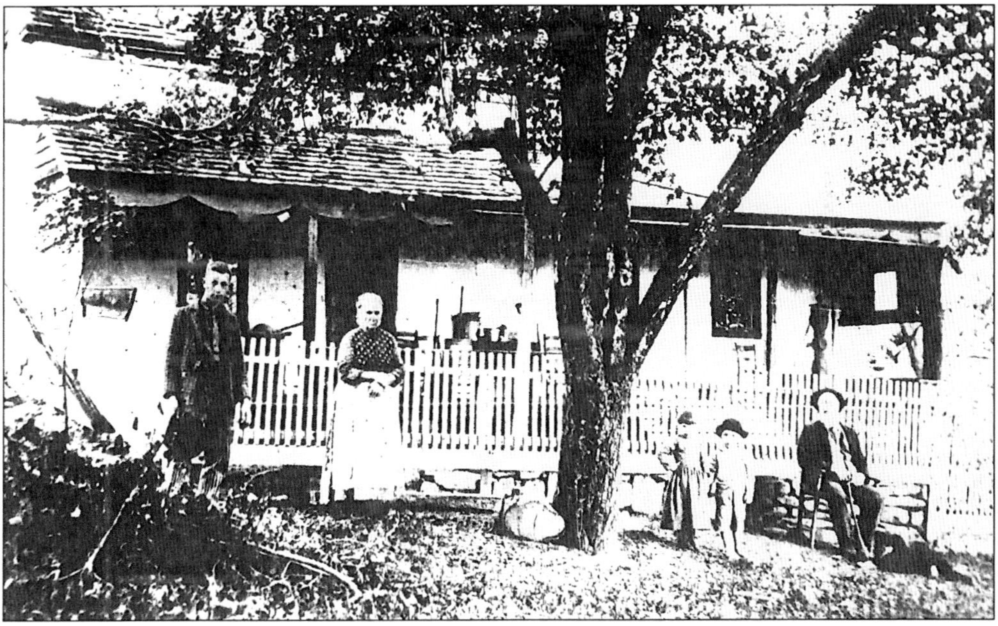

The Philhower homestead. Early settlers in the Tewksbury area were largely northern Europeans who came here looking for land to farm. In 1760 Philip Philhower found his land and built his homestead along what is now Longview Road, at some distance from the South Branch of the Raritan. Other area settlers bore the names Apgar, Hoffman, Trimmer, Dufford, Sutton, Cole, Burd, Weis, Neighbor, and Beam. Some 130 years later, Philip's descendents gathered in the yard in front of his house to have their picture taken: (from left) Charles, Harriet, and David Philhower, and two children, Hattie and Israel. The clan holds regular reunions today. (Califon Historical Society photo.)

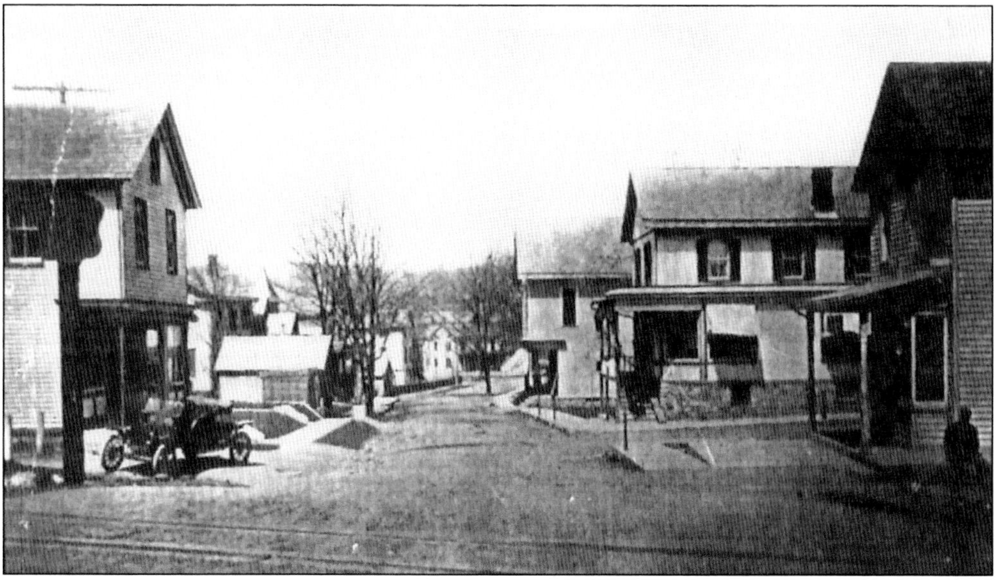

Main Street, Califon. In the tiny borough of Califon on the west edge of Tewksbury Township, a Hupmobile is parked on the unpaved Main Street. It belonged to Harry Geist, a former mayor and rural mail carrier. (Califon Historical Society photo.)

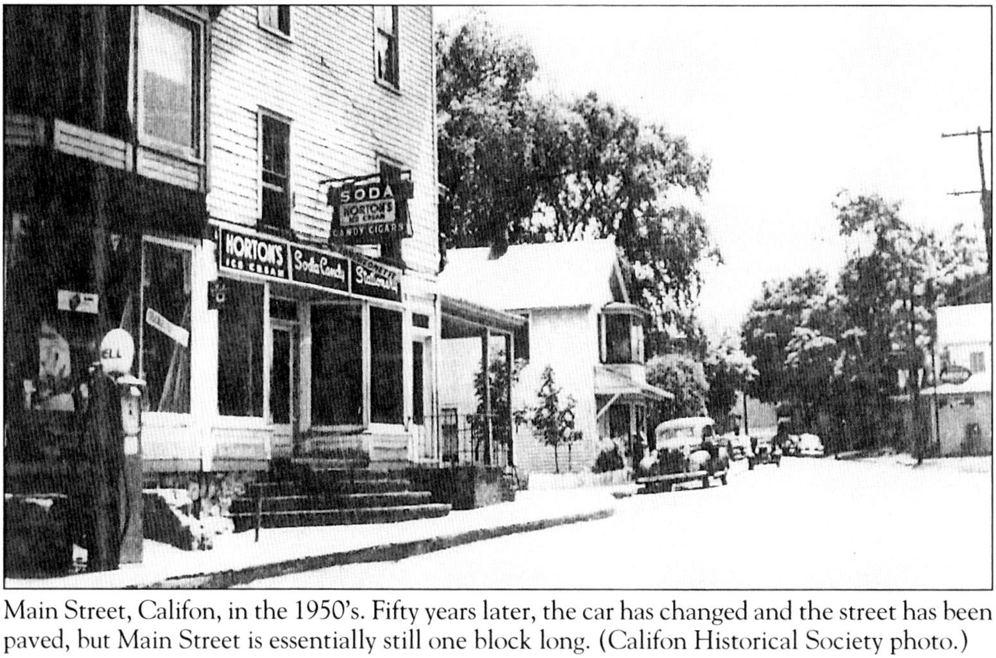

Main Street, Califon, in the 1950's. Fifty years later, the car has changed and the street has been paved, but Main Street is essentially still one block long. (Califon Historical Society photo.)

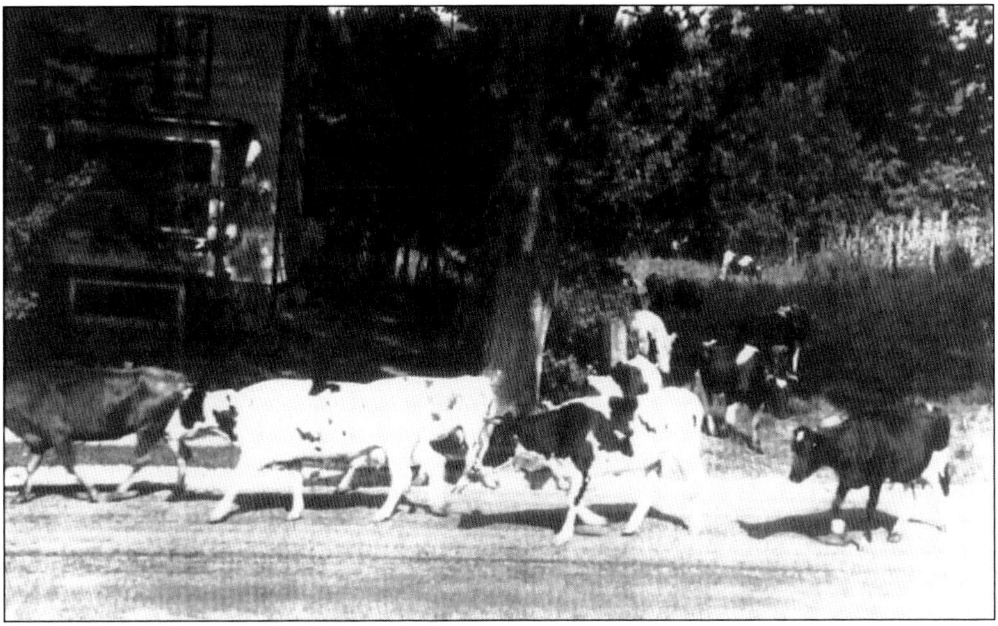

A herd of cows were brought home from pasture every night, up Main Street and across the bridge to their owner. Apparently, no one objected. (Califon Historical Society photo.)

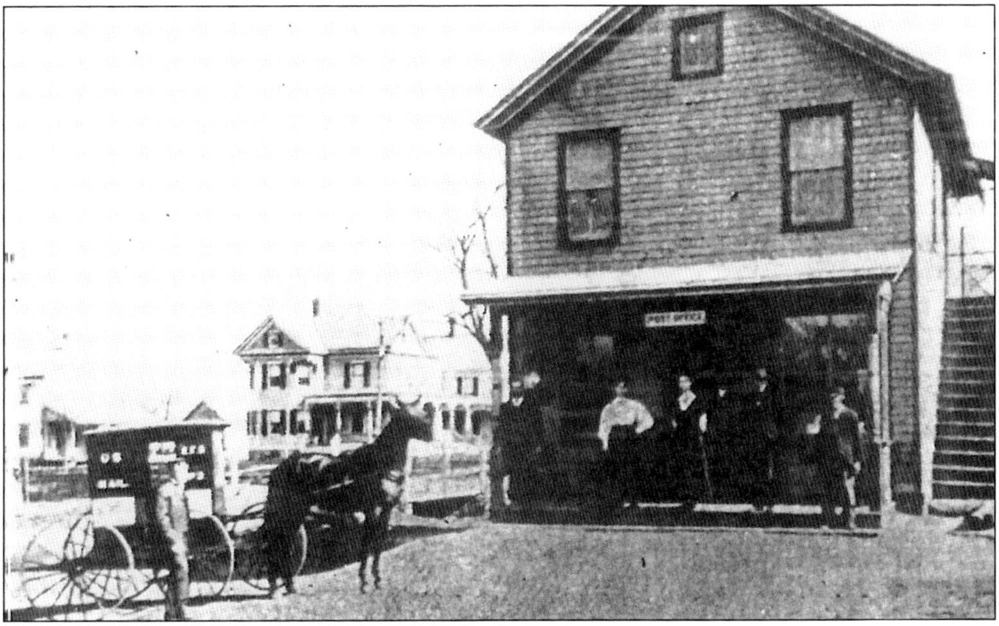

Califon Post Office. In pre-Hupmobile days, the rural mail carrier drove a horse and buggy. There was a heating stove inside the buggy, and two lanterns outside for use when the mail carrier got back late from his rounds. (Califon Historical Society photo.)

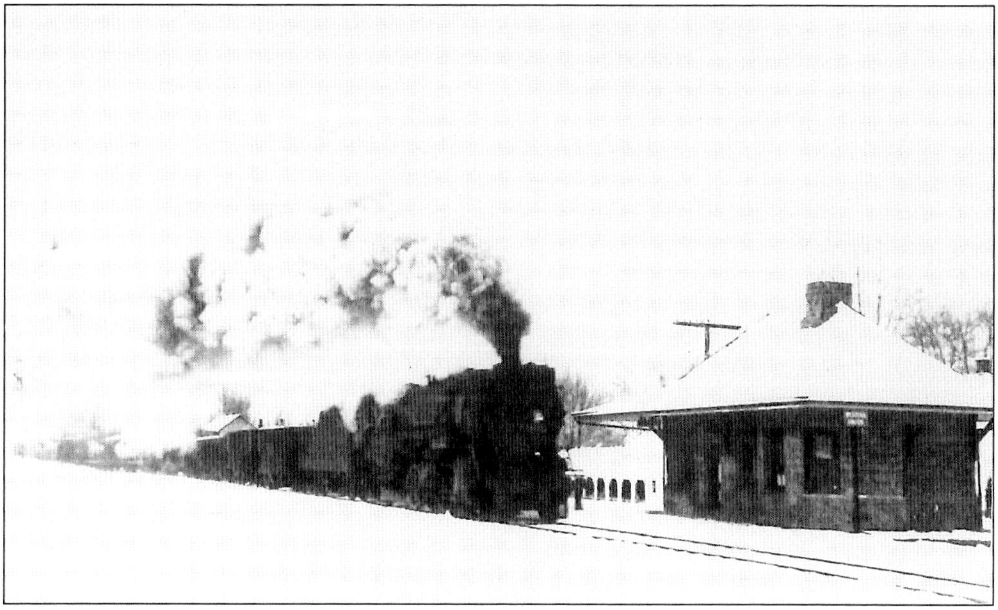

Califon railroad station. Califon's name was shortened from California when the longer name wouldn't fit on the new railroad station sign! This snapshot of a train arriving at the station one winter's day was taken by A. Isak. (Califon Historical Society photo.)

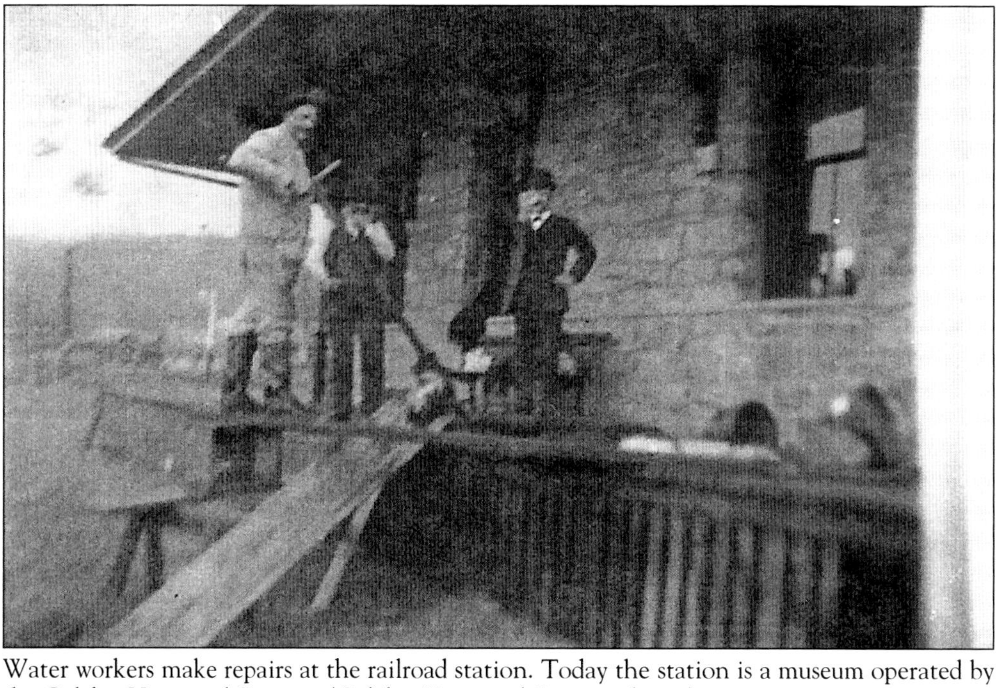

Water workers make repairs at the railroad station. Today the station is a museum operated by the Califon Historical Society. (Califon Historical Society photo.)

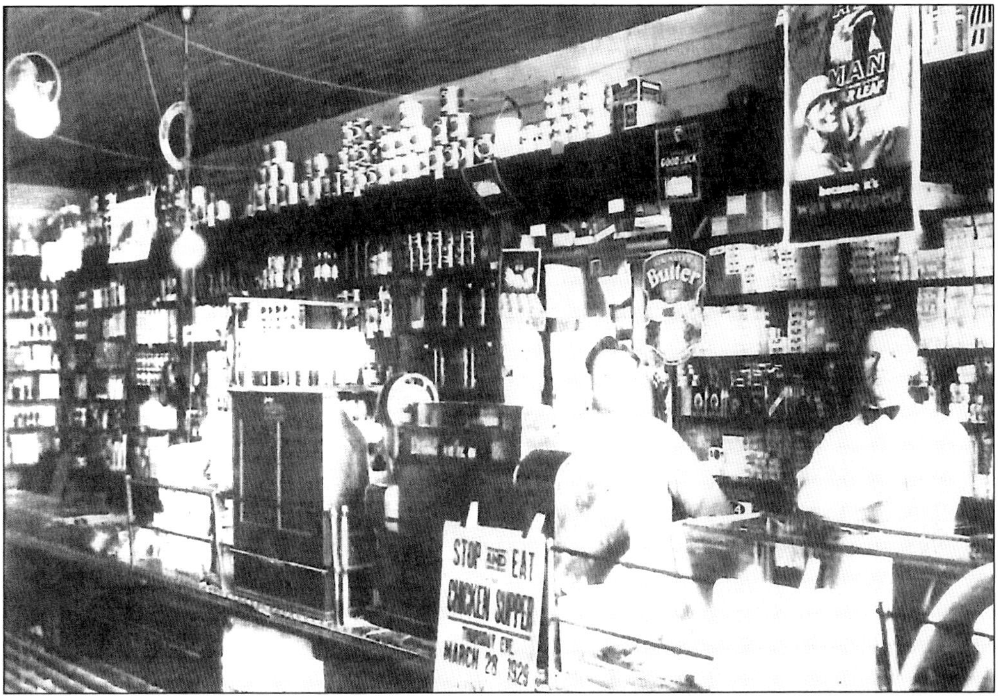

Philhower Grocery. In 1929, one of Philip Philhower's descendents, William Philhower, operated a grocery store on Califon's Main Street. Earlier, Abraham Philhower ran one where Rambo's is now. (Donald Freiberg collection.)

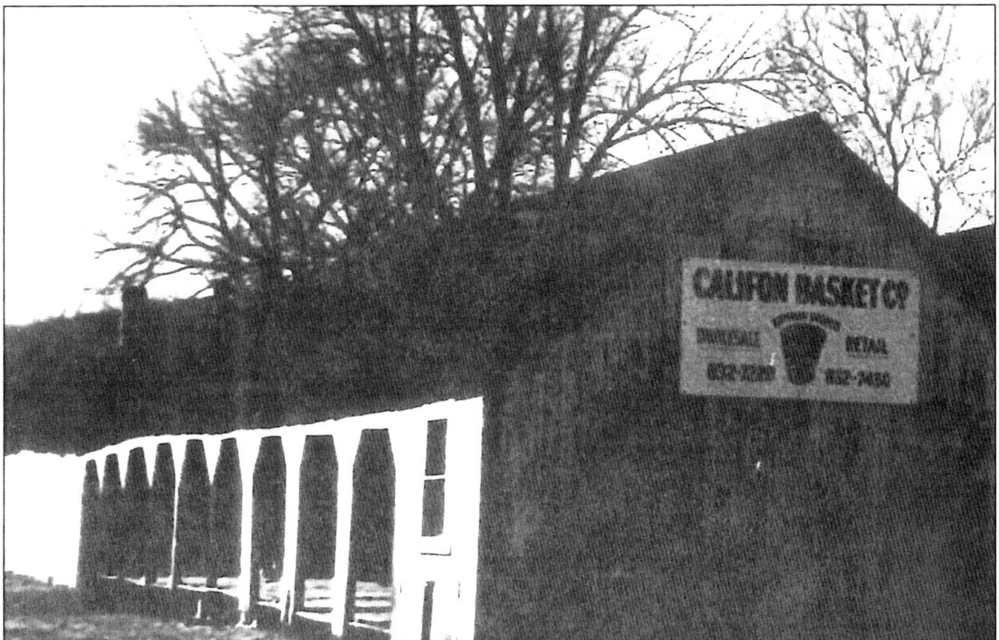

Califon Basket Company. Apples and peaches have always been popular crops in Hunterdon County. The Califon Basket Company's products were much needed for shipping peaches to the New York City area in the late 1800s. (Califon Historical Society photo.)

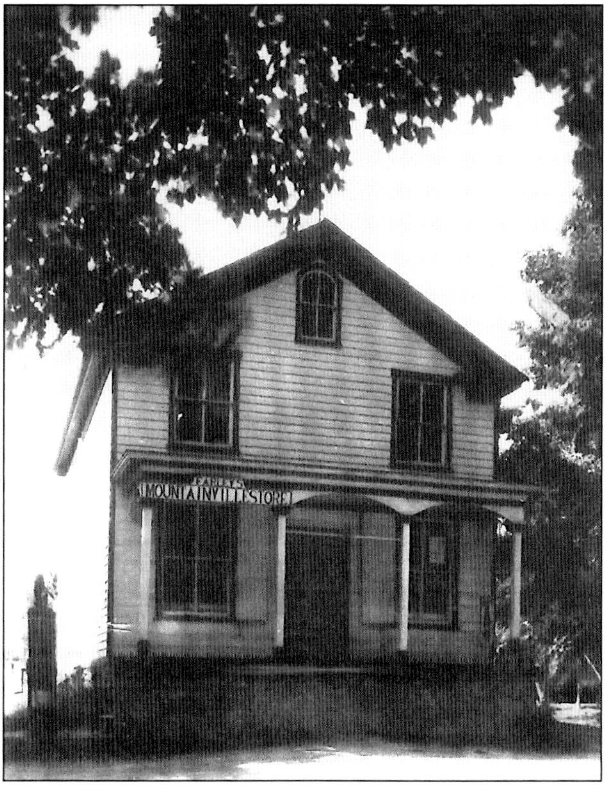

Mountainville General Store is still the center of activity of its unincorporated hill town community of one hundred people. Other businesses there today are mostly antique shops and realtors.

Oldwick, another of Tewksbury's unincorporated hill towns, had rutted dirt roads when this picture was taken from its west boundaries near the turn of the century. The fenced field in the foreground is now George Melick's apple orchard.

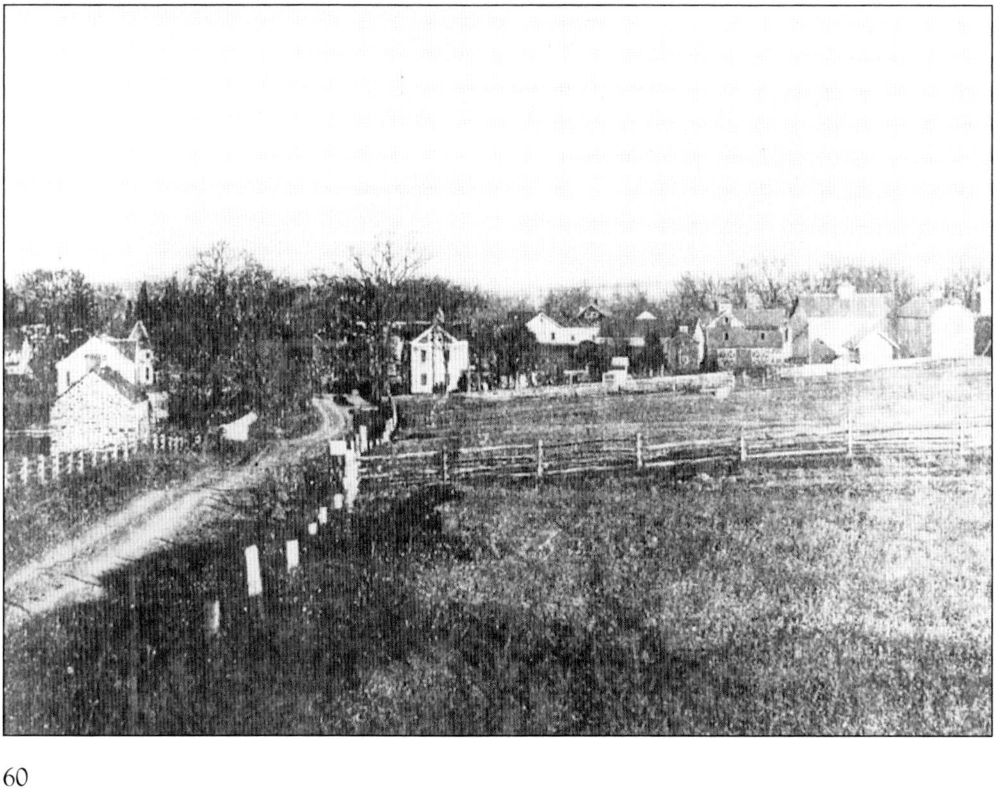

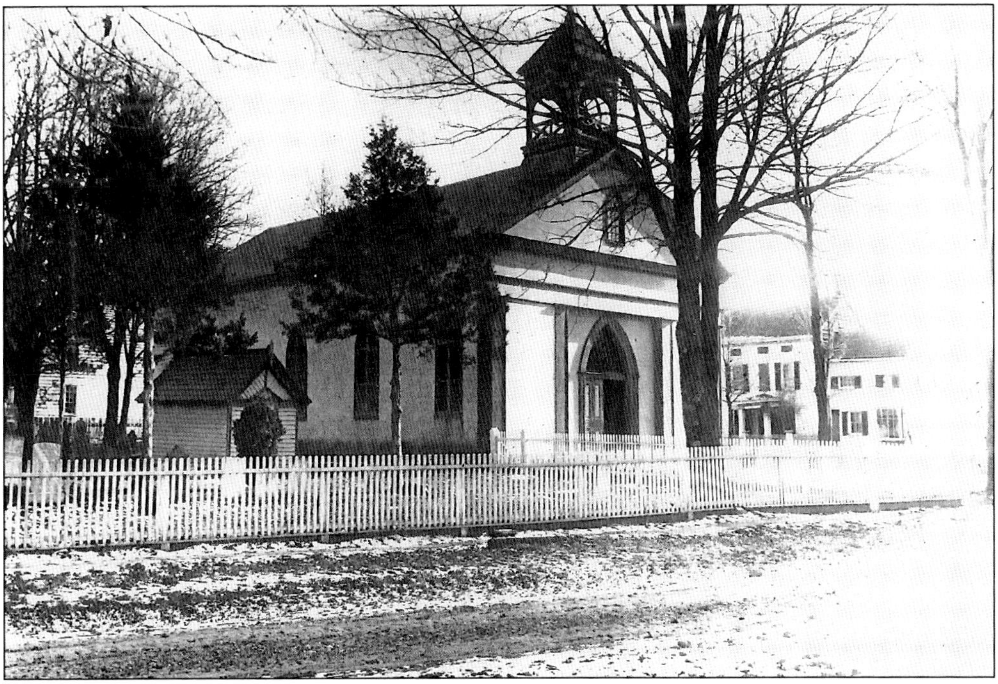

Zion Lutheran Church. Oldwick was called New Germantown when it grew up around Zion Lutheran Church, erected in part in 1749. German members built homes on 7 acres of land originally purchased by the congregation.

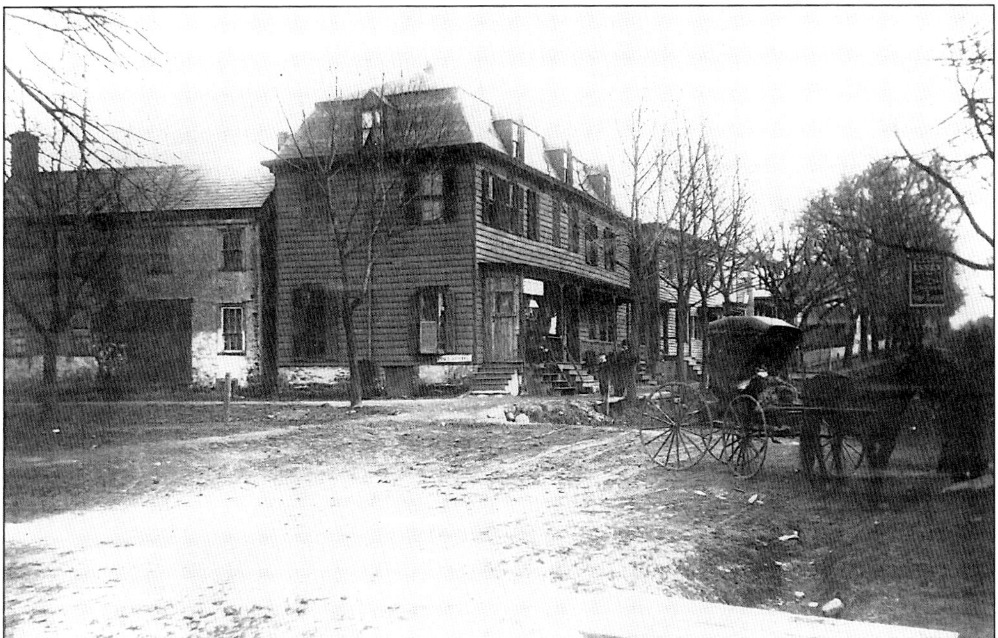

Oldwick Main Street. Across the street looking south from Zion Church along Main Street are shops which have today become mostly offices and antique stores. A buggy is parked in front of what is now Oldwick General Store on the west side of Main Street.

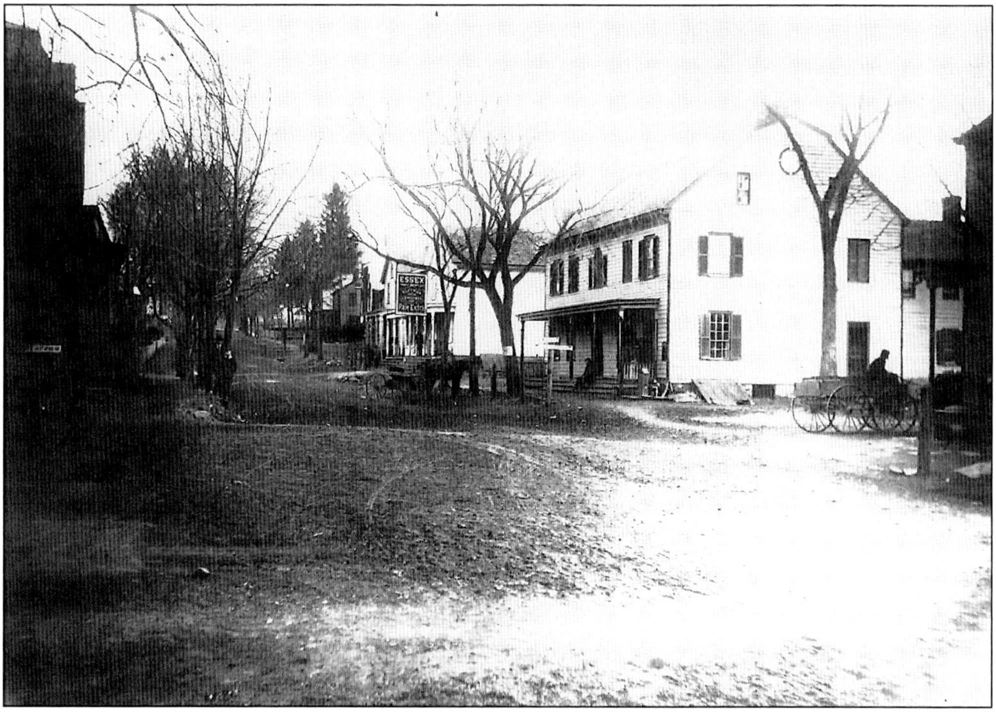

Another view of Oldwick Main Street. At the right edge of the picture is Tewksbury Inn, where a farm wagon has stopped. These buildings are on the west side of Main Street across from Zion Lutheran Church.

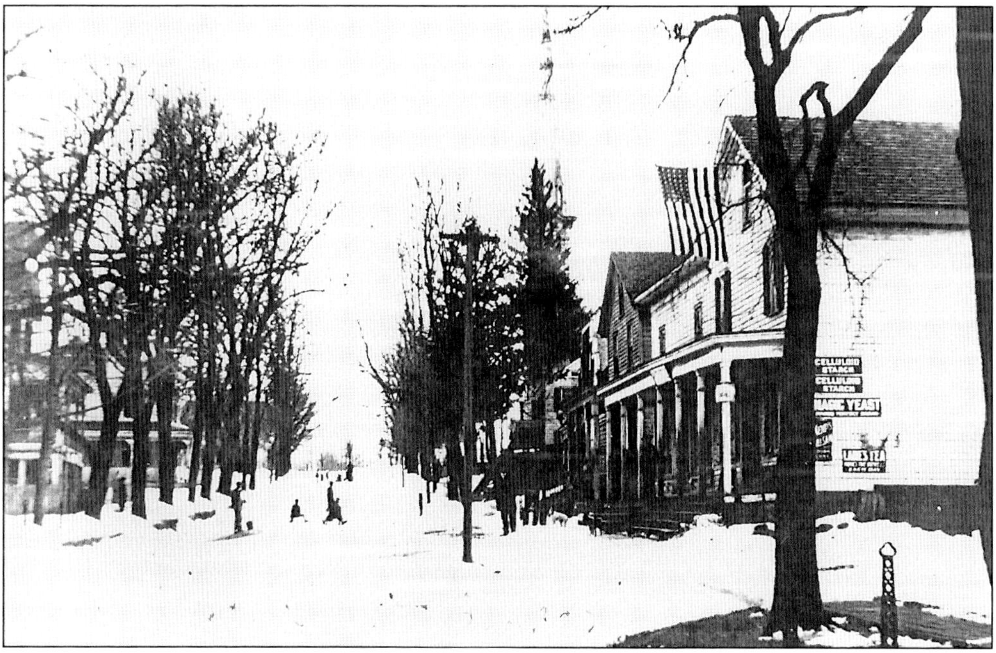

Oldwick in winter. Children played in the middle of Main Street on a snowy day when there was much less traffic than Oldwick draws today. The building on the right was then the town's general store. Now it is occupied by dentists' offices.

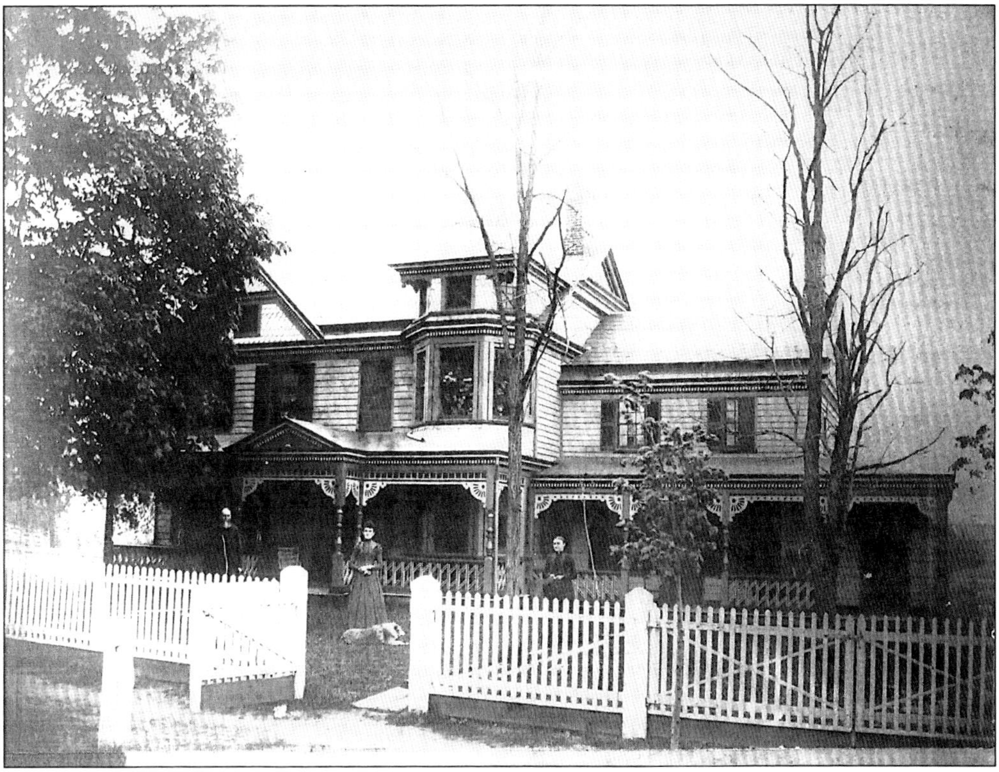

The Walter Melick farmstead is located across from George Melick's orchard on the west side of town. Oldwick's present general store and its parking lot are out of the picture on the right.

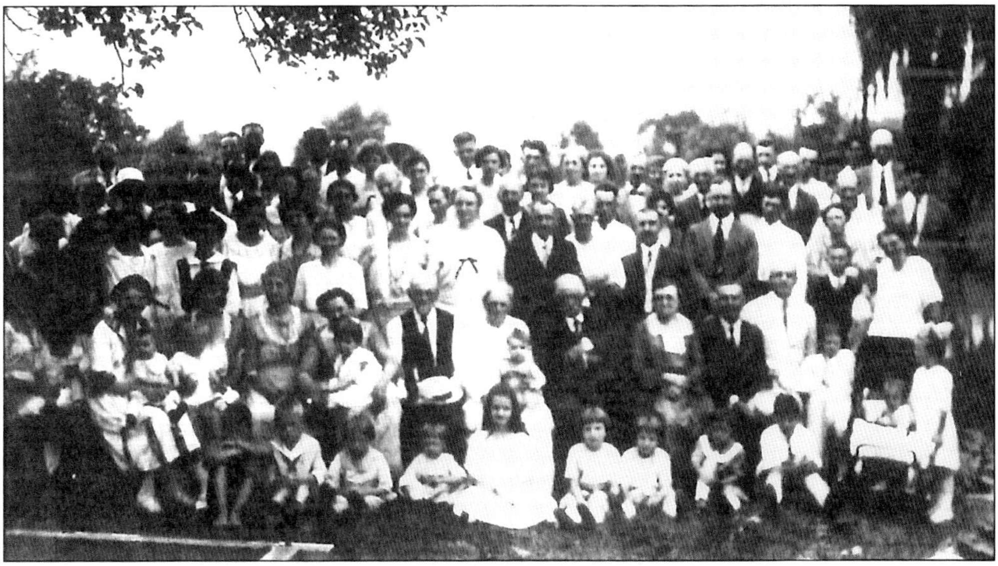

A family reunion. Like many Hunterdon children, George Melick spent holidays at his grandparents' farms. In this photograph he and his cousins are down in front at a family reunion at the J. Alfred Rinehart farmstead, northeast of town.

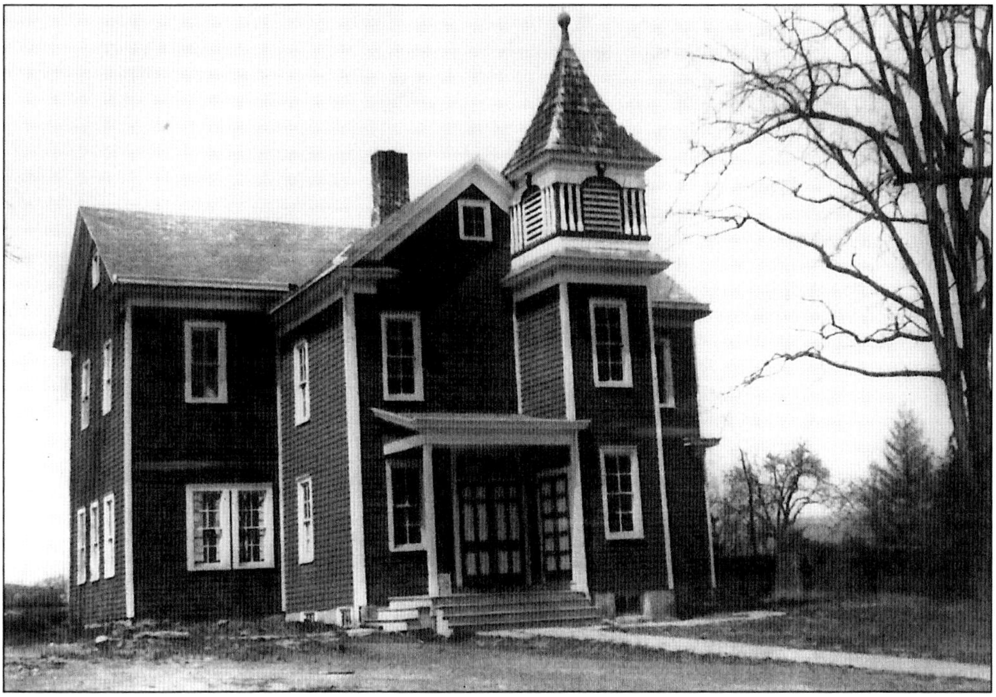

Barnet Hall Academy, Oldwick's fourth school, was erected in 1807 on Main Street. The upper floor held a community hall. The academy closed in 1951 when a new school was built. Today it is the Oldwick Community Center.

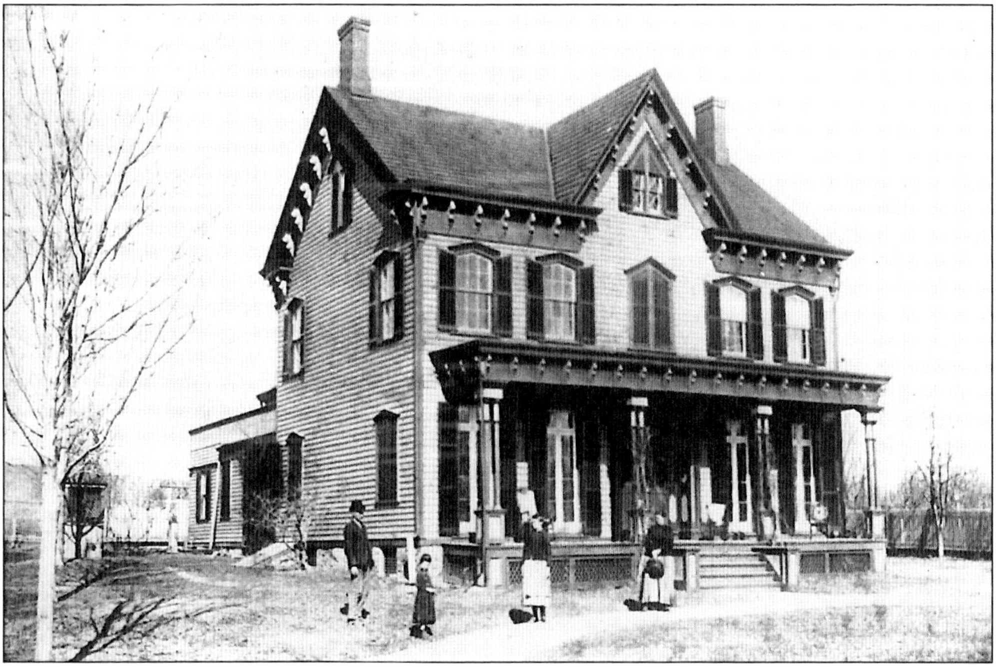

One of the many beautiful Victorian buildings on Main Street in Oldwick is the Eick family's home. Trees were scarce in the area in the 1800s; many had been burned for firewood or to fuel limestone kilns for fertilizer.

Six

Small Town Childhood

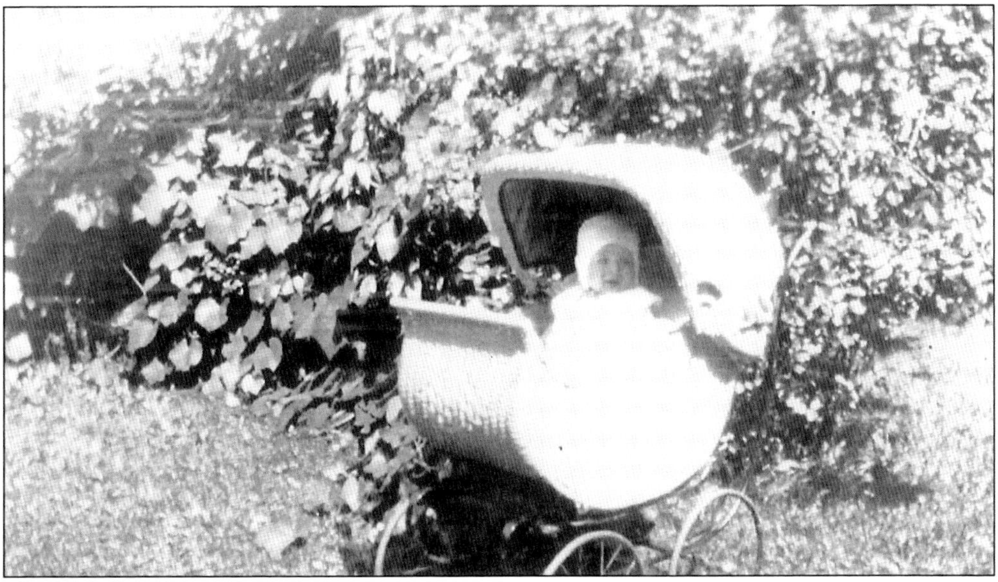

Clinton, Flemington, and Lambertville, as well as the hill towns of Tewksbury, provided the classic ideal setting for a growing child in the late 1800s and early 1900s. From the time he or she was born, the child was free to breathe unpolluted country air, to play beside rippling streams and run on green lawns; to climb a tree, steal its apples, or hold a doll tea party on a blanket beneath it; to build a dirt road for a toy horse or car, or make mud pies after rain. Frank Shepherd, peering from his wicker carriage in Clinton, could have had no idea of the delights that awaited him in his small town childhood. (Clinton Historical Society photo.)

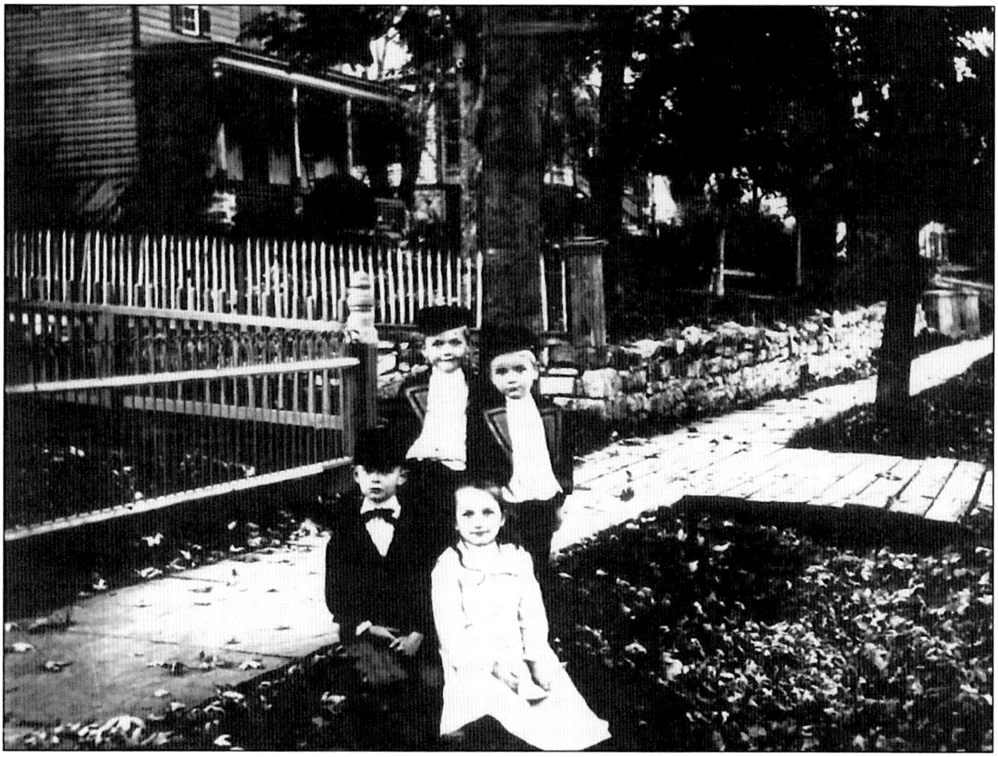

Clinton children. Two brothers in matching coats and their playmates take a break from their games to pose for a picture. Neighborhood children in small towns often played group games like "Run, Sheep, Run" and "Kick the Can." (Clinton Historical Society photo.)

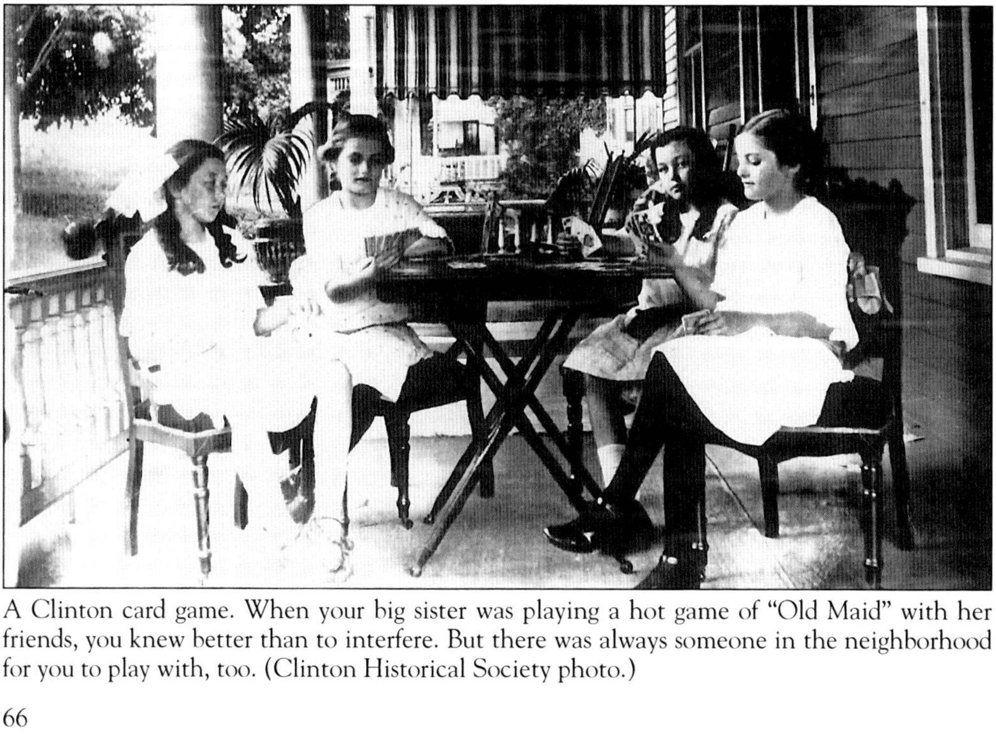

A Clinton card game. When your big sister was playing a hot game of "Old Maid" with her friends, you knew better than to interfere. But there was always someone in the neighborhood for you to play with, too. (Clinton Historical Society photo.)

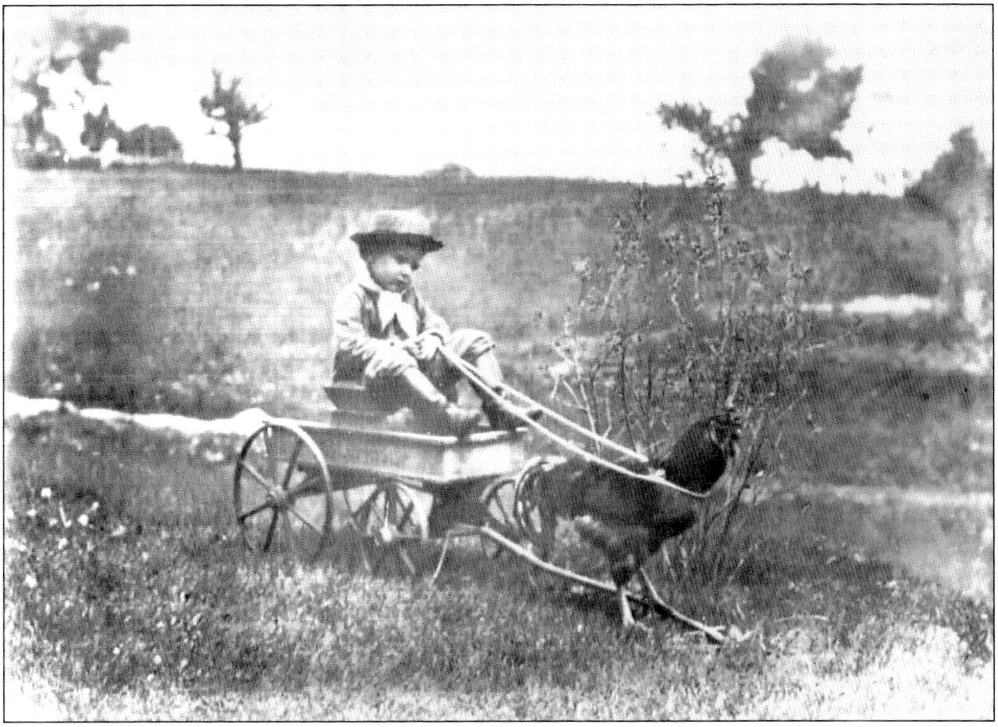

Grownups had time to spend with children when commuting didn't take hours out of life. Someone hitched a rooster to this boy's wagon, just for fun. (Clinton Historical Society photo.)

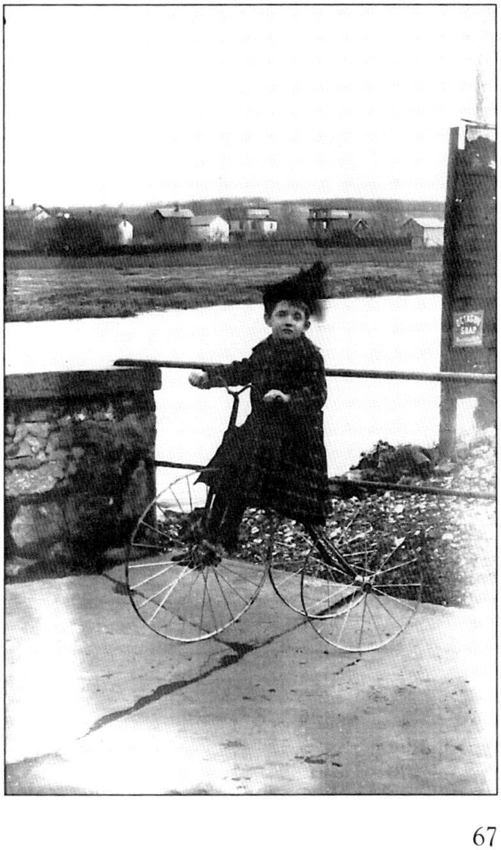

A new tricycle was an exciting event! This new owner posed with her proud possession at the west end of Clinton's Main Street bridge. The cow pasture across the river is now a commercial area. (Clinton Historical Society photo.)

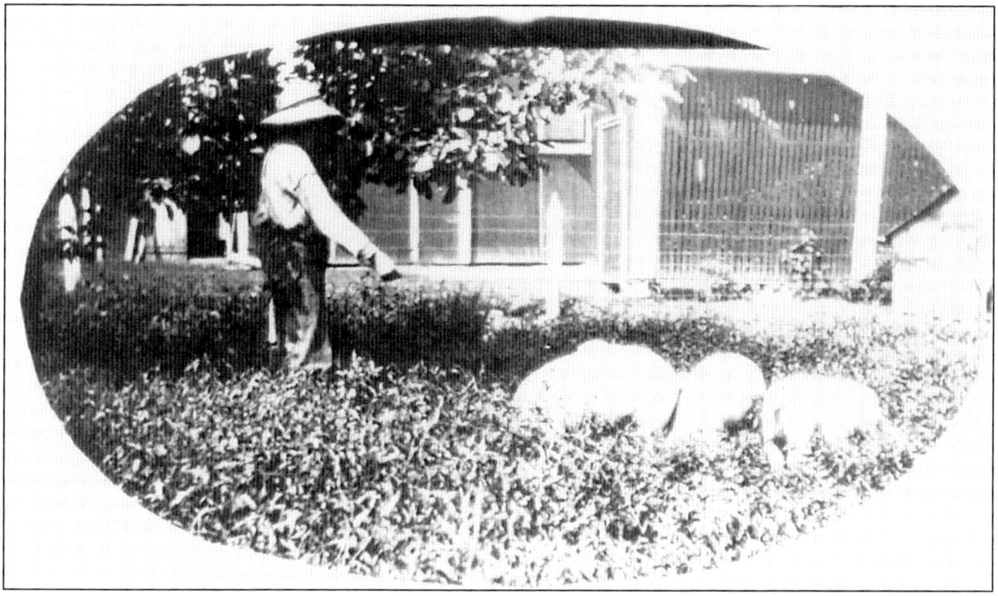

A visit to grandpa's farm could hold all sorts of wonders, like these baby pigs. Small town children knew much from personal experience that today's children can only read about or see in films. (Clinton Historical Society photo.)

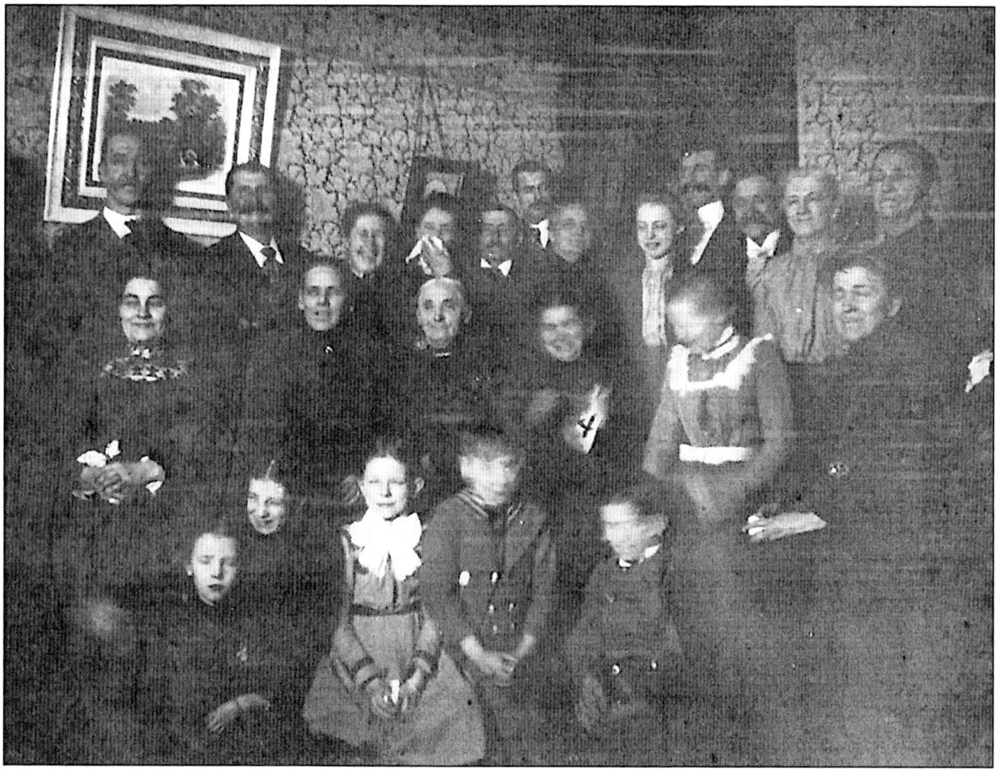

A Clinton family. One of the delights of life was being part of an extended family that lived nearby. You didn't have to travel far to see your cousins, aunts, and uncles. You got together often, like the Shepherds gathered here. (Clinton Historical Society photo.)

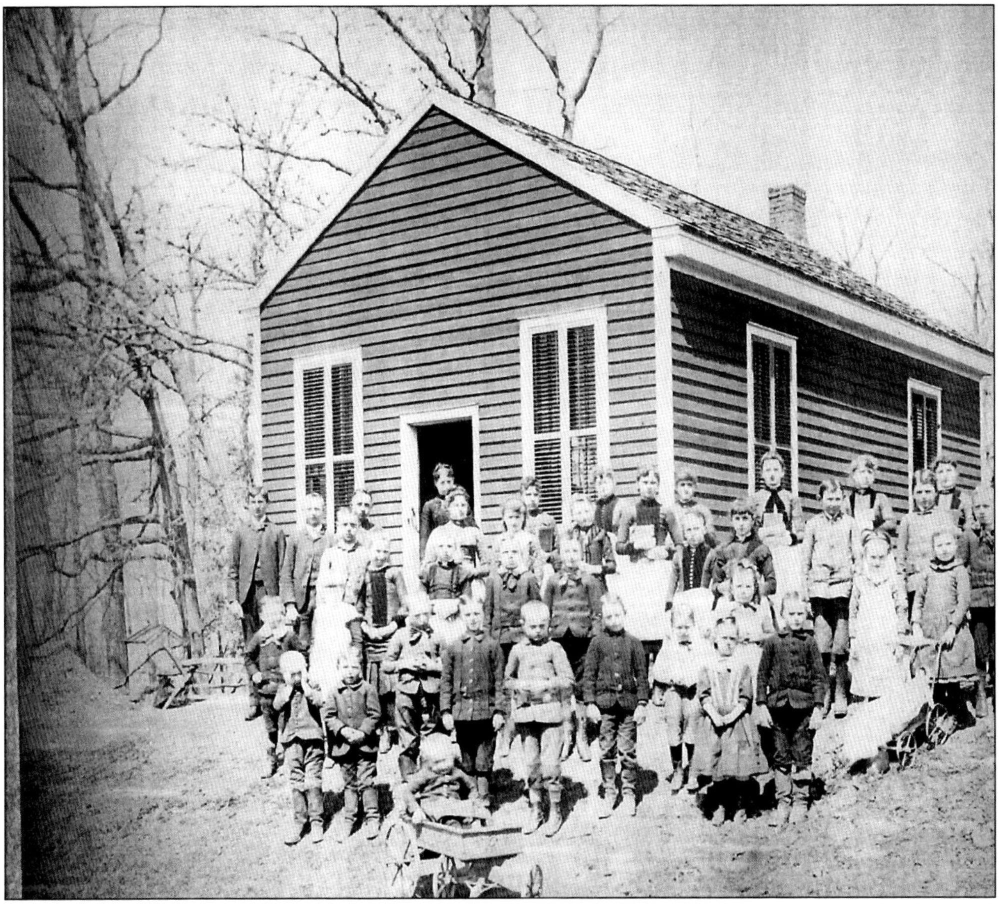

In the early years, school was a single room where children of all grades were taught. In 1891 Ada Bell Hoff (top right) posed with her classmates at Bunker Hill School, now on the grounds of the Clinton Museum. (Clinton Historical Society photo.)

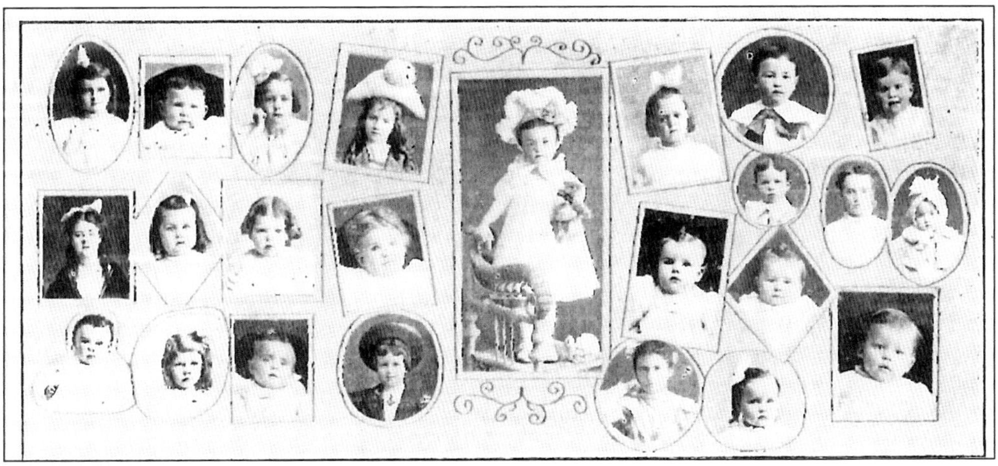

A Flemington photographer's advertisement. In Victorian times, children were sentimentalized as well as "seen but not heard." Photography was still new; a child's photograph was a perfect gift for doting grandparents, as this Flemington photographer well knew.

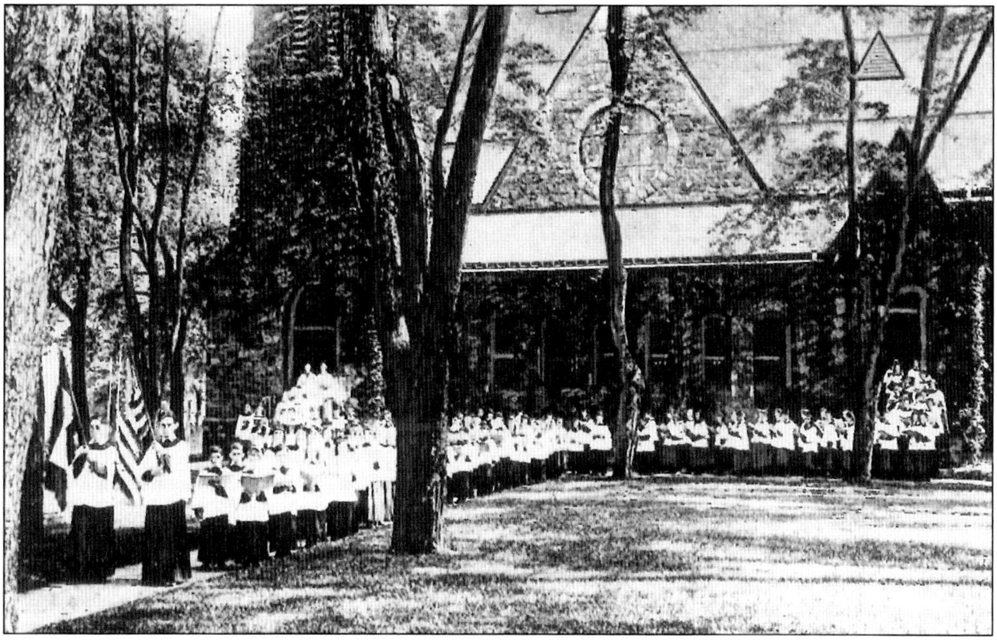

A famous children's choir. Flemington children who could carry a tune and learn to read music could join the "Two Miss Bessies'" five-church junior choir school. One pupil was the well-known bass-baritone, Paul Robeson. The school was operated between 1895 and 1958.

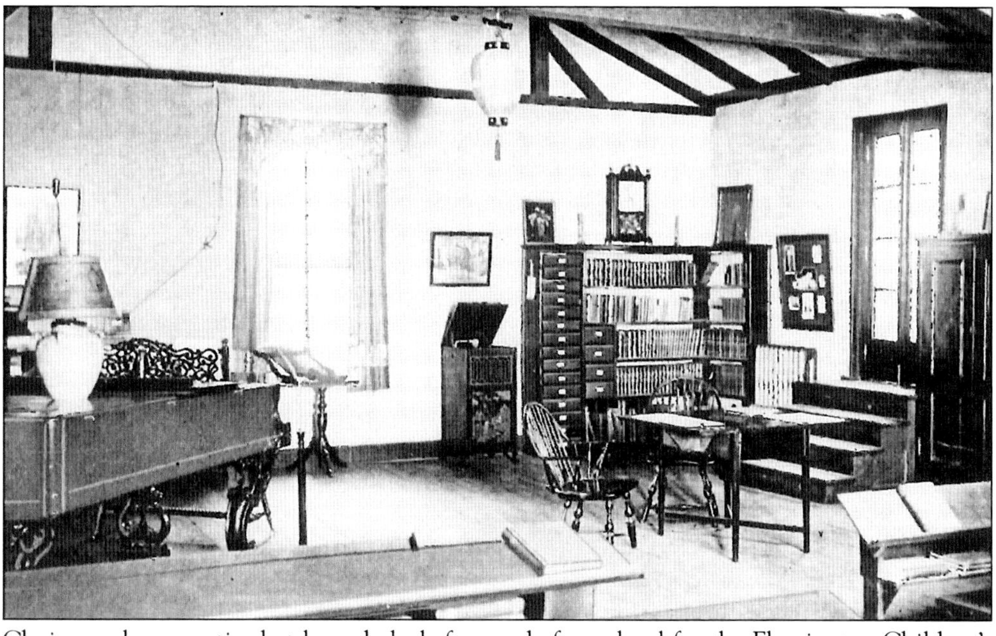

Choir members practiced at long desks before and after school for the Flemington Children's Choir performances. The beloved "Two Miss Bessies"—Elizabeth Vosseller and Elizabeth Hopewell—exacted good behavior from pupils. Techniques from the school are still used in junior choirs today.

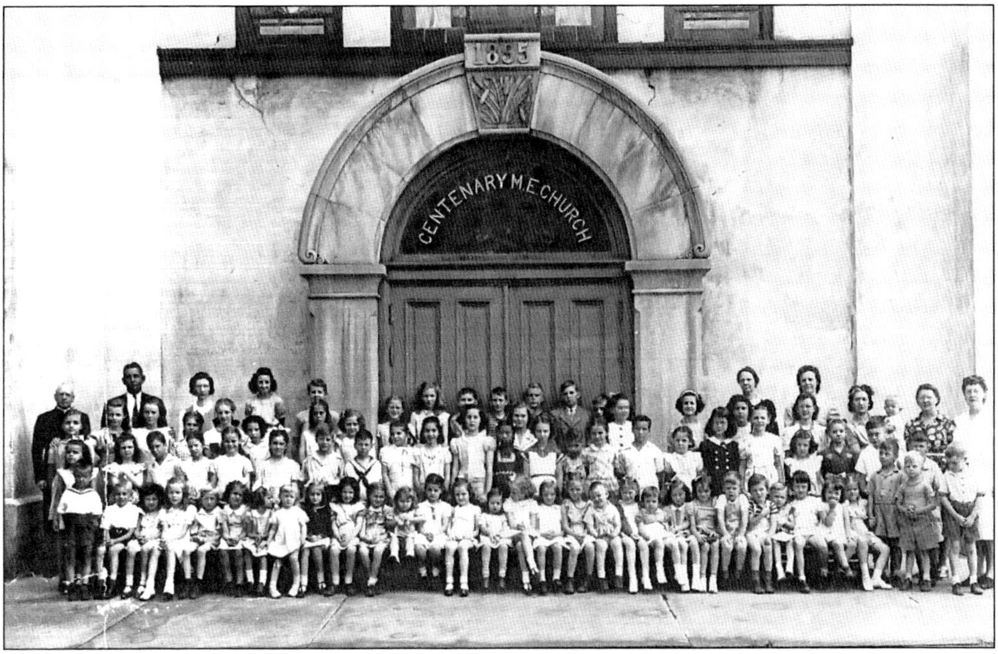

Lambertville children may not have had a choir school, but they did have busy Sunday schools. This sizable group attended Centenary Methodist Episcopal Church in 1945. The church was built in 1895. (Lambertville Historical Society photo.)

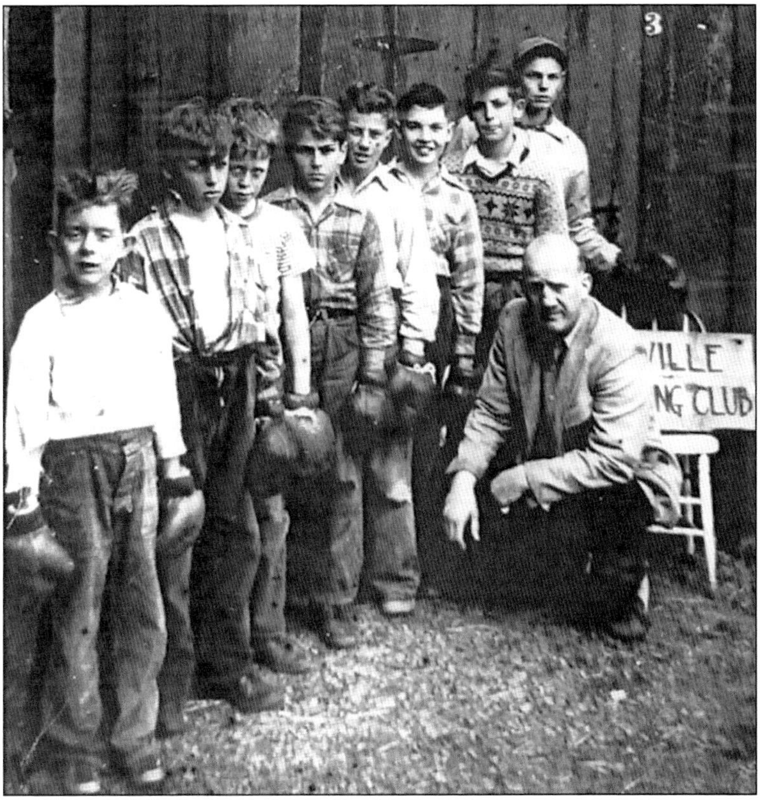

Non-Sunday school types had some fun things going, too—like this Lambertville Boxing Club. It was organized in 1948 at Highfields Farm, Goat Hill, for boys who saw themselves as "tough guys." (Lambertville Historical Society photo.)

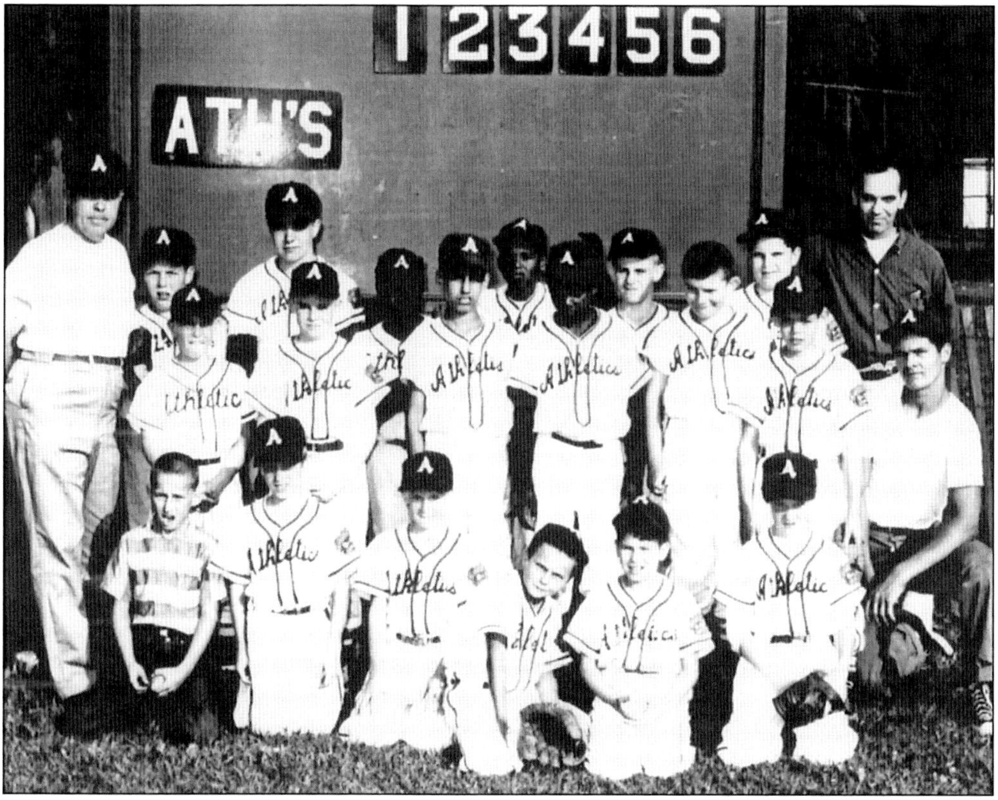

Every spring there was baseball, the great American game. Coaches Frank Bohren (left) and Frank McGuire (right) headed the Lambertville Athletics Team in June, 1960. (Lambertville Historical Society photo.)

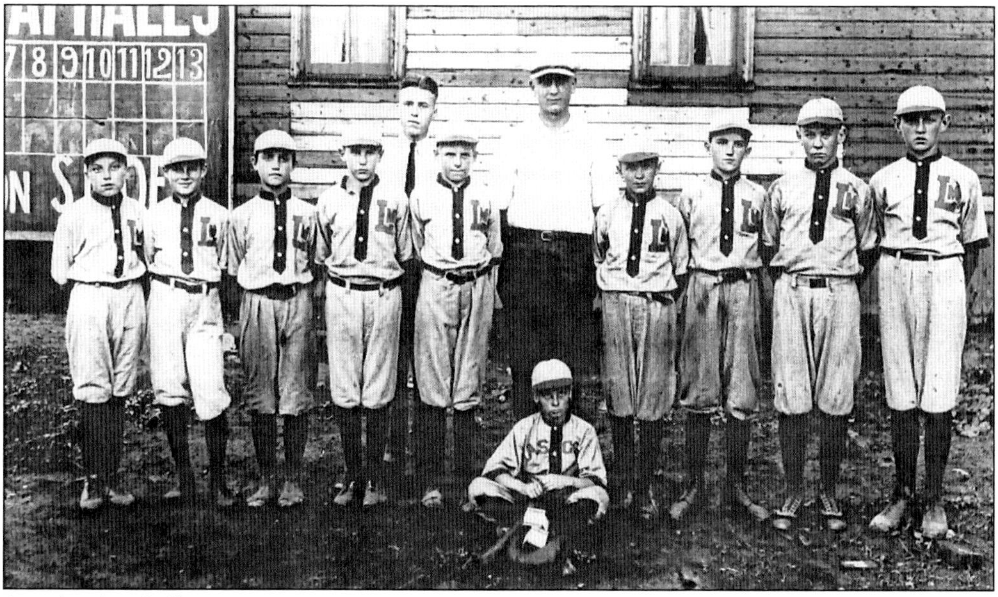

Another baseball team. Manager Eugene Narducci was in charge of this Lambertville team of grade school age baseball players in 1921/2. (Lambertville Historical Society photo.)

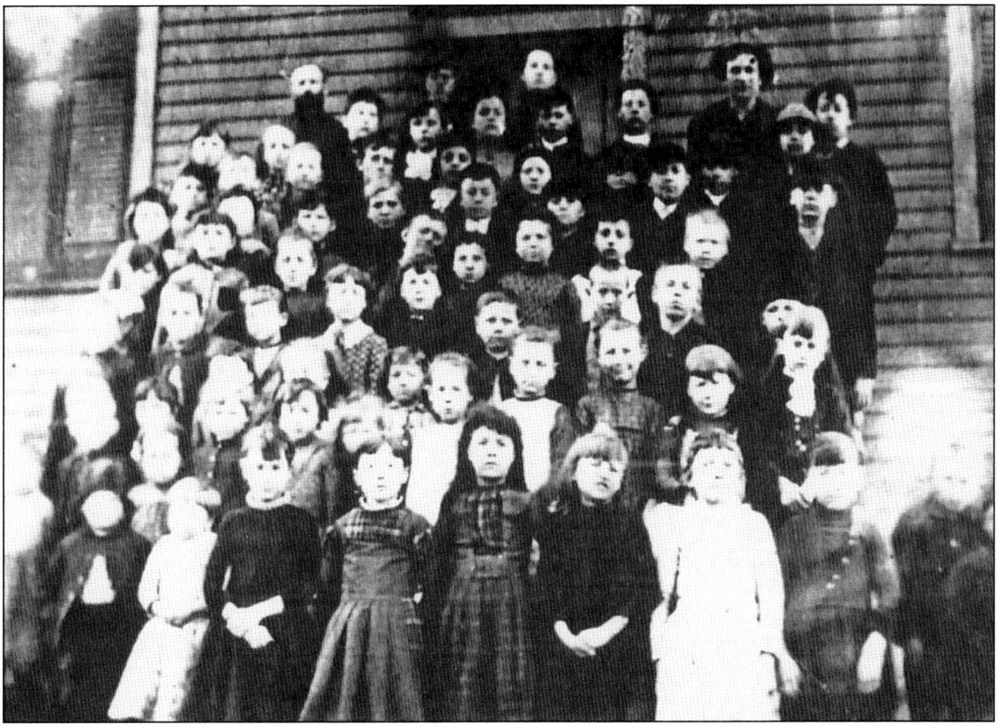

Califon's grade school was more than a single room at the turn of the century when this class picture was taken. But it was still small enough so that you knew everyone in school—and they knew you, and would tell on you, unfortunately. (Califon Historical Society photo.)

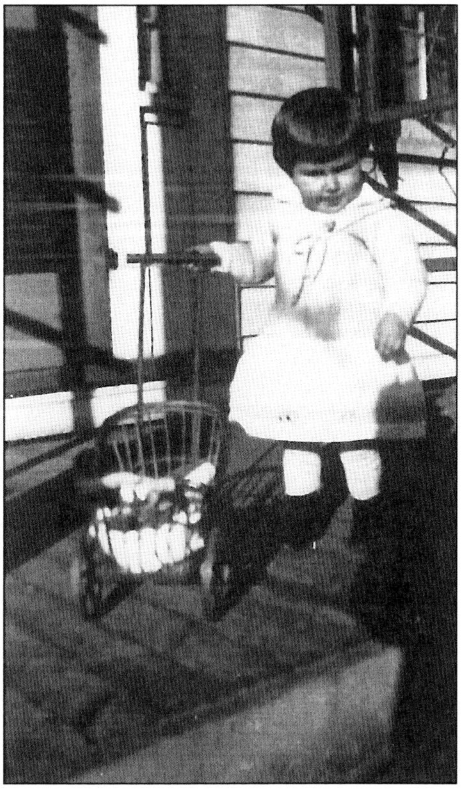

Such problems were far in the future, though, for little Dorothy and her dolly in the wicker go-cart. Dorothy was part of the Melick clan in Oldwick.

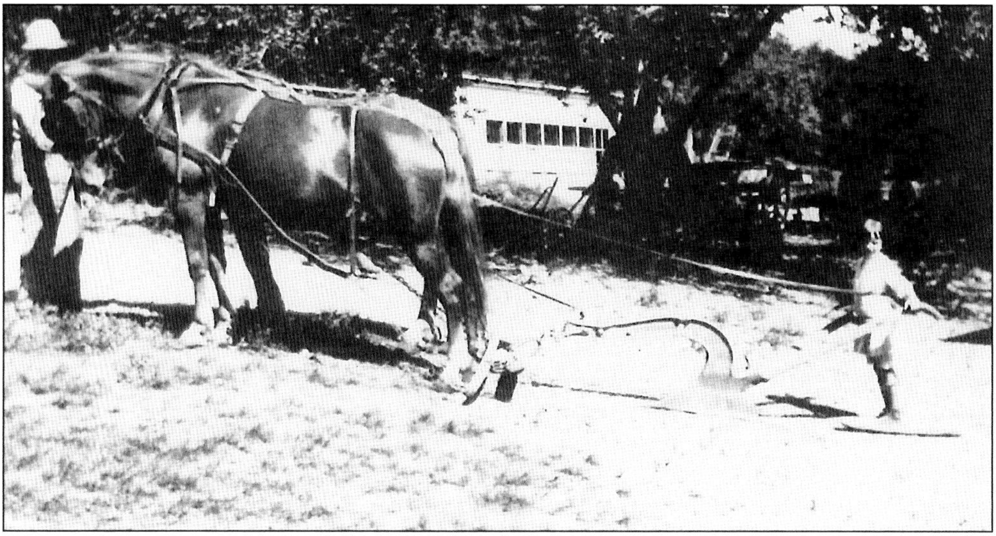

A young plowman. Children still longed to be farmers in Hunterdon County at the turn of the century. This little Califon boy could see himself plowing his own field behind his own faithful plowhorse some day in the future. (Donald Freiberg collection.)

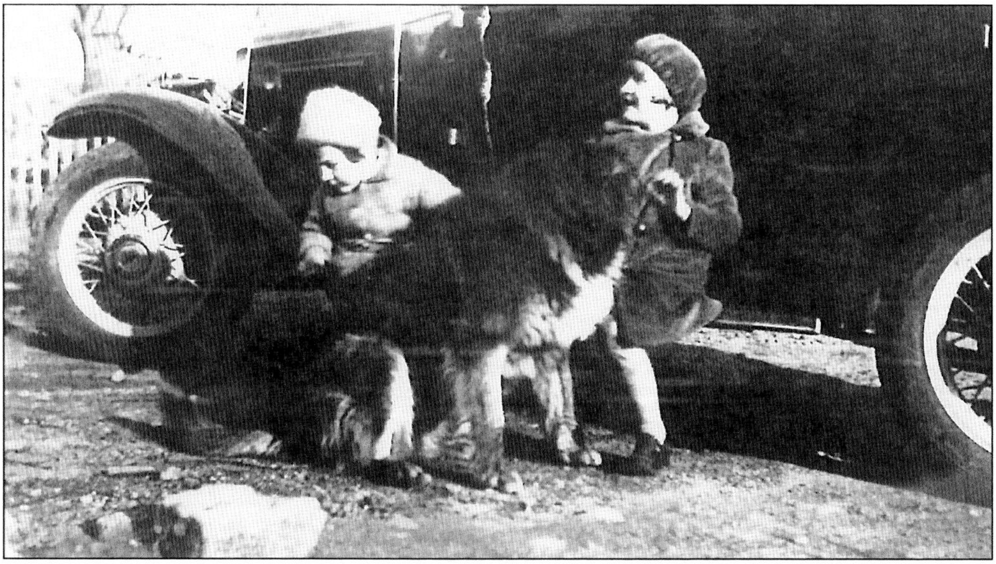

Meanwhile, there was childhood to be enjoyed. And, at a given moment, nothing was more fun for children like Genevieve and Marilyn Jean Philhower than sitting on the fender of your father's car and having your picture taken with the family dog. (Donald Freiberg collection.)

Seven

The Workaday World

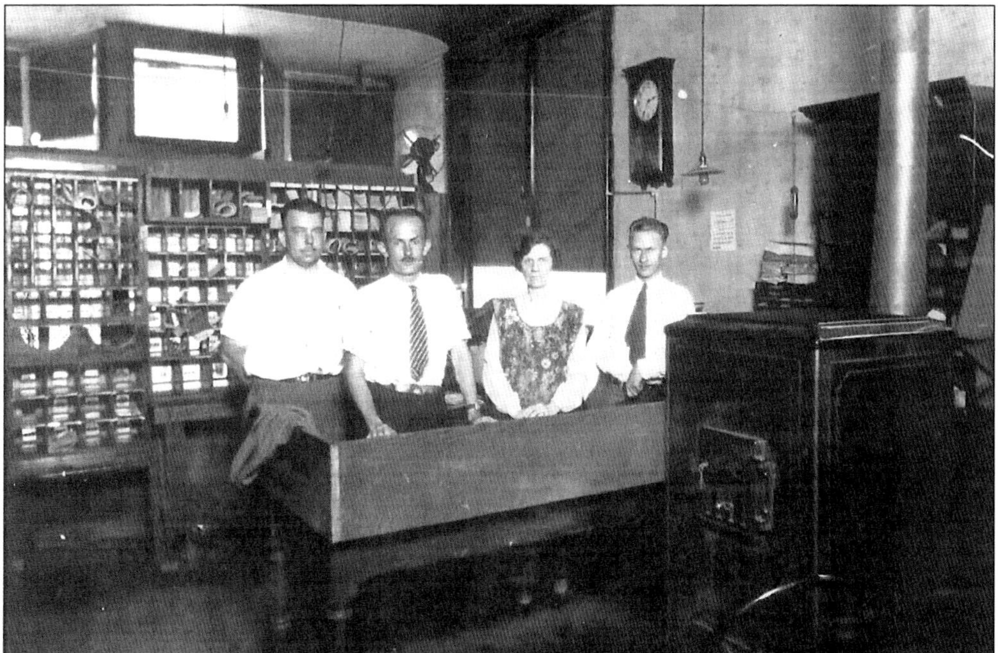

Clinton Post Office. Life was real and earnest for the adult working population of Hunterdon County's small towns. Three men and one woman staffed the Clinton Post Office in the 1920s. A wood stove kept them warm as they sorted mail into the pigeonhole boxes behind them. While the major occupation of the area was farming, many different jobs had to be filled to service the agriculture industry and also those who worked in it.

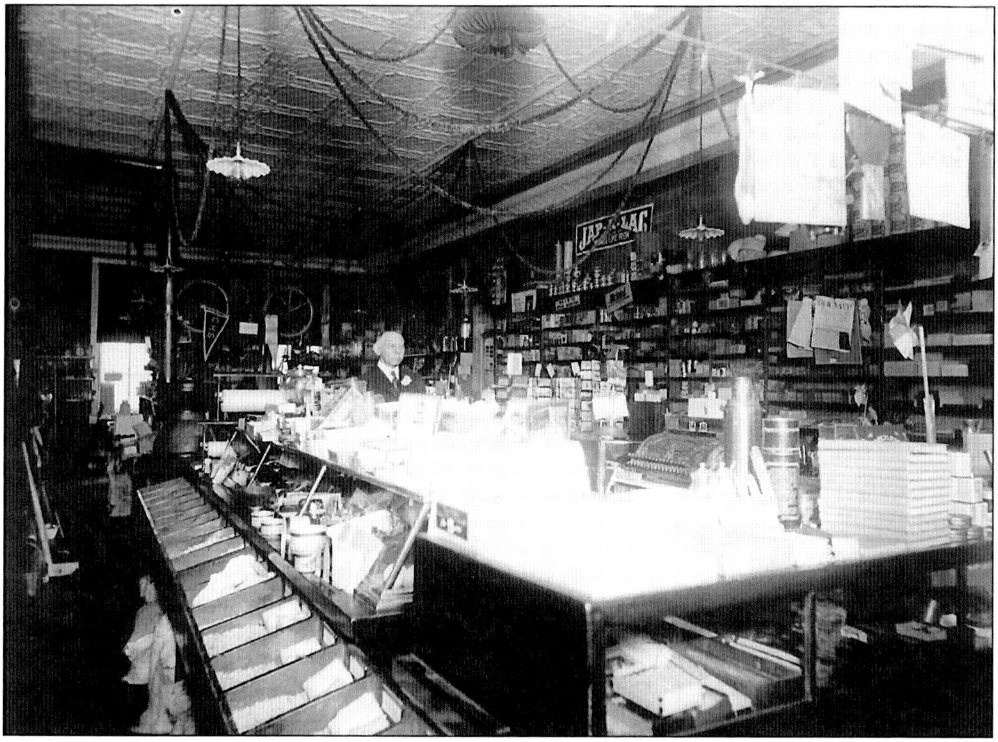

Clinton's Leonard Brewer Bellis and his son, John Young Bellis II, ran a variety store, judging from the items offered for sale. Note the pinwheel and stick candy in the foreground, the cigars under the counter, and the bicycle on the rear wall. (Clinton Historical Society photo.)

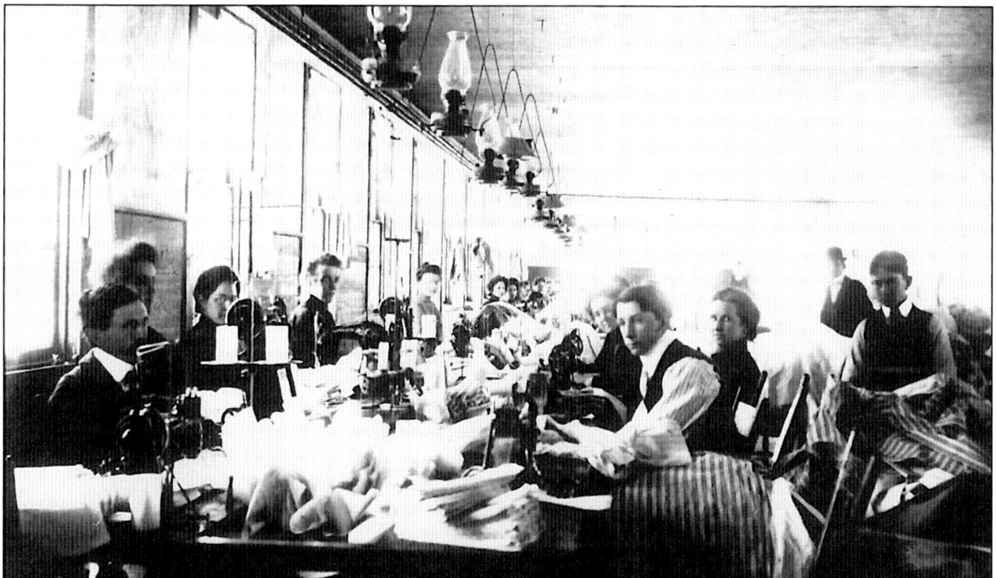

The Clinton Shirt Factory hired both men and women to work at its sewing machines. Elias Howe patented the first practical sewing machine in 1846, and the Singer Sewing Machine Company added electrical power in 1889. (Clinton Historical Society photo.)

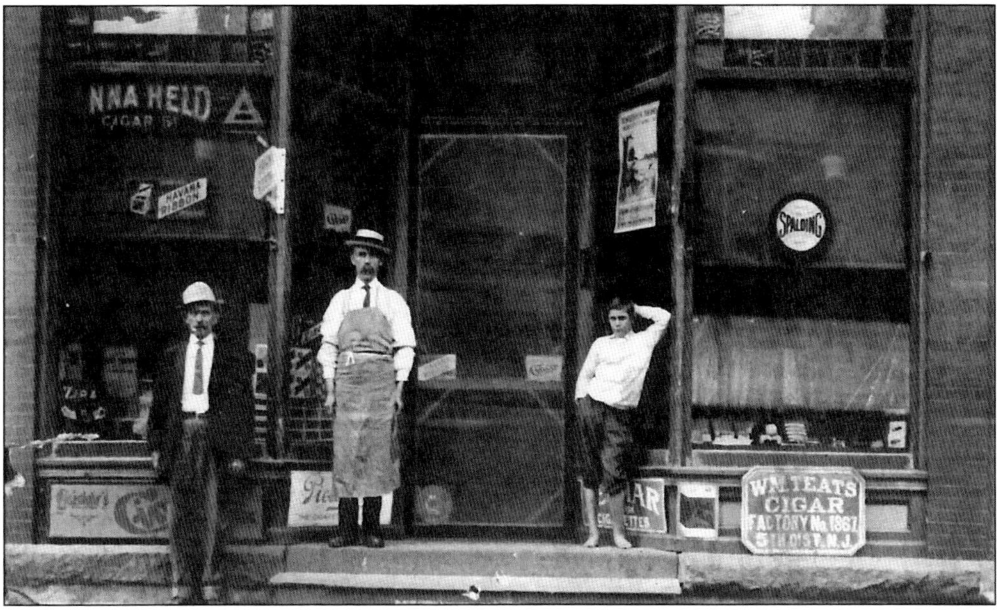

William Teats (in apron) owned the Clinton Cigar Store in the late 1900's. He also sold housewares, toiletries, and candy. Later he merged his business with that of the town's other cigar store owner, William Carey. (Clinton Historical Society photo.)

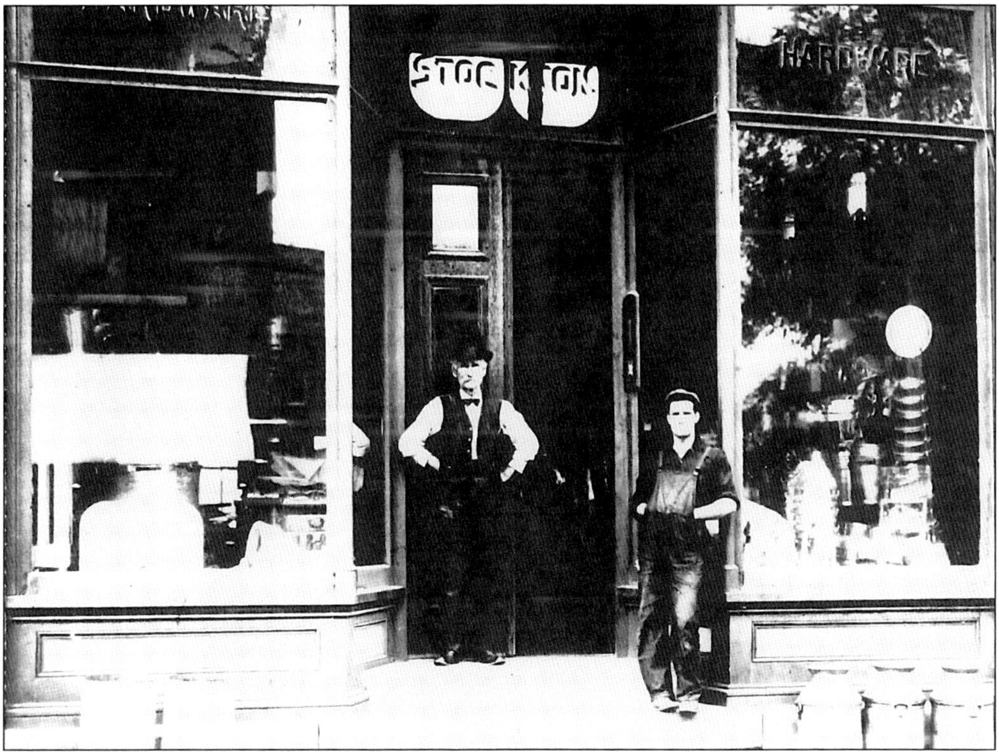

Stockton Hardware was two doors east of Teats' cigar store on Main Street in Clinton. Its owner sold goods to everyone from householders to plumbers and farmers; note the milk cans in the lower right-hand corner of the photograph. (Clinton Historical Society photo.)

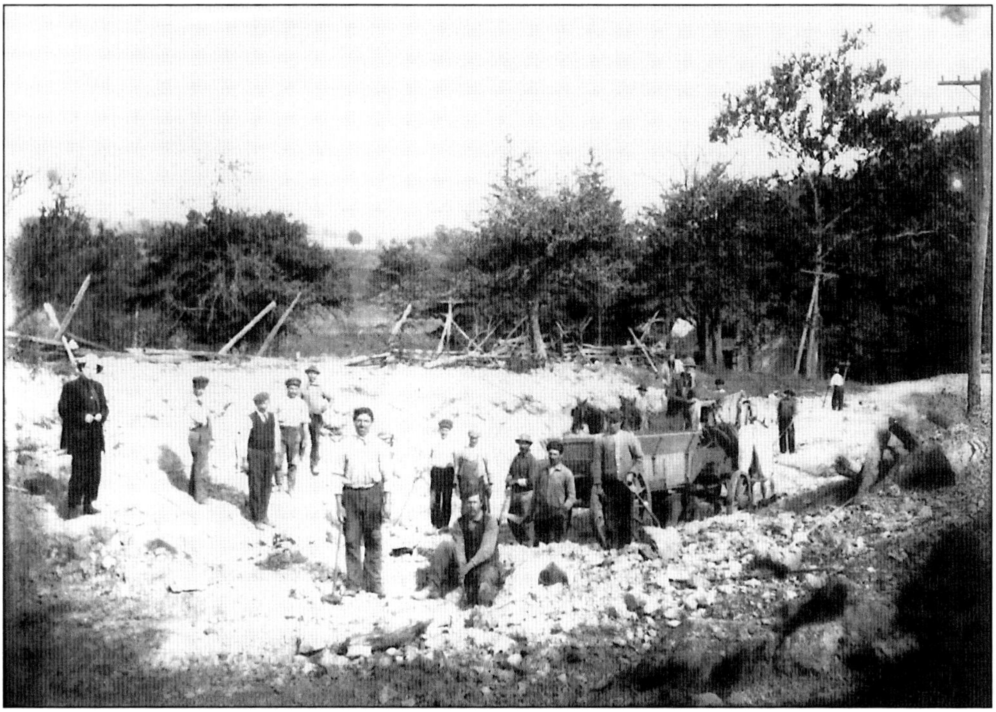

If you had just come to this country and needed a job, you could always work on the roads. Here a crew of Italian immigrants attacks the job of constructing a highway, possibly Pattenburg Turnpike, *c.*1910. (Clinton Historical Society photo.)

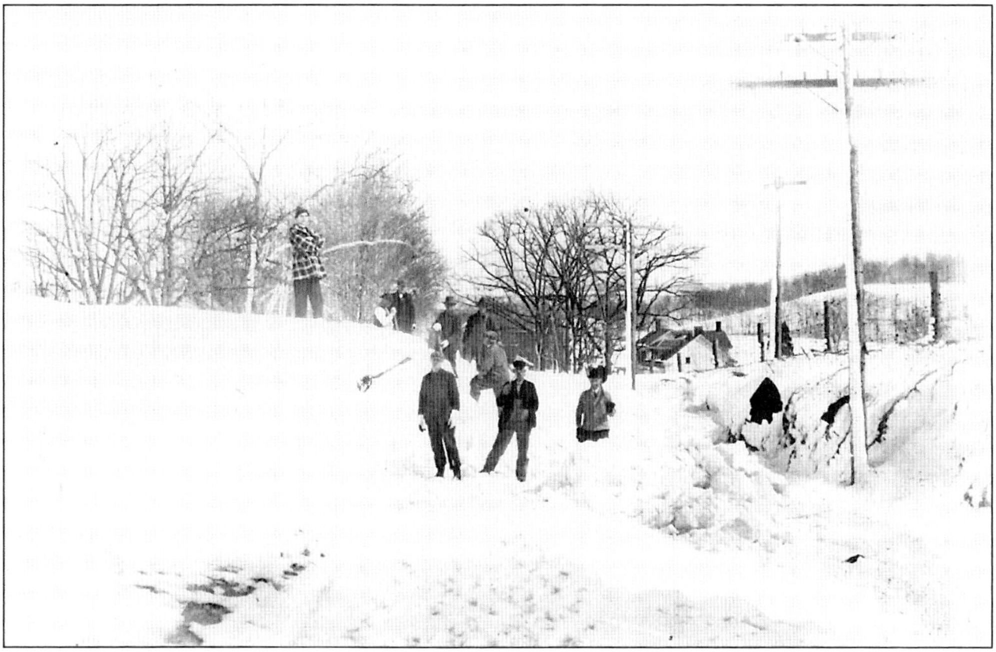

Everyone had to pitch in to clear the roads after a major blizzard. Here the road is Center Street, part of the old Easton-Brunswick Turnpike. In the background is the old Seale farm. (Clinton Historical Society photo.)

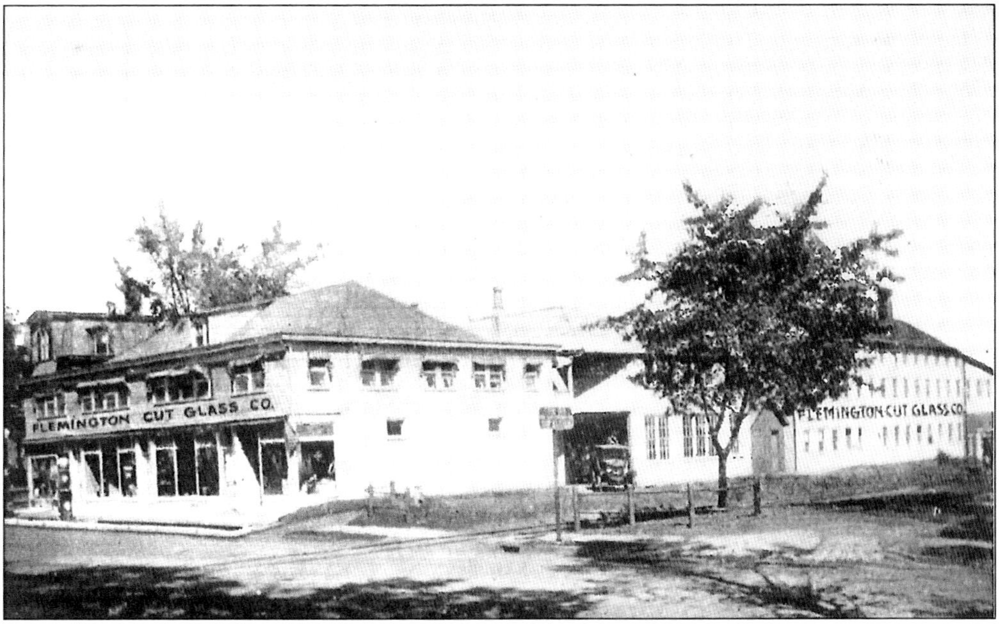

Lured by a $1,000 backing from the local board of trade in return for promising a $100 weekly payroll for four employees, Alphonse Muller and Charles McMullen opened Flemington Cut Glass in 1908. By 1987 eighty people were employed, and the payroll was $10,000 a week.

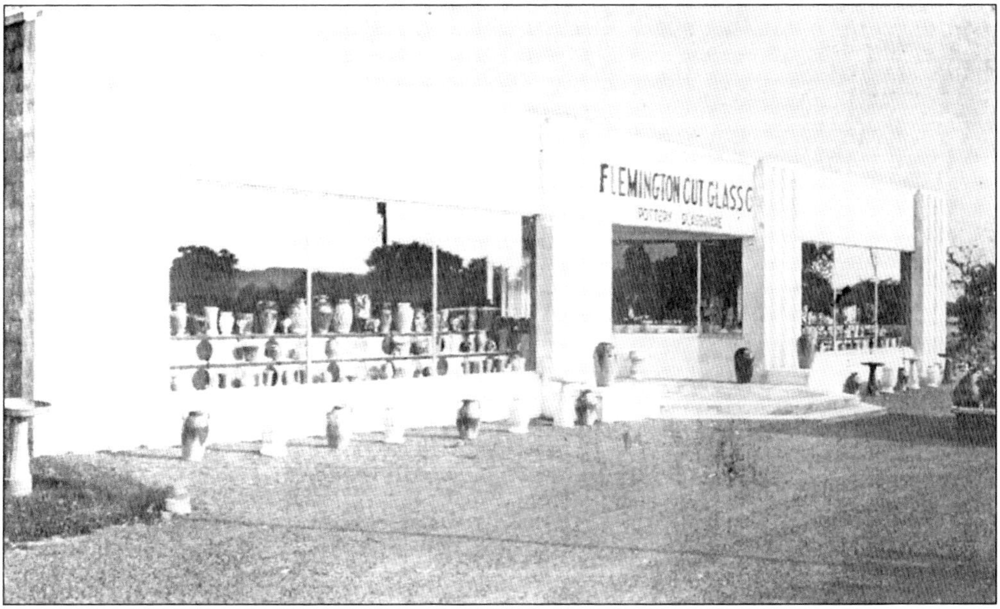

Part of the Flemington Cut Glass complex is its showroom. The company is one of the largest retail glass factories in the country. McMullen and Muller split up in 1940, Muller retaining the glass company and emphasizing its retail trade.

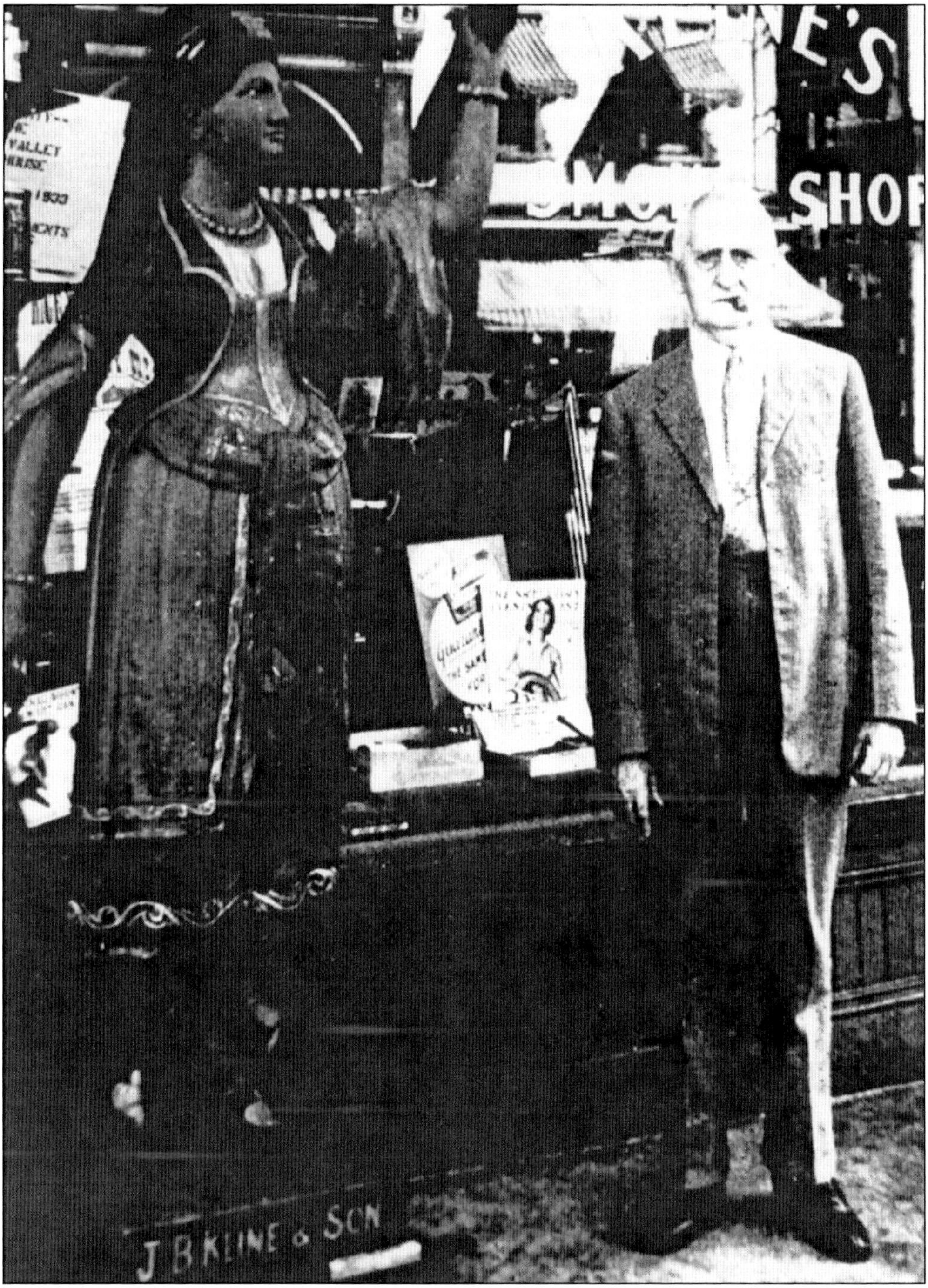

J.B. Kline of Lambertville imported this "cigar store Indian," called The Princess, from the Black Forest of Germany in 1888 to stand outside and attract customers to his Bridge Street store, the J.B. Kline & Son Smoke Shop. (Lambertville Historical Society photo.)

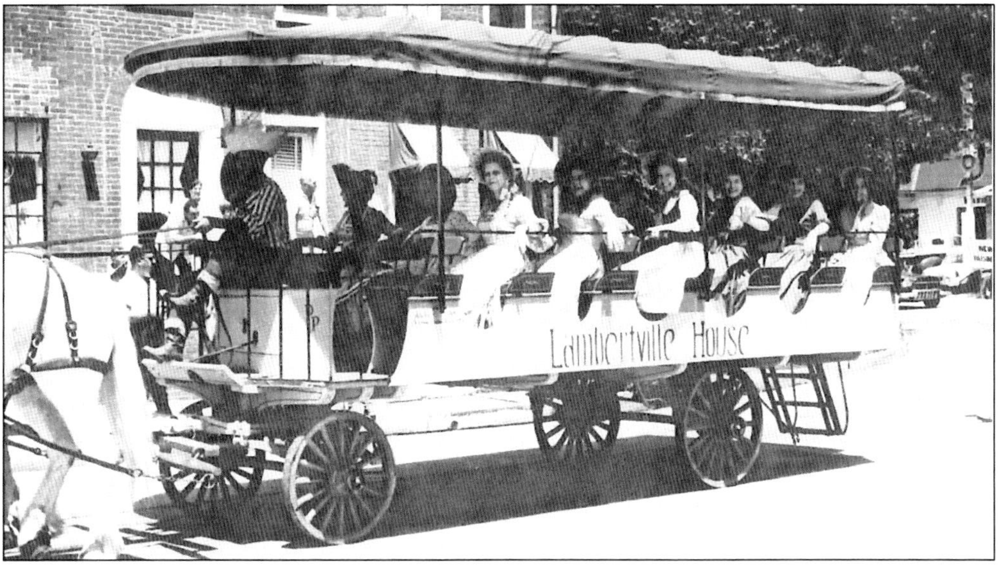

In August, 1849, waitresses of the Lambertville House restaurant got a break in their job routine when they rode in this horse-drawn trolley to advertise their employer in Lambertville's Centennial Parade. (Lambertville Historical Society photo.)

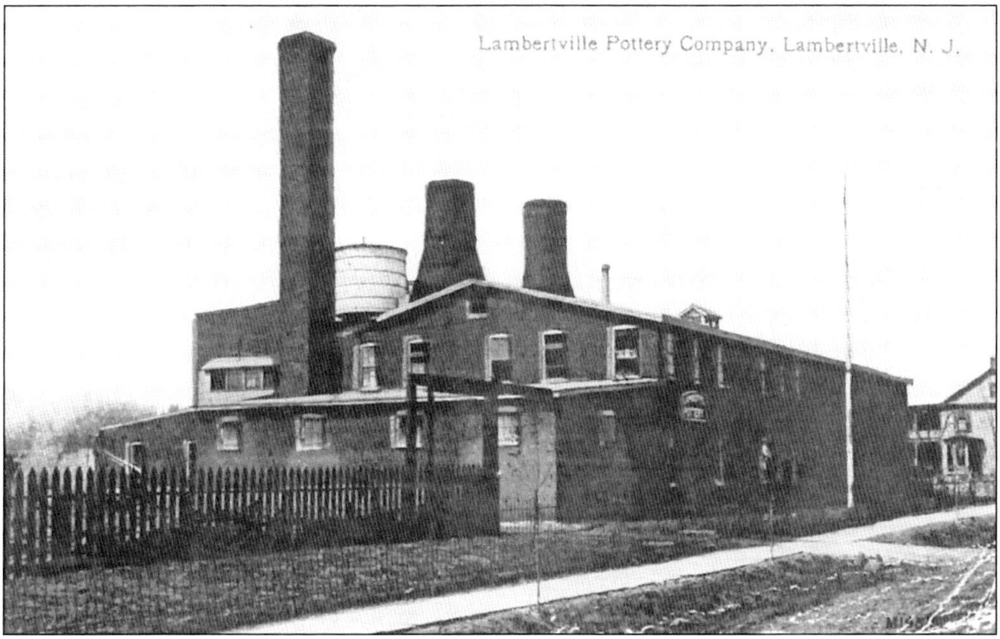

Its smokestacks a familiar sight on the horizon, Lambertville Pottery made toilets, tanks, and related porcelain and ceramic products from 1922 until the country's economic crash in 1929. (Lambertville Historical Society photo.)

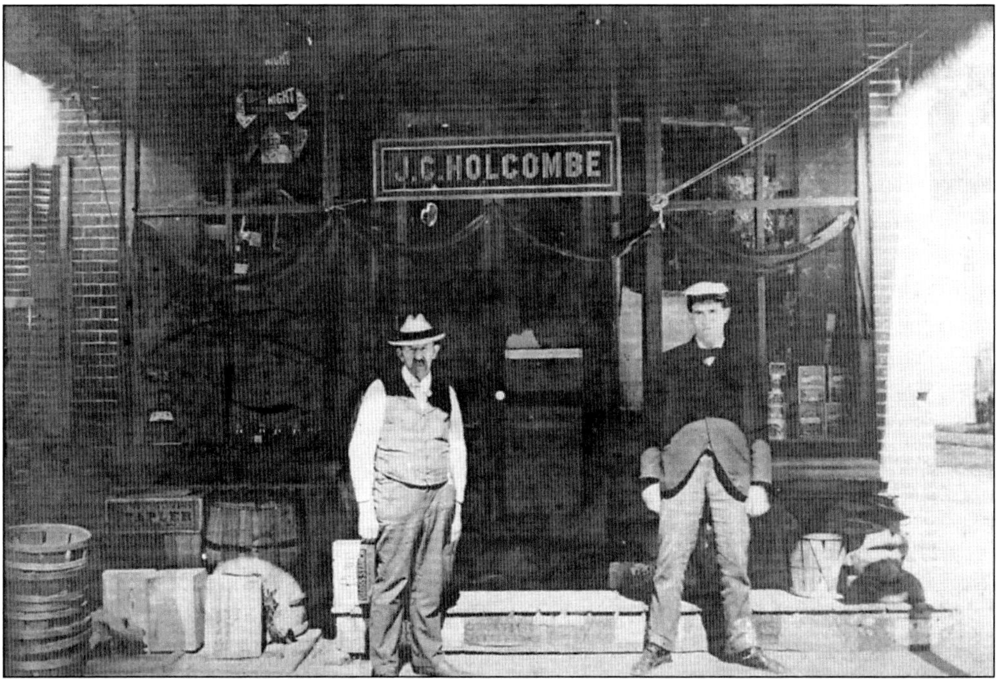

John C. Holcombe and his son, Frank, ran a general store on North Union Street at the turn of the century. It was an earlier John Holcombe who, soon after 1707, was one of the area's first settlers. (Lambertville Historical Society photo.)

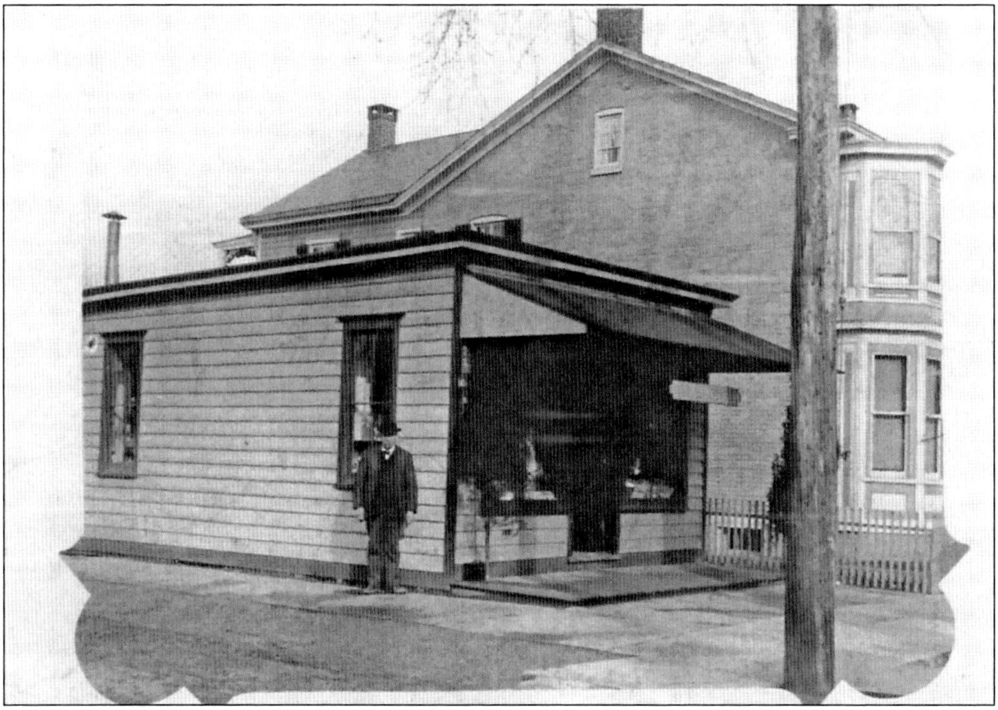

Another Holcombe, named Johan, ran a store at the corner of Perry and George Streets in Lambertville. (Lambertville Historical Society photo.)

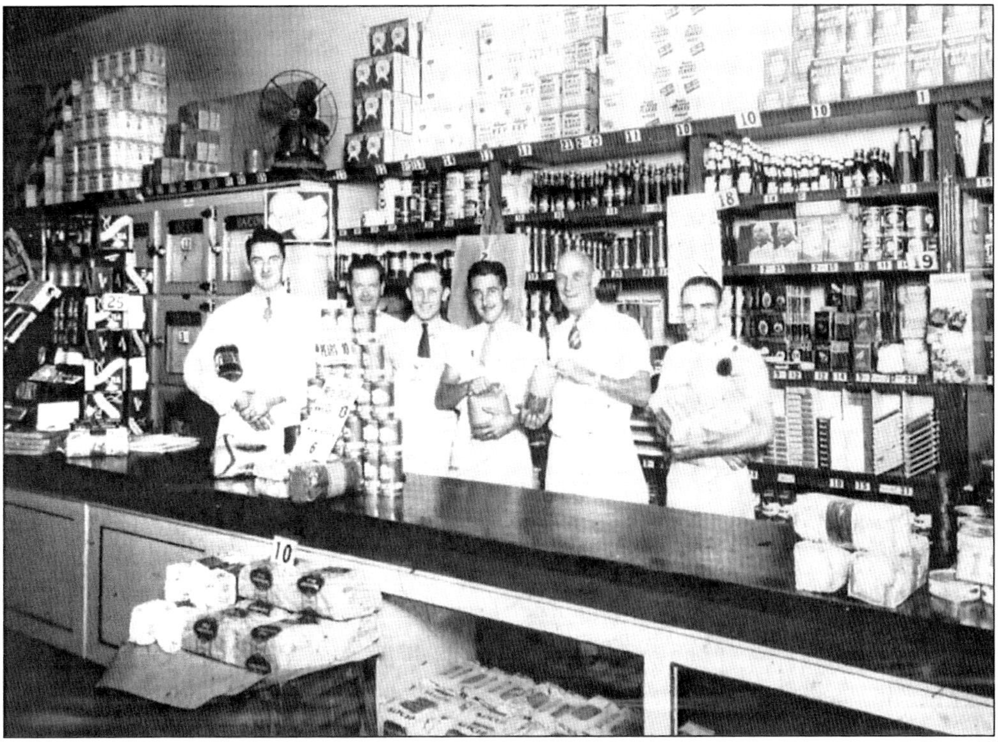

In later times, Ray Wilson (second from right) managed an A & P grocery store at Bridge and Union Streets. Clerks included: (from left) unknown, Ed Reardon, unknown, Ray Skillman, Ray Wilson, and Shorty Musselman. (Lambertville Historical Society photo.)

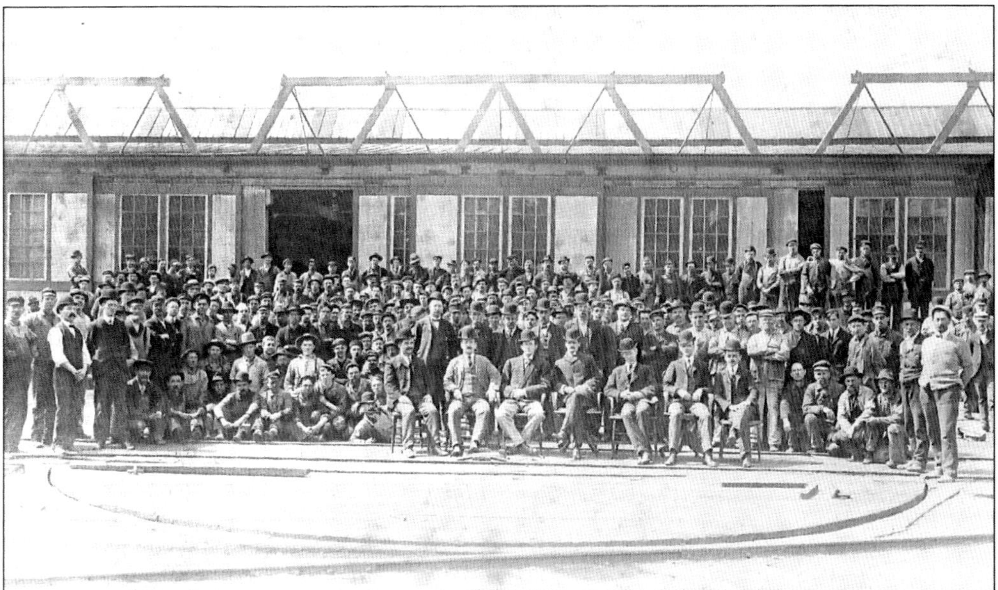

One of the biggest employers in Lambertville was the Belvidere-Delaware Railroad. The Pennsylvania Railroad took over the Belvidere-Delaware line in 1871, about the time this roundhouse picture was taken. (Lambertville Historical Society photo.)

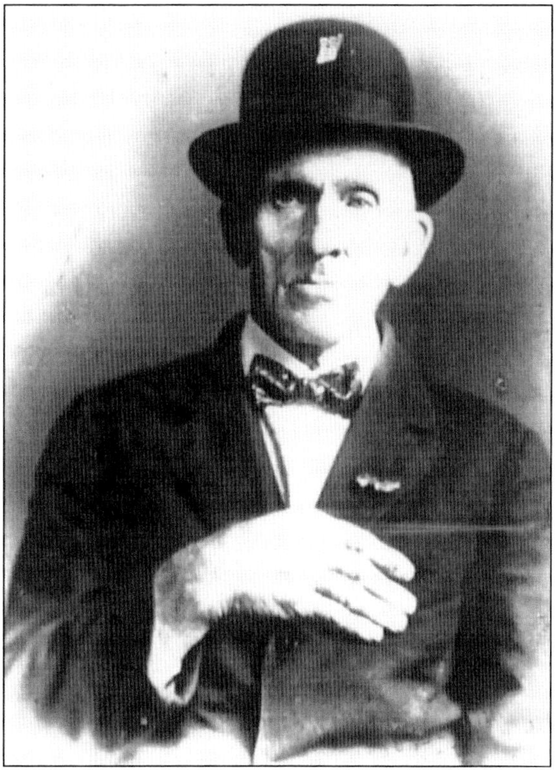

Frederick Philhower, a descendent of the early settler, Philip Philhower, made his mark in Hunterdon County by building handsome stone bridges over creeks throughout the countryside. (Donald Freiberg collection.)

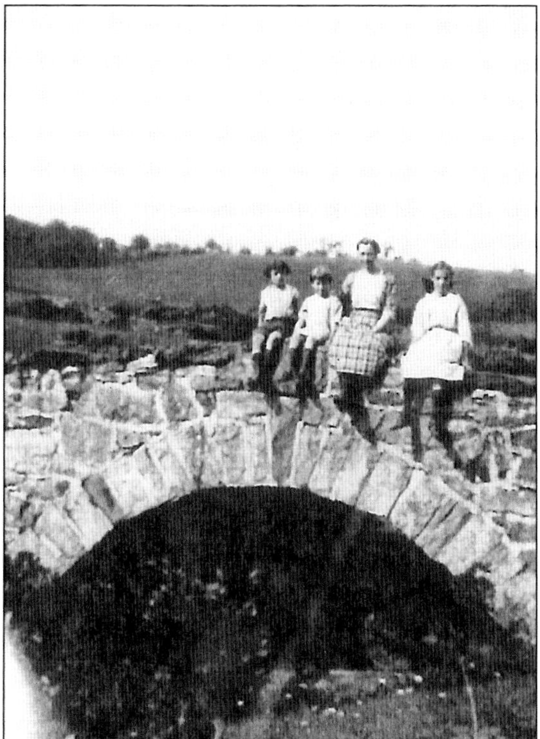

One of Frederick Philhower's bridges spans a creek on Longview Road, close to the homestead Philip Philhower established in 1760. The tall girl (second from right) is also a Philhower. (Donald Freiberg collection.)

Eight

HAVING FUN

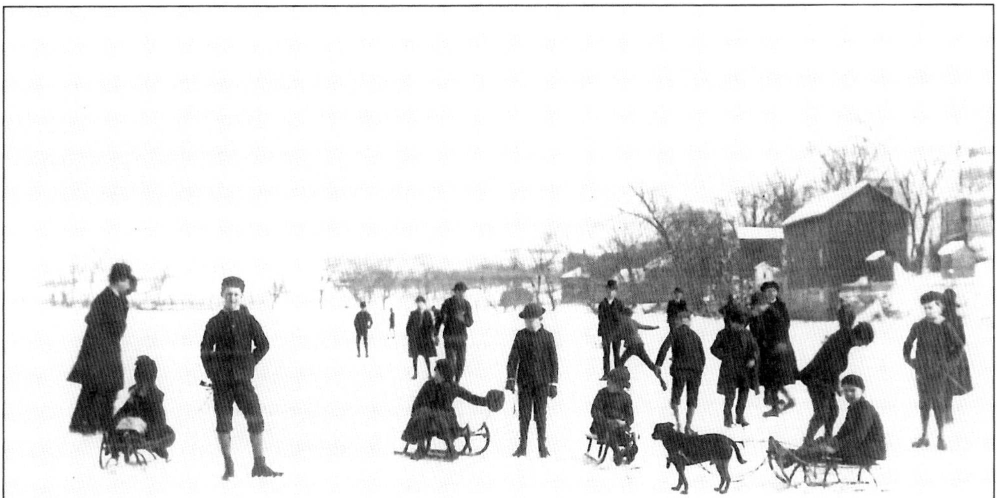

In the aptly named "Gay Nineties," having fun after your work was done was a major goal in American life, and the people of Hunterdon County were no slouches. Collections of old photographs record many instances of fun times, from camp-outs to crazy parades. On a bright winter day, a favorite activity along the South Branch of the Raritan was playing on the ice, on skates or sleds. Clinton residents—including the dog pulling the sled at right—gamboled on the ice in front of the carriage sheds and privies of Center Street's elegant homes. (Clinton Historical Society photo.)

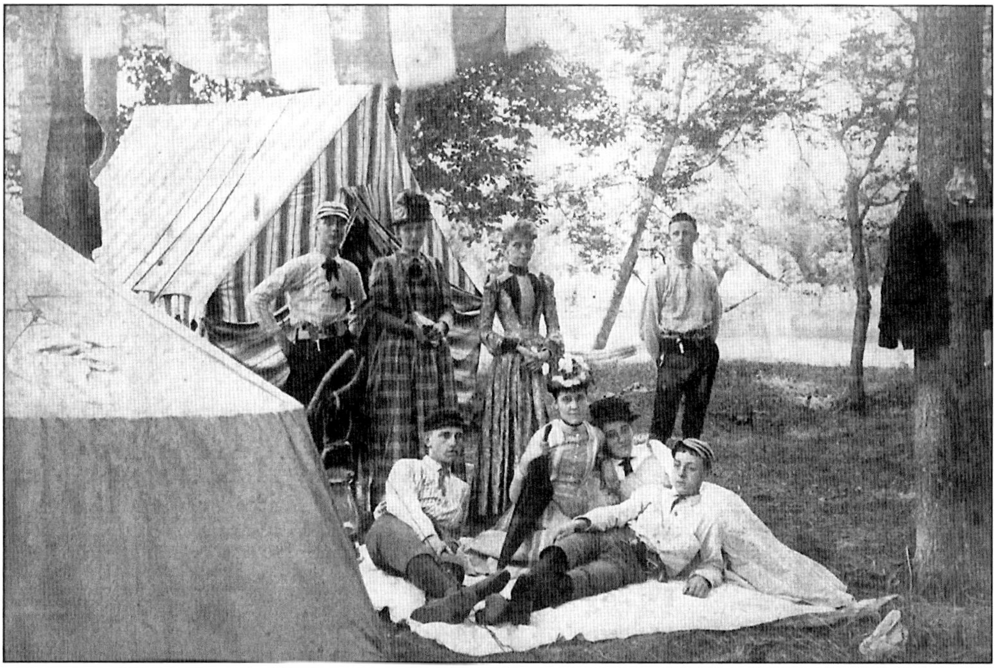

Helen Bonnell Bellis (first girl standing at left) and her friends could have been camping out in a Clinton backyard or at a New Jersey or Pennsylvania resort area. Wherever it was, you can be sure they were chaperoned. (Clinton Historical Society photo.)

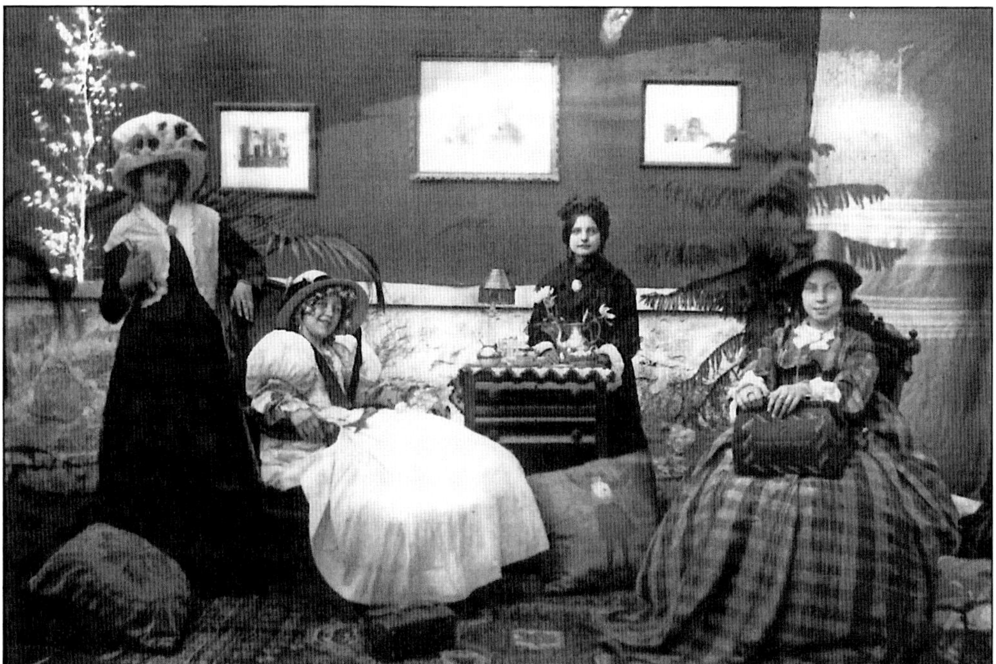

"Putting on a show" was always fun, for children and grownups alike, whether in a local hall, a parlor, or in somebody's backyard with a blanket on a clothesline for a stage curtain. (Clinton Historical Society photo.)

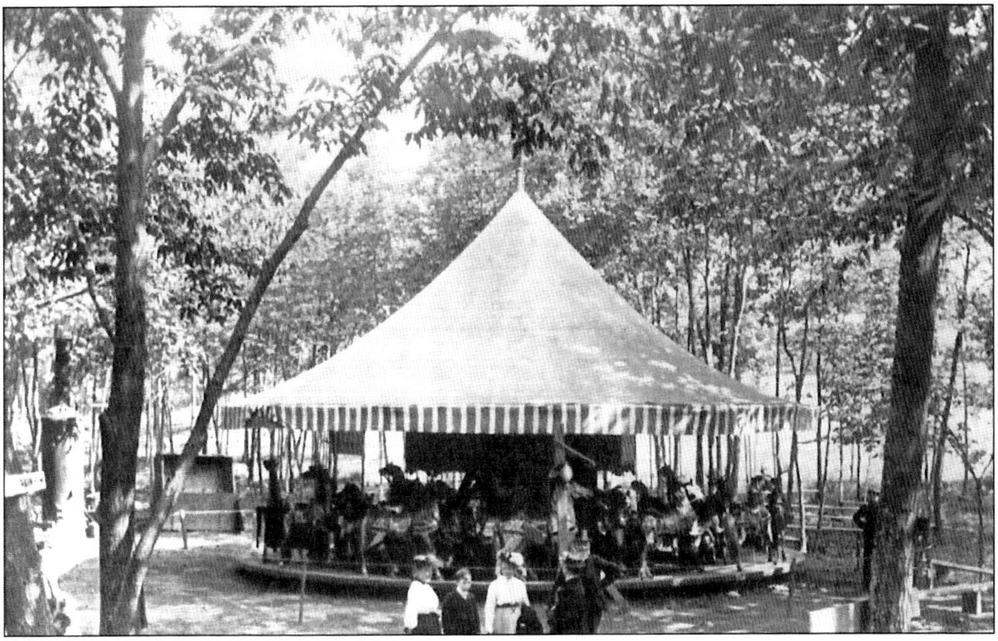

A ride on the "full menagerie" carousel at Bellewood Park, Pattenburg, was a treat for Clinton youngsters. Bellewood was built by the Lehigh Valley Railroad partly as a goodwill gesture to area farmers whose land it intruded and partly as a profitable excursion train stop. (Clinton Historical Society photo.)

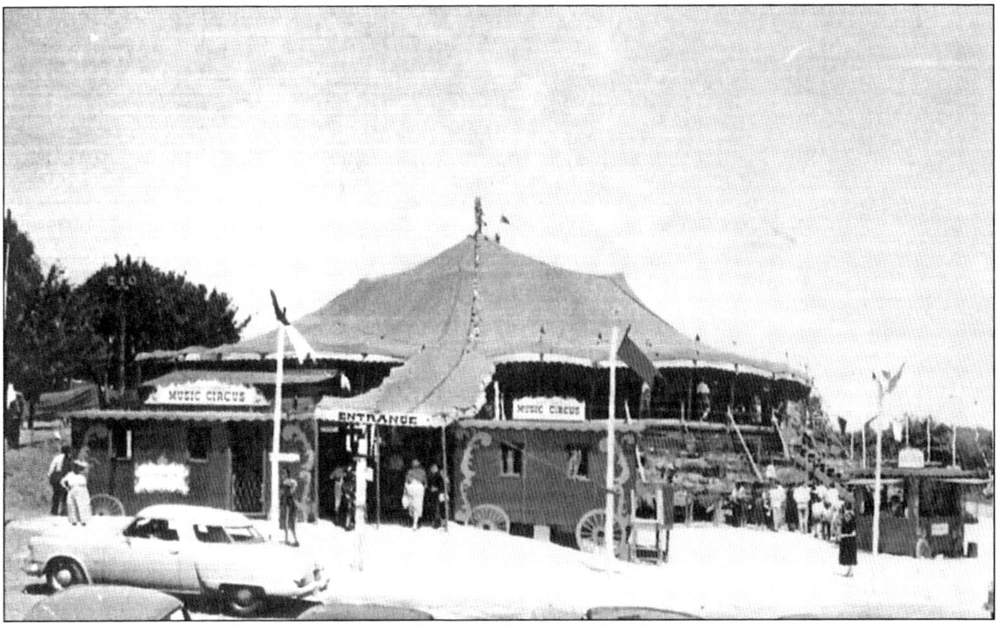

An outing for Lambertville families was to St. John Terrell's Music Circus atop Music Mountain. The music circus was the country's first tent theater, where operettas and musical comedies were presented on summer evenings. (Lambertville Historical Society photo.)

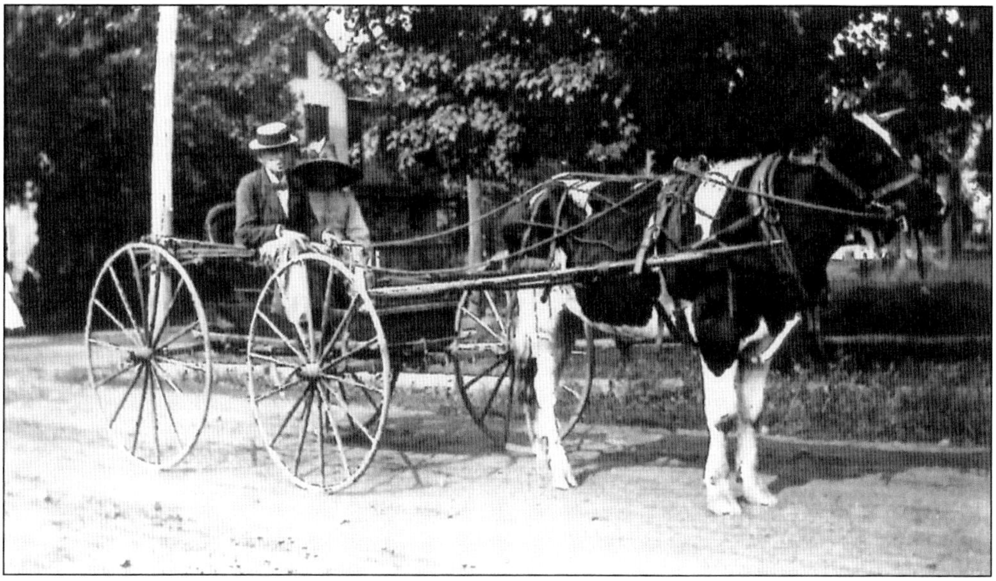

A "crazy parade" was a part of the Flemington Firemen's Carnival the year this buggy driver replaced his horse with a steer. The annual carnival was a big event in Flemington (see Section 12.)

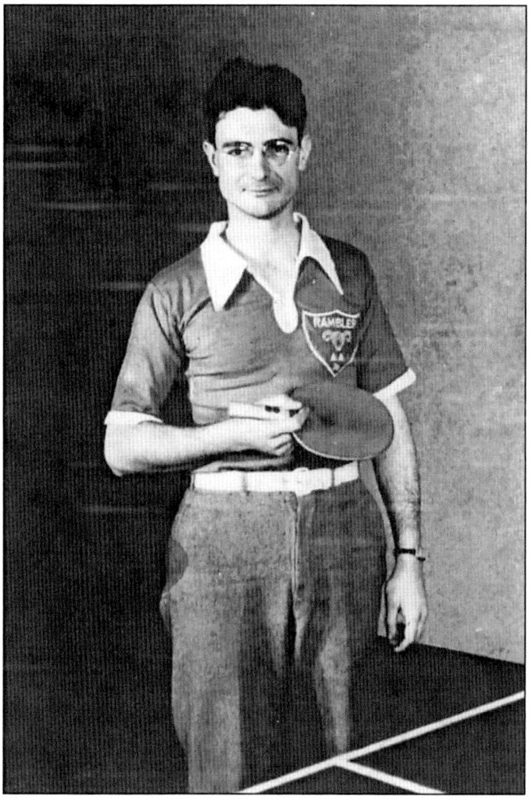

Of course sports were always part of the fun. Francis Monteverde's sport was table tennis. He was a Lambertville champion in 1919. (Lambertville Historical Society photo.)

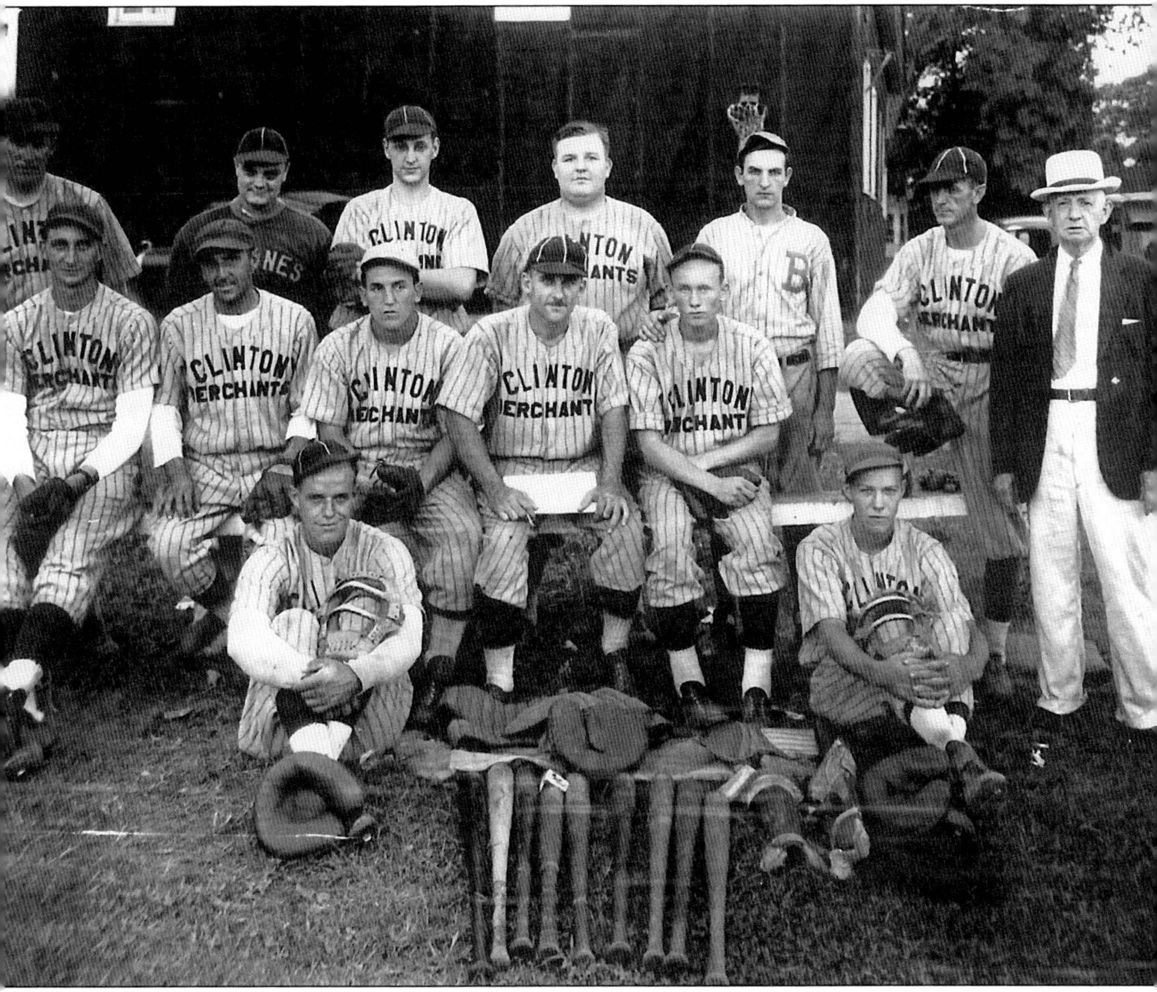

Baseball was a summertime game in the United States not so long ago. The Clinton Merchants' team from the 1930s included: (back row, from left) John Lea, Paul Lance, Frank Cramer, Ed Smith, unknown, Les Kershaw, Jim Trewin; (bench) Jack Ramsey, unknown, Joe Dughi, unknown, Joe Kephart; (front) Jim Bell and Harry Fields. Trewin was probably the manager. The whole town would come out to see the team play. (Clinton Historical Society photo.)

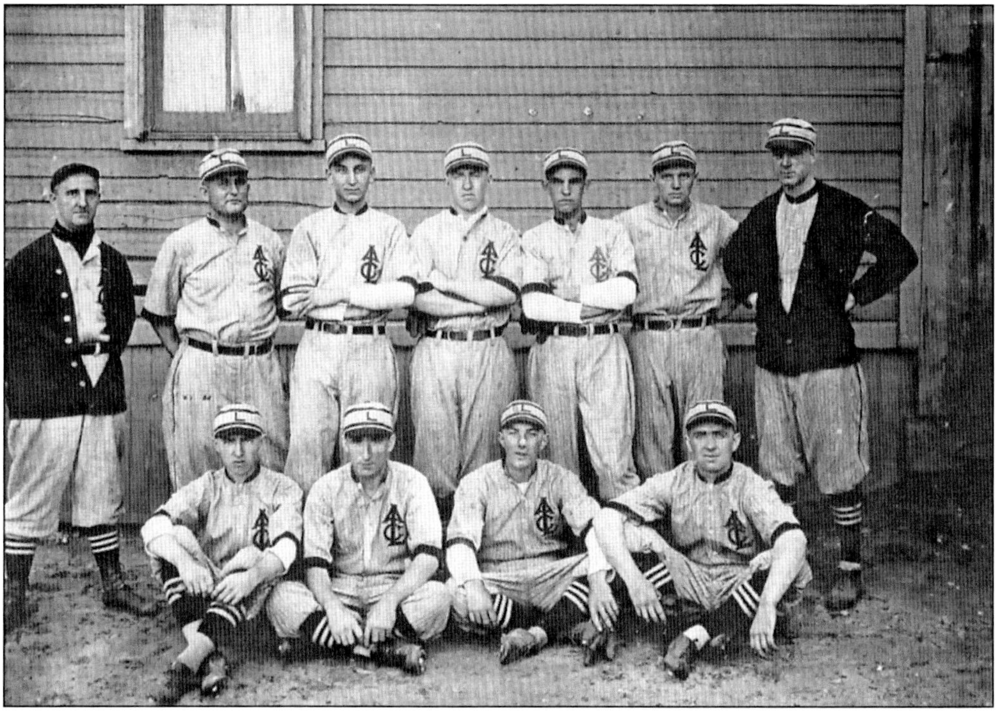

A popular Lambertville baseball team in the summer of 1917 was the Men's Athletic Club, flanked here by its two managers. (Lambertville Historical Society photo.)

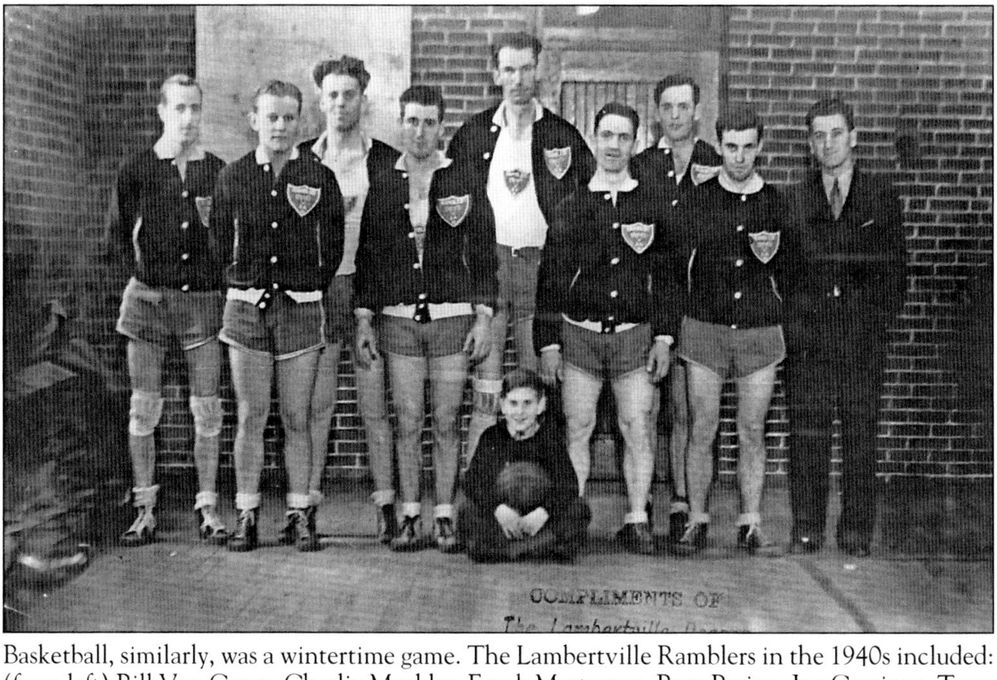

Basketball, similarly, was a wintertime game. The Lambertville Ramblers in the 1940s included: (from left) Bill Van Camp, Charlie Mackler, Frank Masterson, Russ Perine, Joe Corrigan, Tony DeVitt, Johnny Lake, Vincent Kelty and Lou Welsh. Their mascot held the ball. (Lambertville Historical Society photo.)

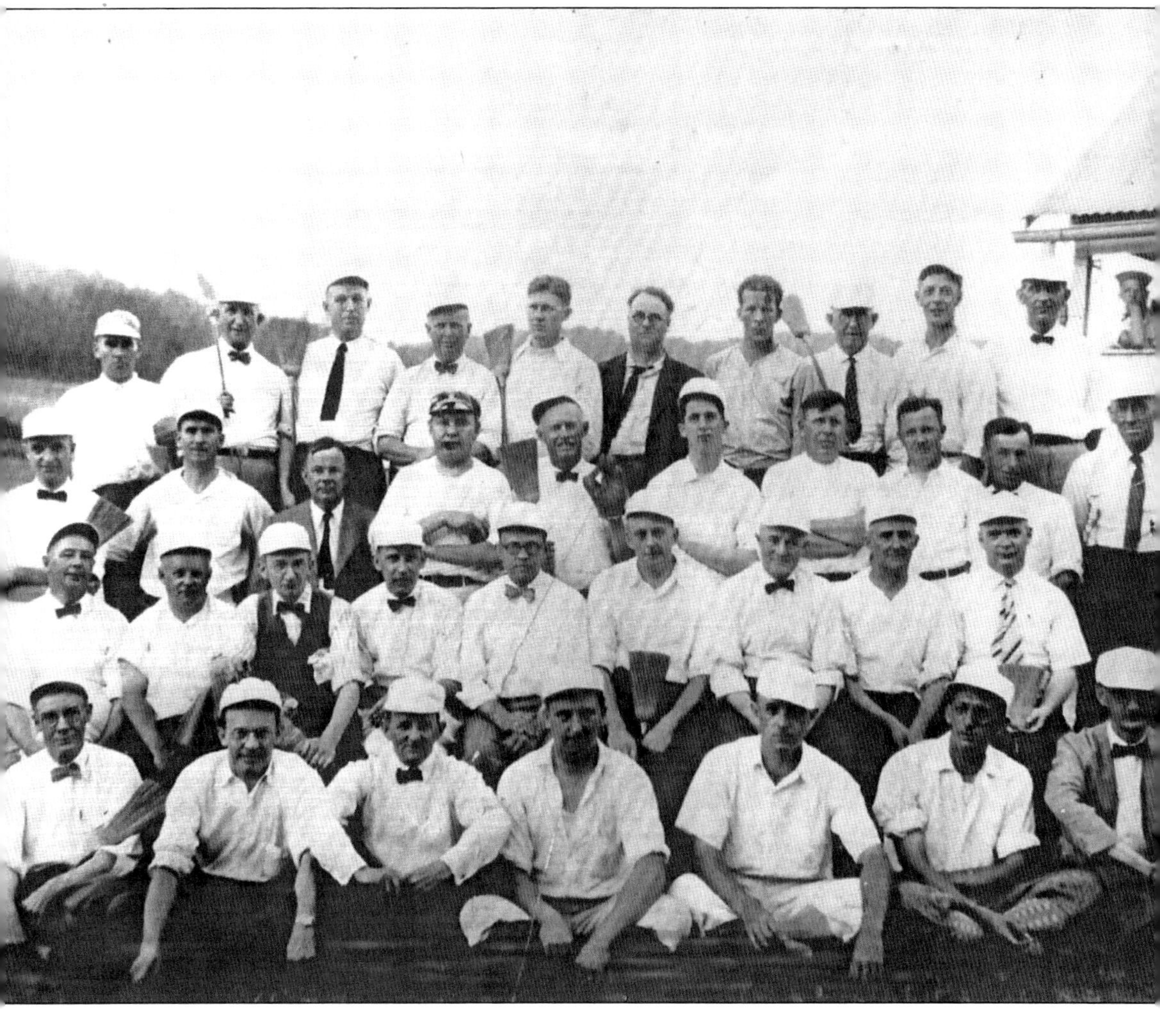

A Lambertville Kiwanis and Rotary Club outing at Raven Rock, NJ in 1927 included: (back row, from left) Vincent Smith, Hervey Holcombe, Gus Brown, Ed Moonan, John Allen, Ben Turner, Watson Janney, Wimmiam Hambleton, George Larison, Walter Reif; (second row) Clarence Lugar, Albert Mathews, James Whiteley, Ralph Rinck, J.P. Borden, John Hazen, Joseph Smith, C.E. Wagg, George Whitney, Harry Worthington; (third row) Byron Wollaston, F.R. Whiteley, Thomas Walker, Andrew Holcombe, Morris Mackler, L.R. Stout, Harry Van Horn, George Kline, Samuel Whitely; (front) Charles Dilts, Thomas Kilroy, William Kachline, Bradley Sine, Frank Kramer, Charles McCracken and Neilson Rittenhouse. (Lambertville Historical Society photo.)

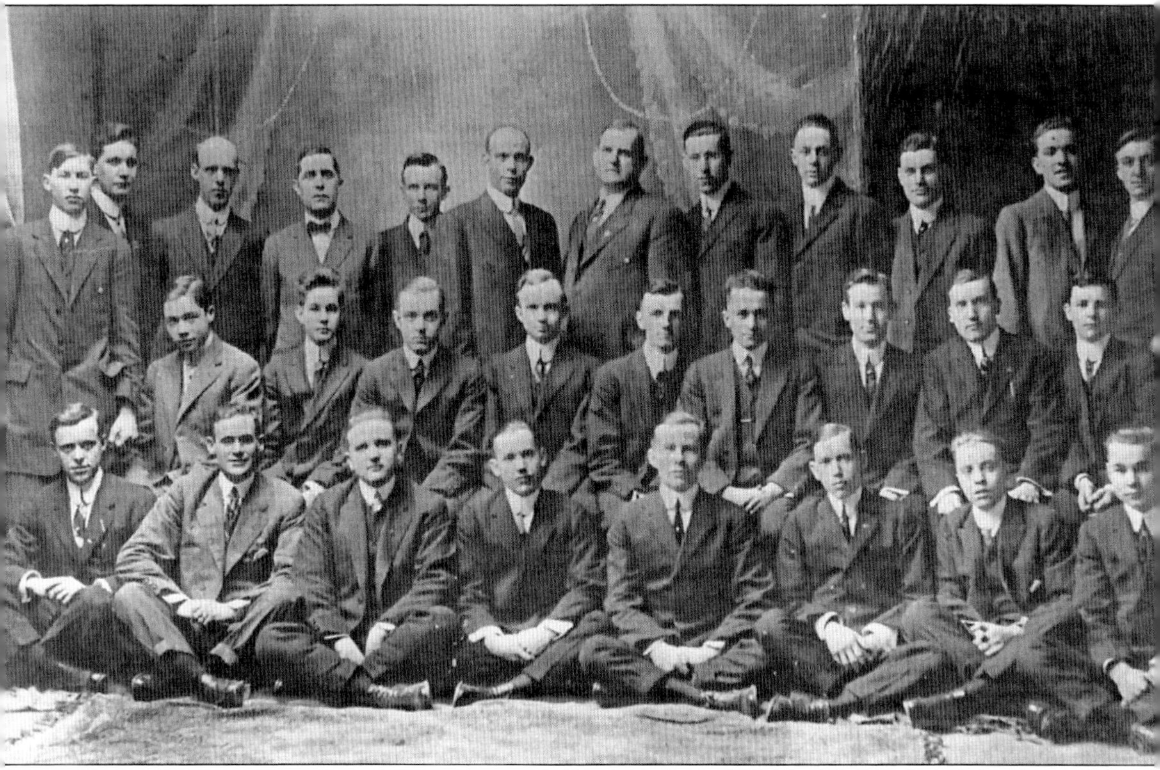

The Lambertville Old Reliance Men's Club met at 8 Bridge Street in 1910. Included were: (back row, from left) Leon Abbott, Bill Bacorn, Frank Bailey, John Dilley, Arthur Miller, Dory Skillman, John Johnson, Harold Dilley, Carlon Hooker, Welland Thorn, Earl Barcroft, Zeke Van Camp, Albert Mathews; (center row) Tony Thorn, Joe Stockton, Frank Kramer, Egbert Price, Bill Wilmot, Don Park, Bill Calloway, Jack Butler, George Zigler, Frank Walton; (front) Welland Reading, Steve Brady, John Ennis, Herbert Holcombe, Andrew Black, Jake Holcombe, Fred Lugar and John Stockton. (Lambertville Historical Society photo.)

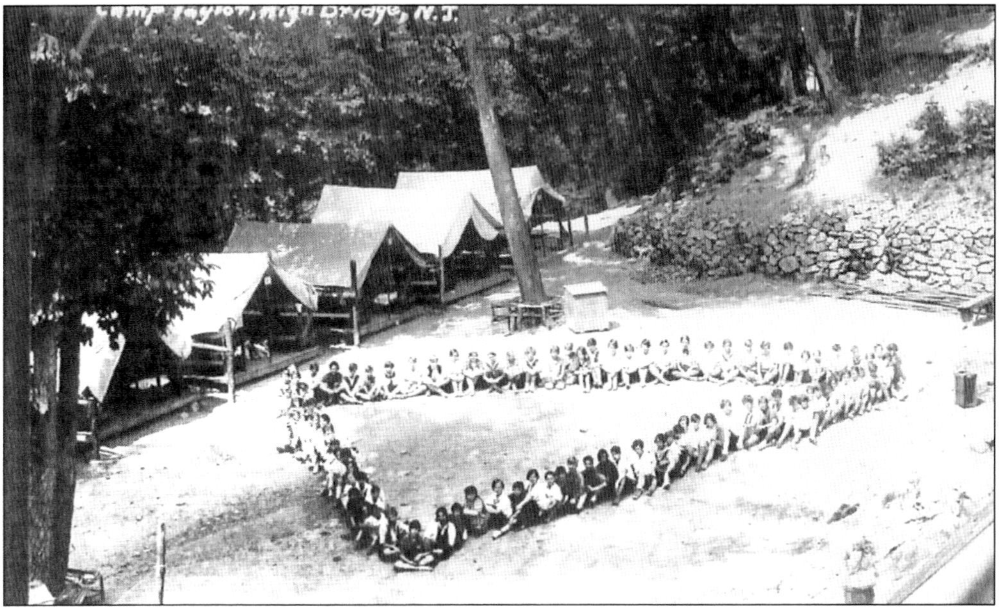

When they weren't picnicking with friends, boating on Hunterdon's rivers, or going on family vacations in summer, the girls of Tewksbury and Clinton could attend YWCA Camp Taylor outside the nearby village of High Bridge.

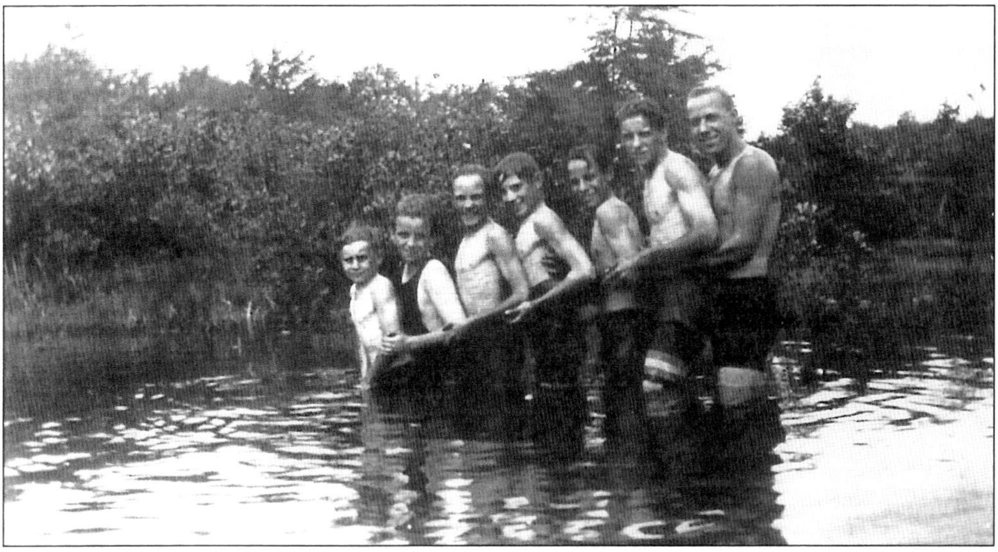

Boys and men swimming in the Philhower farm's creek in Tewksbury Township were horsing around when they decided to form a "chorus line" in the stream. (Donald Freiberg collection.)

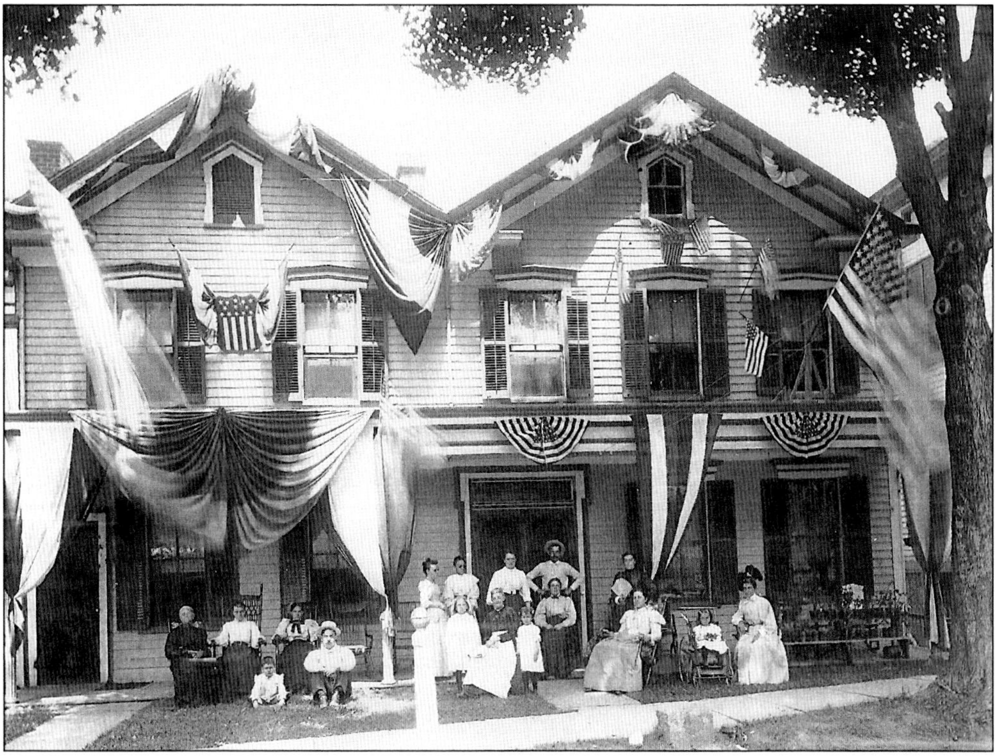

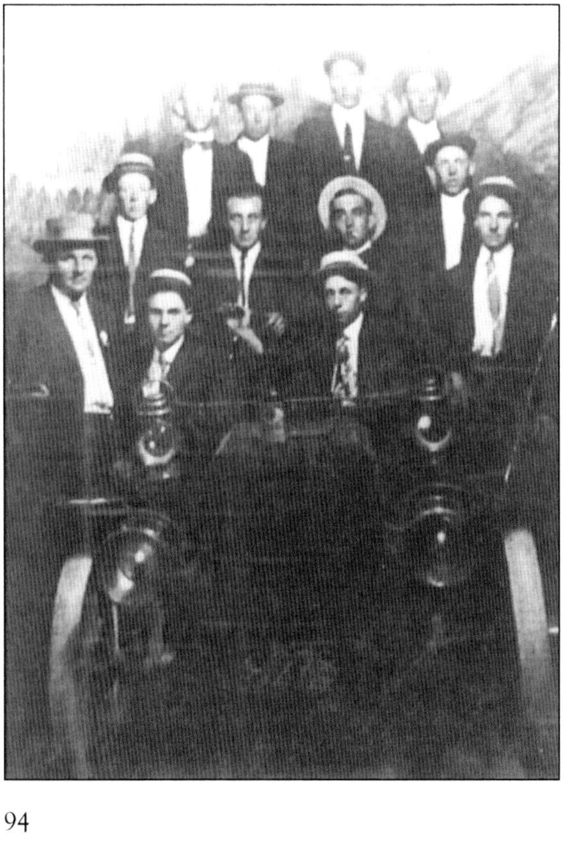

Oldwick relatives gathered at this Center Street home in Clinton to watch a parade. Residents didn't stint on decorations on such an occasion. The child in the wheelchair, blind from birth, could only hear the festivities.

Arnold Philhower, Donald Freiberg's grandfather, is second from left in front of the group who swarmed over this car. Freiberg, recently married, had bought the Philhower homestead to live in. (Donald Freiberg collection.)

Nine

Styles of the Times

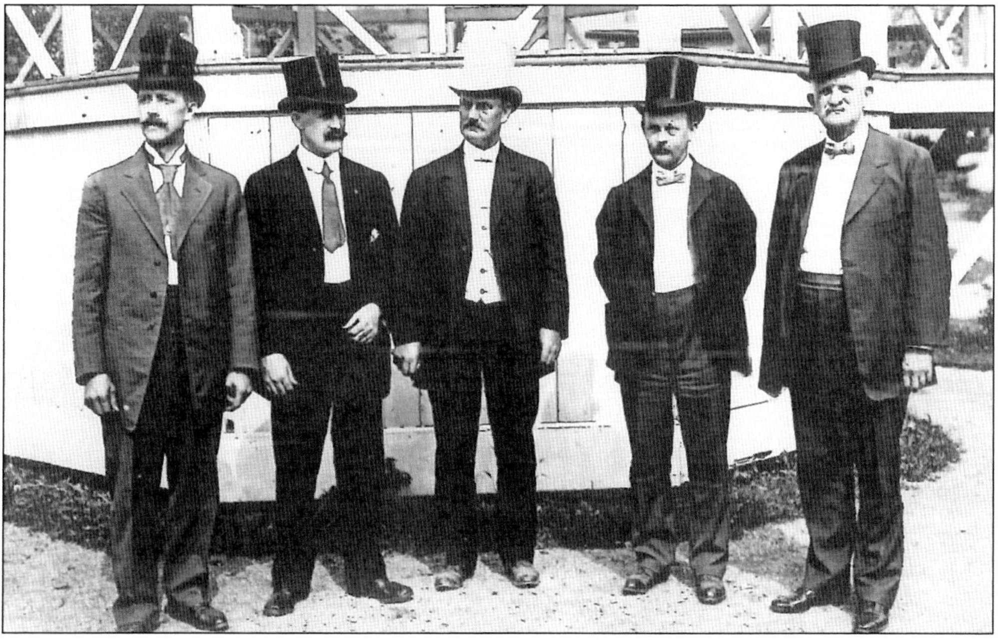

Hunterdon County styles were always changing—women's skirts were lowered and raised; men wore beards and mustaches for a while and then went about clean-shaven; even children's clothes varied from decade to decade. It is amusing to look back upon the clothes and hairstyles of former times, if only to be happy that we today are not expected to cope with such things as wasp-waist corsets and wind-blown top hats. The top hats do add a touch of savoir-faire to these members of Flemington's first borough council in 1910: (from left) John Kunsman, William E. Corcoran, Mayor A.C. Hulsizer, Charles V. Weiler, and Daniel McPherson.

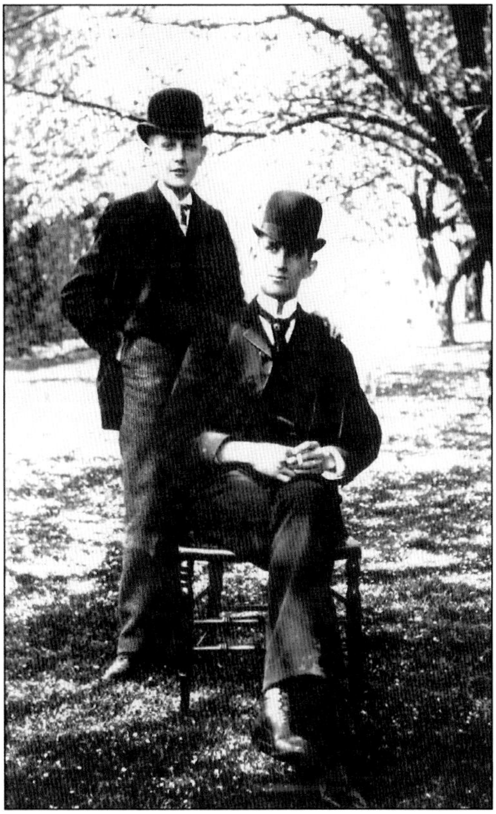

Bowlerhats gave a distinguished look to this father and son pair, believed to be Bloomfield Van Syckel Leigh Sr. and Jr. Leigh Jr. later moved to the West Orange, NJ area, and with him the last of the Leighs in Clinton. (Clinton Historical Society photo.)

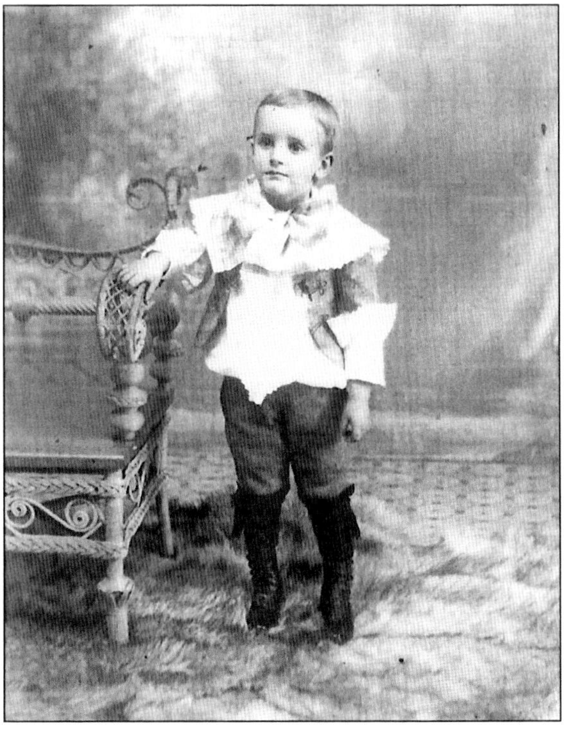

Elegance was not confined to the adult population at the turn of the century, as this young man in his first Lord Fauntleroy suit shows. (Clinton Historical Society photo.)

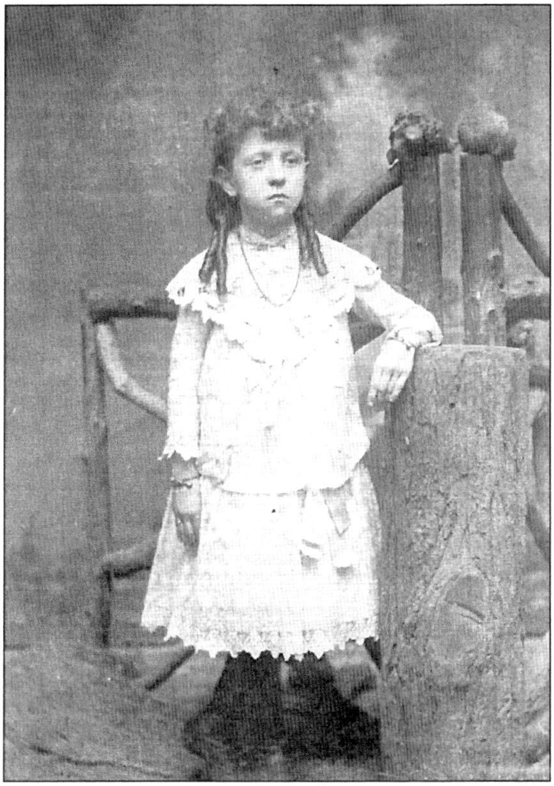

Ribbons and lace adorned this young miss's white party dress. Corkscrew curls and a bead necklace completed the turn-of-the-century look for little girls. (Clinton Historical Society photo.).

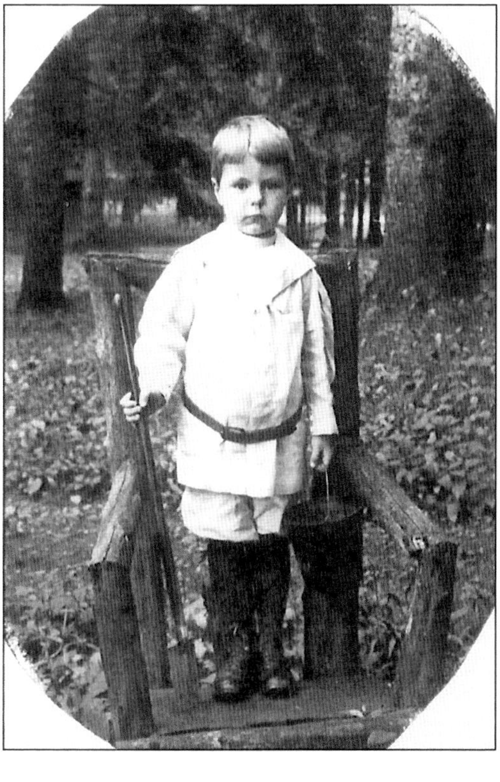

A sailor suit was part of every well-dressed young boy's wardrobe, along with black stockings and copper-toed boots. Note this boy's pail and shovel. (Clinton Historical Society photo.)

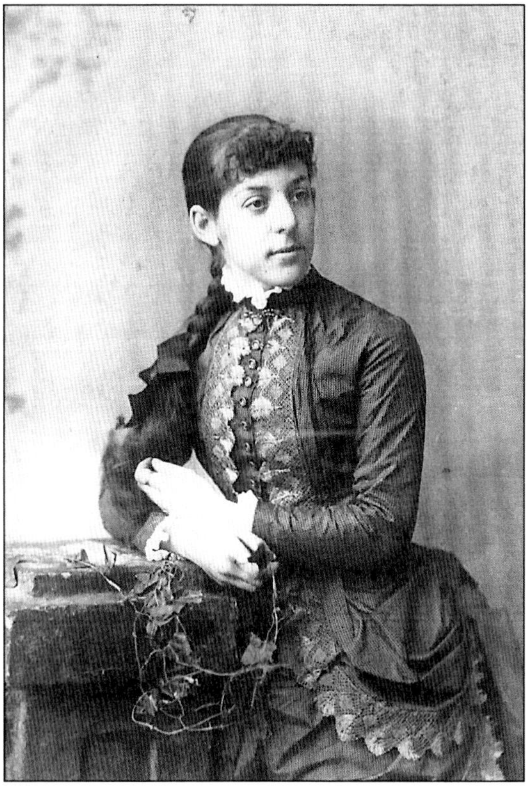

This young lady of Oldwick is holding her hat in her hand to show off her fringe of bangs. Her braid-trimmed dress was very fashionable.

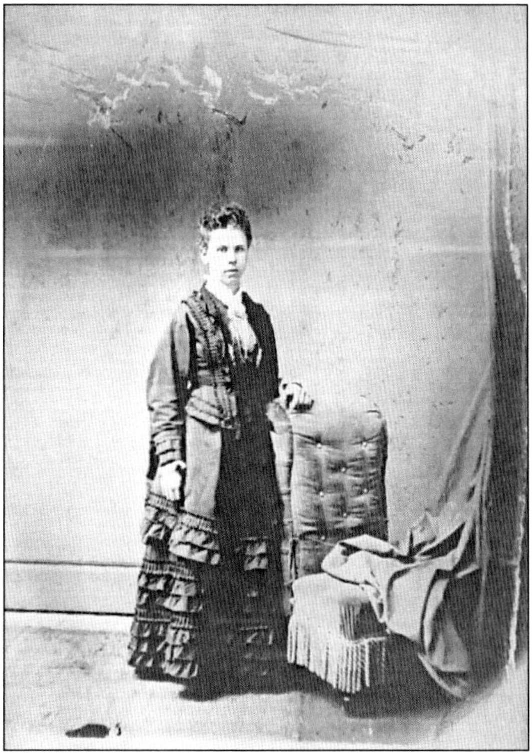

A dress much decorated with layered tucks and ruffles reliably provided feminine elegance at the turn of the century in Lambertville as elsewhere in the country.

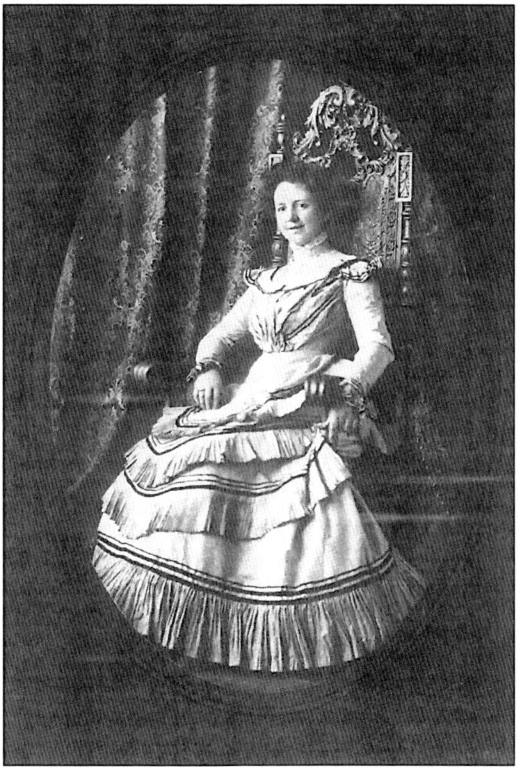

Mrs. Alexander Probasco (Ella Hall) of Clinton looked lovely in her white ruffled party dress. Born in 1848, she died in 1890. (Clinton Historical Society photo.)

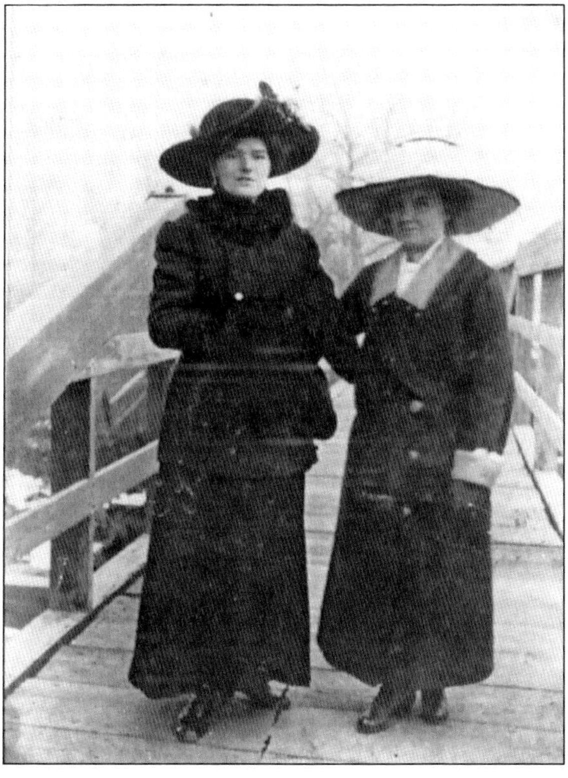

Wasp waists and bustles had given way to loose comfort by 1917 when Mrs. Alice Narducci (left), founder of the Lambertville Historical Society, strolled with Mrs. Alice Leary along the canal. (Lambertville Historical Society photo.)

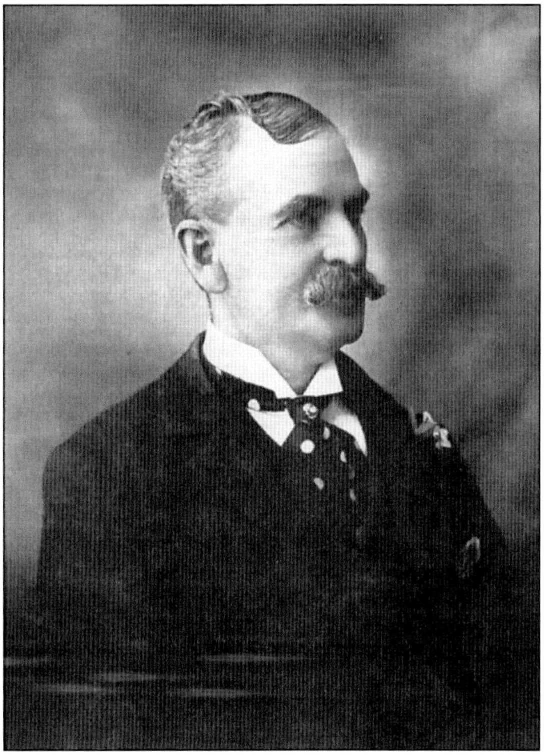

Alexander Probasco, Ella's husband, had a fine flowing mustache, if thinning hair, when this portrait was made. (Clinton Historical Society photo.)

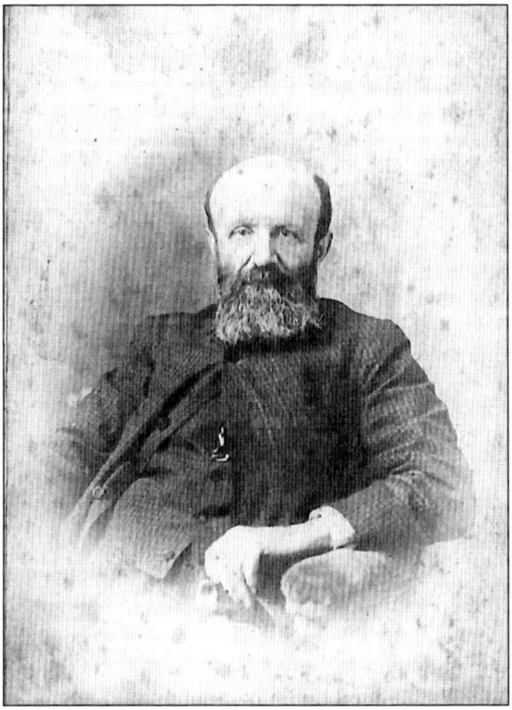

The squared-off beard on this Oldwick gentleman was not unusual in the late nineteenth century, when men's facial hairstyles took a wildly original turn.

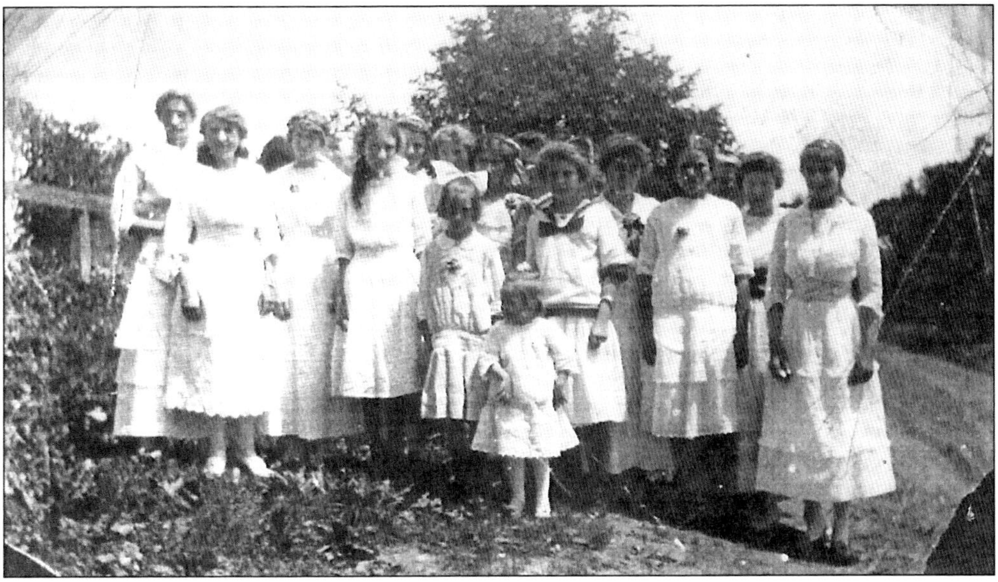

A party at the Mohnseys'. White was the color for party dresses, as shown by this worn Califon snapshot. Alice May Landon is second from the right.

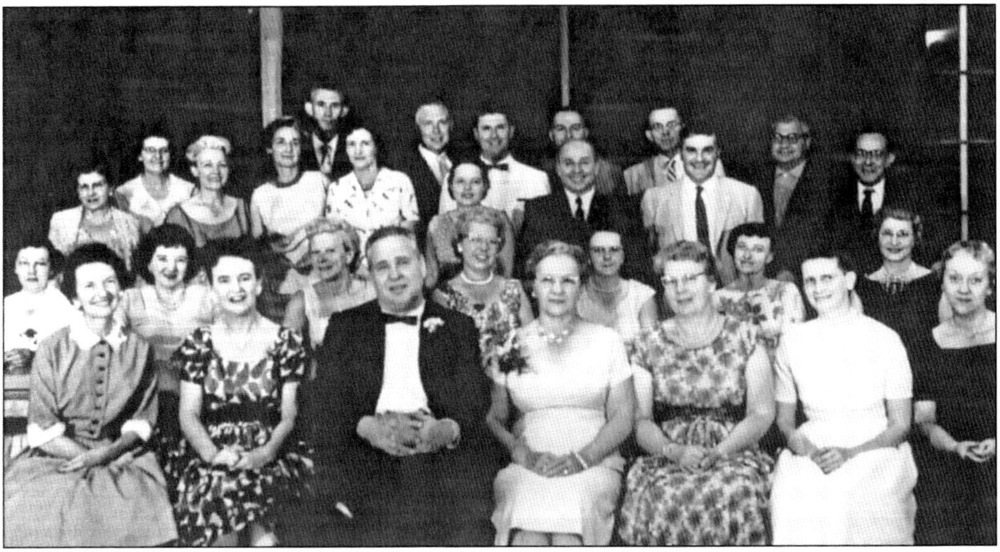

Prints and basic blacks outnumbered white dresses among the women of the Lambertville High School Class of 1930 when they held a reunion some thirty years later. (Lambertville Historical Society photo.)

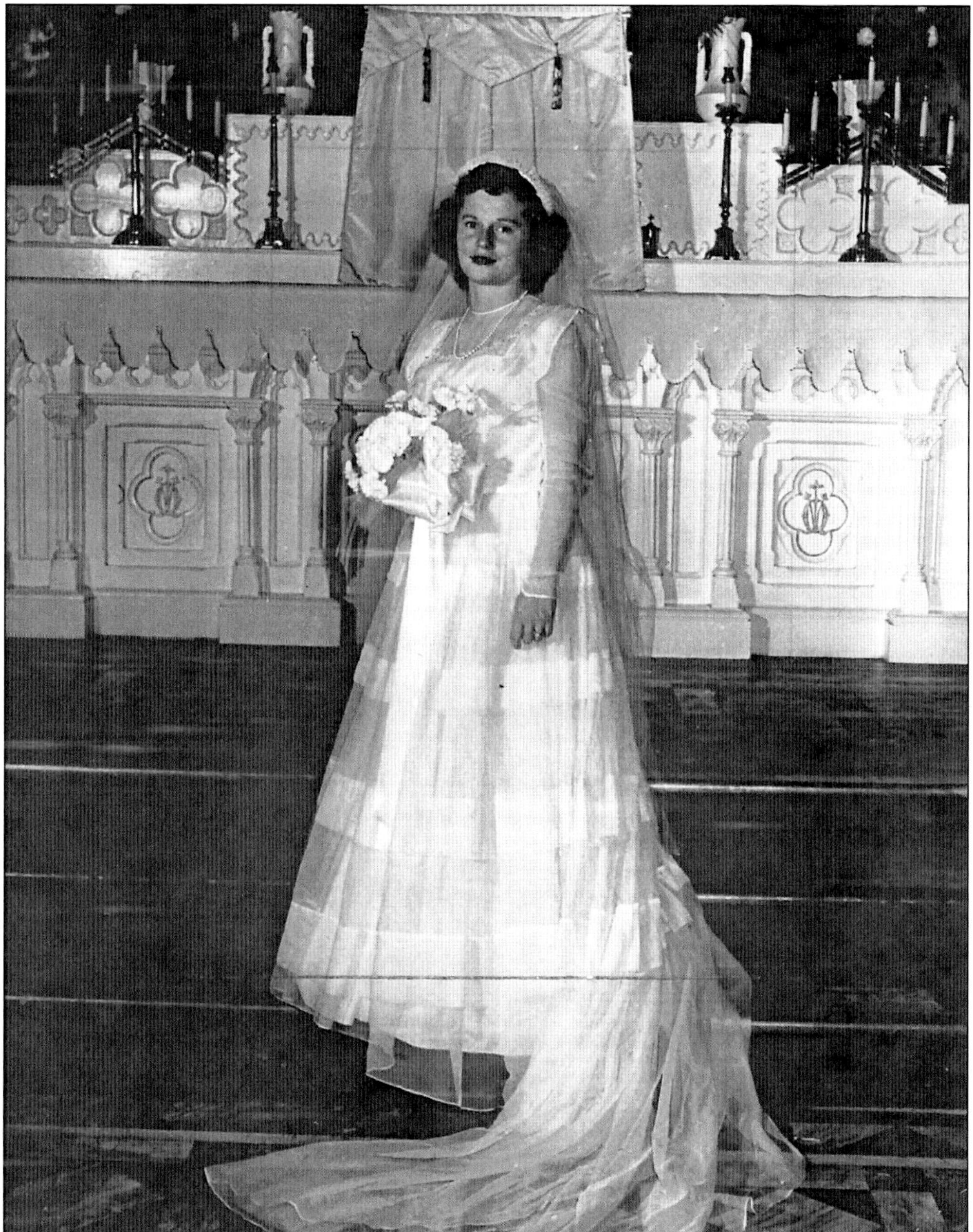

Marion Edwards Garefino was a beautiful bride at the altar of St. John the Evangelist Church, Lambertville, on August 27, 1949. (Lambertville Historical Society photo.)

Ten

FAME AND NOTORIETY

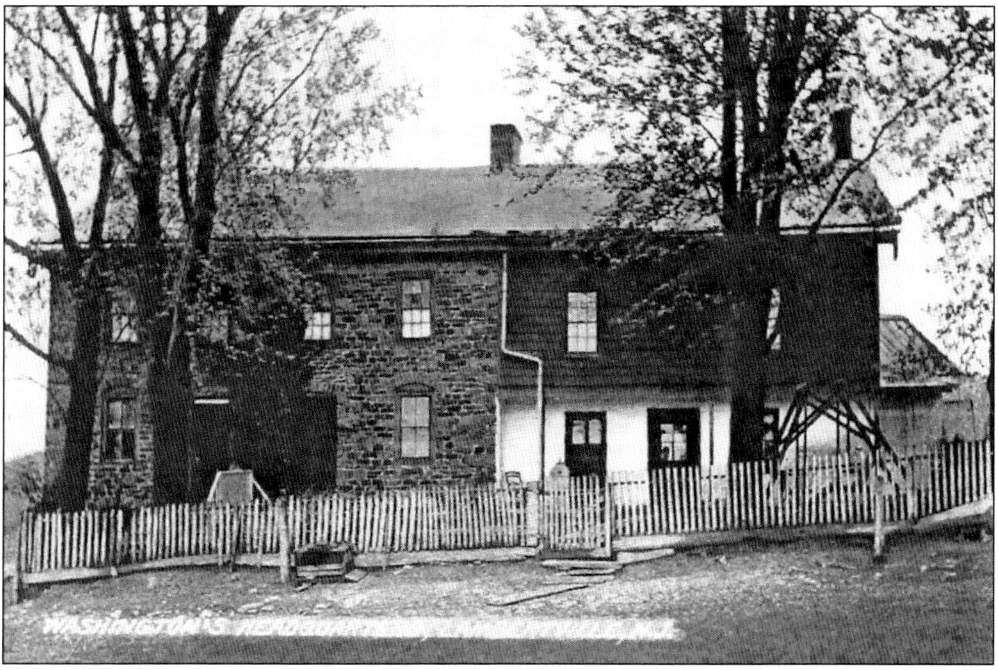

World attention has been focused on the Hunterdon County area several times over the years. This happened in Flemington during the 1935 trial of Bruno Hauptmann for the kidnapping-murder of the son of aviator Charles A. Lindbergh. A gentler fame came to Stockton in the 1930s when Richard Rogers and Lorenz Hart wrote the song, "There's a Small Hotel" at Colligan's Inn. James Wilson Marshall, whose gold discovery started the 1849 California Gold Rush, was a native of Lambertville. And George Washington really slept in Lambertville's Holcombe House in July, 1777, and June, 1778. (Lambertville Historical Society photo.)

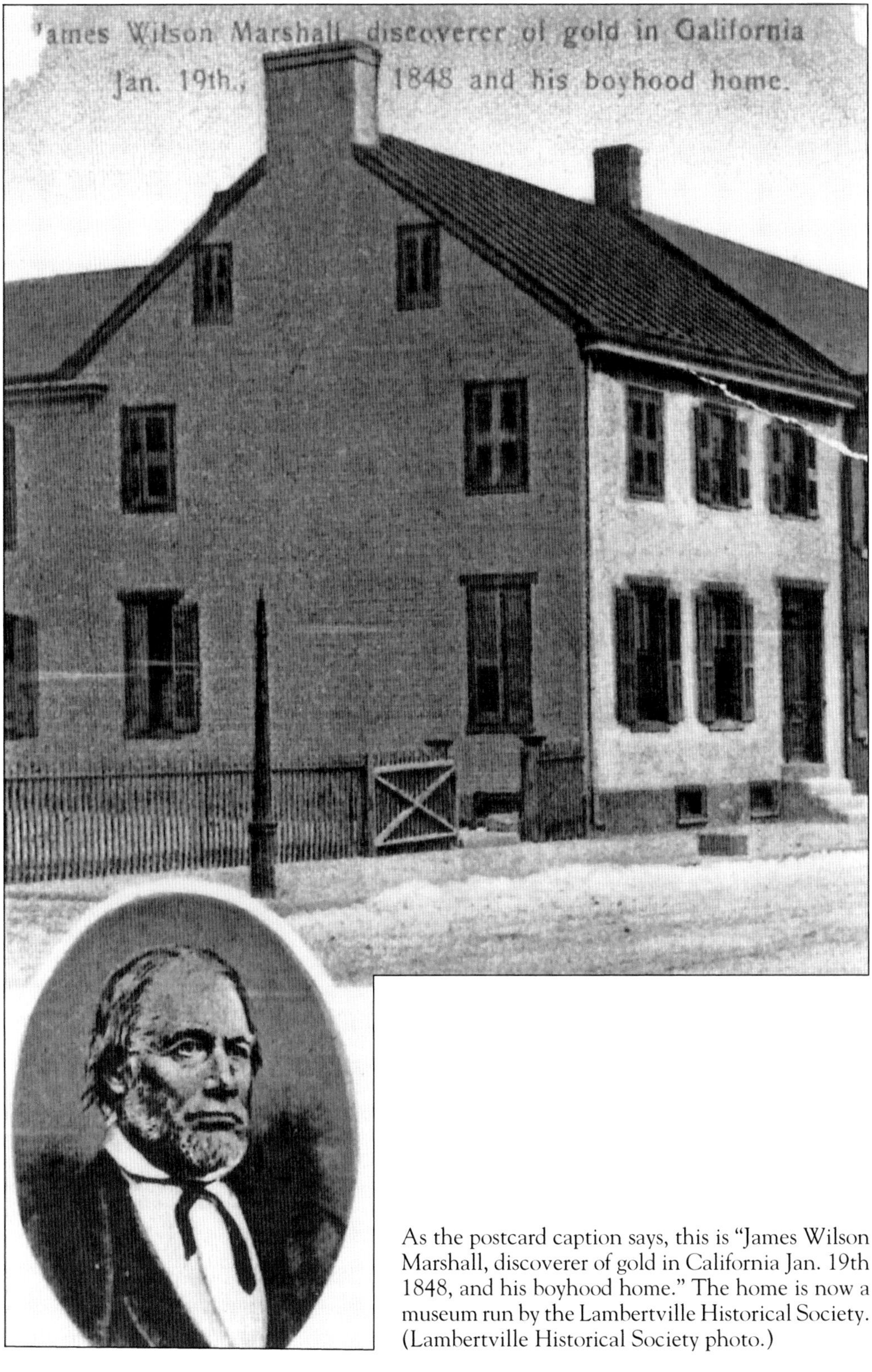

As the postcard caption says, this is "James Wilson Marshall, discoverer of gold in California Jan. 19th 1848, and his boyhood home." The home is now a museum run by the Lambertville Historical Society. (Lambertville Historical Society photo.)

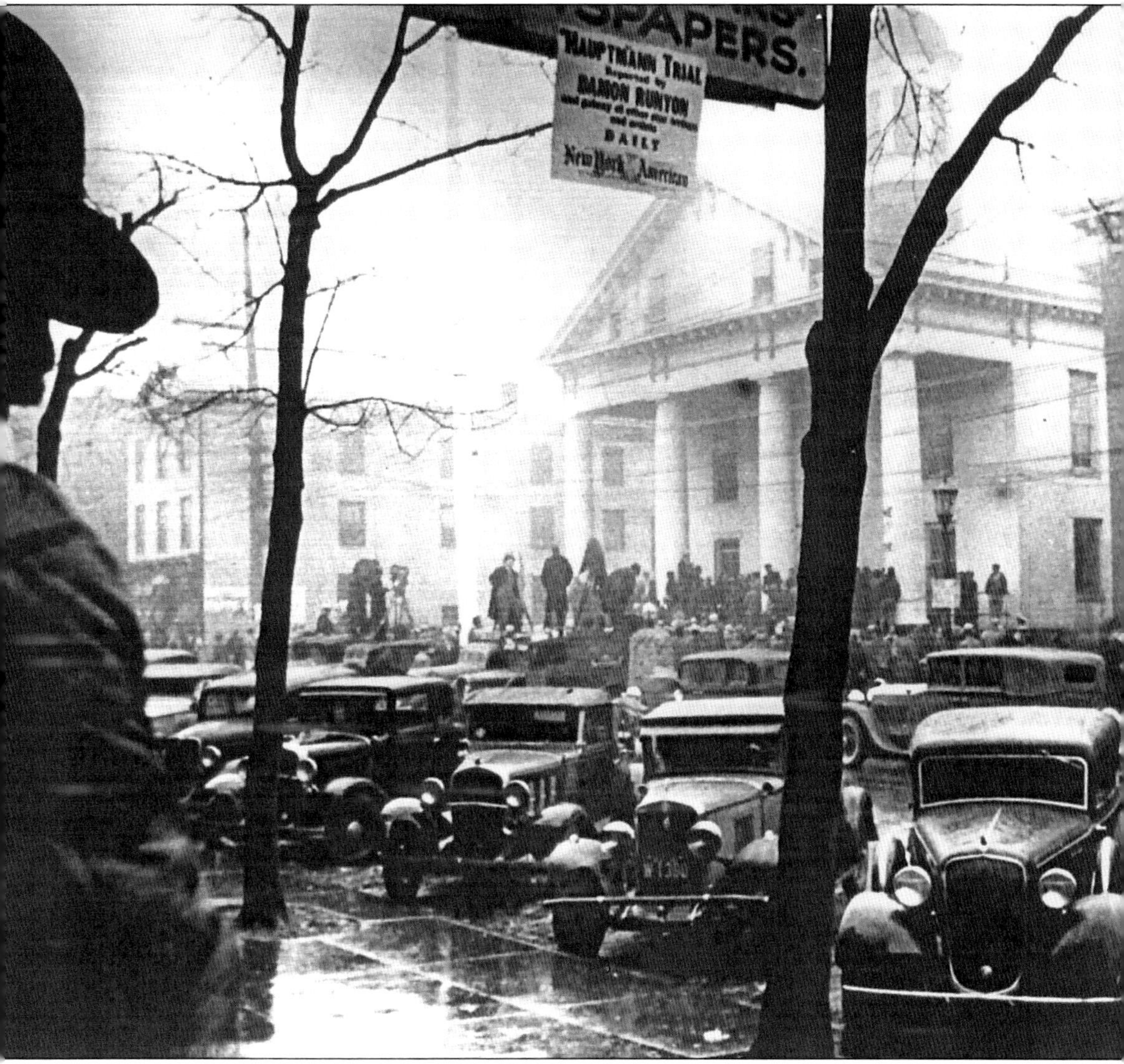

Charles A. Lindbergh had become a hero to the world in 1927 when he was the first man to fly solo non-stop between New York City and Paris. On March 1, 1932, his blue-eyed, curly-haired son, Charles Jr., aged twenty months, was kidnapped from the Lindbergh estate in West Amwell Township. After a forty-three-day trial in January and February, 1935, in Flemington's Hunterdon County Court House, Bruno Richard Hauptmann was convicted of kidnapping and murdering the child. The sign in the upper foreground promotes Damon Runyon's reports on the trial in the old *New York American* newspaper. (Photograph by W.L. "Bud" Armagast. Hunterdon County Democrat photo.)

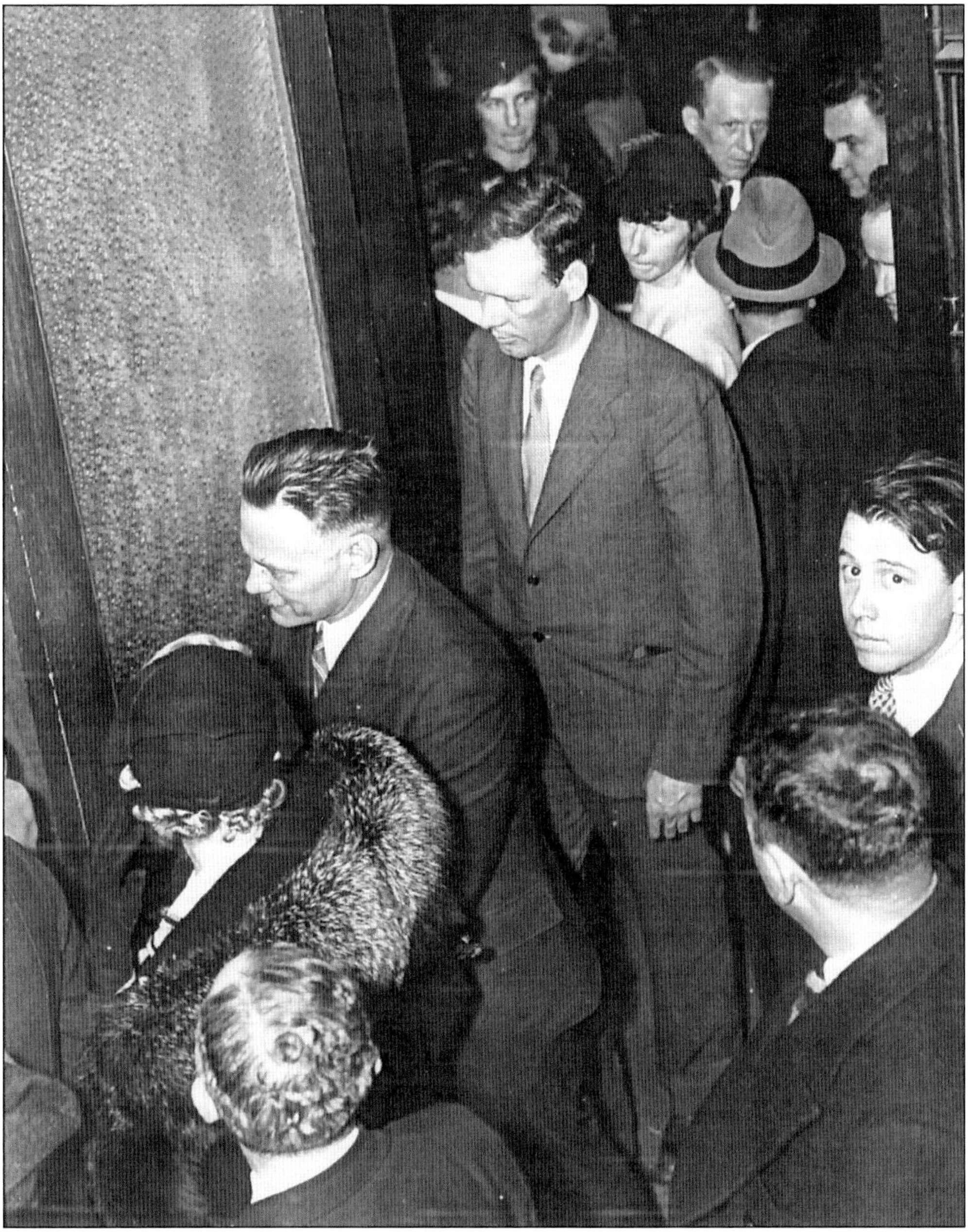

Droves of people milled around as Lindbergh (striped suit) entered the courtroom. Some were there to support Lindbergh and his wife, Anne Morrow Lindbergh; some to do their jobs at the court house. Others were simply curiosity seekers, drawn by the worldwide news reports of the trial. (Hunterdon County Democrat photo.)

Opposite: Lindbergh's house, from which his son was kidnapped while sleeping in an upper story bedroom. An extension ladder was an exhibit at the trial. (Hunterdon County Democrat photo.)

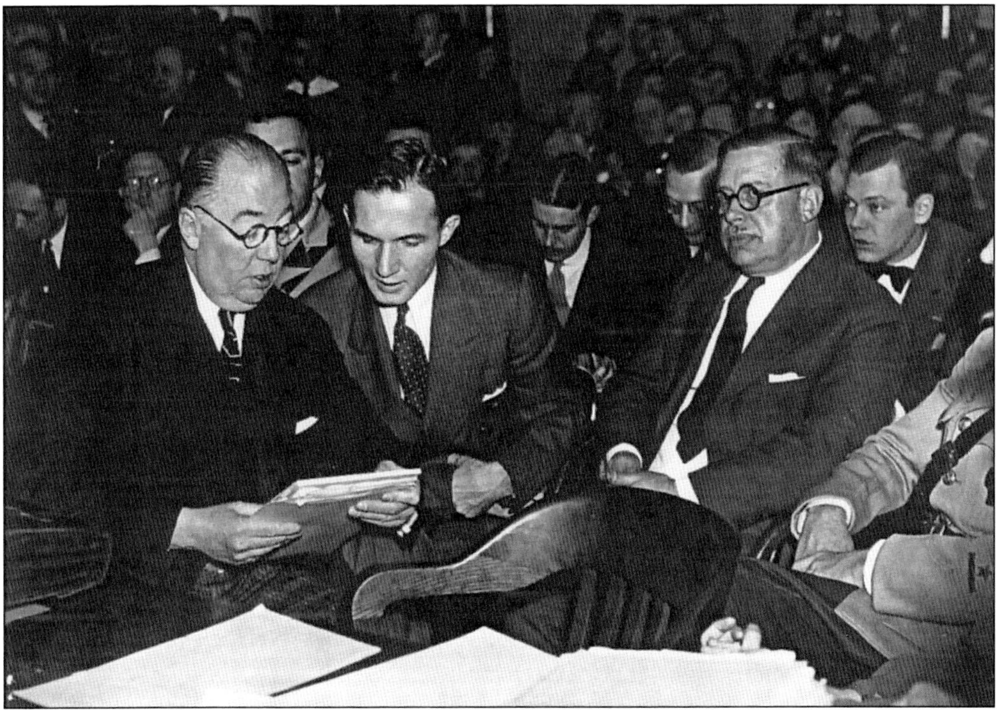

Hauptmann (second from left) consults with his attorney, Edward J. Reilly, and Deputy Sheriff Hovey Low (right). Hauptmann's wife walked their small son back and forth to the court house in his stroller during the trial. (Hunterdon County Democrat photo.)

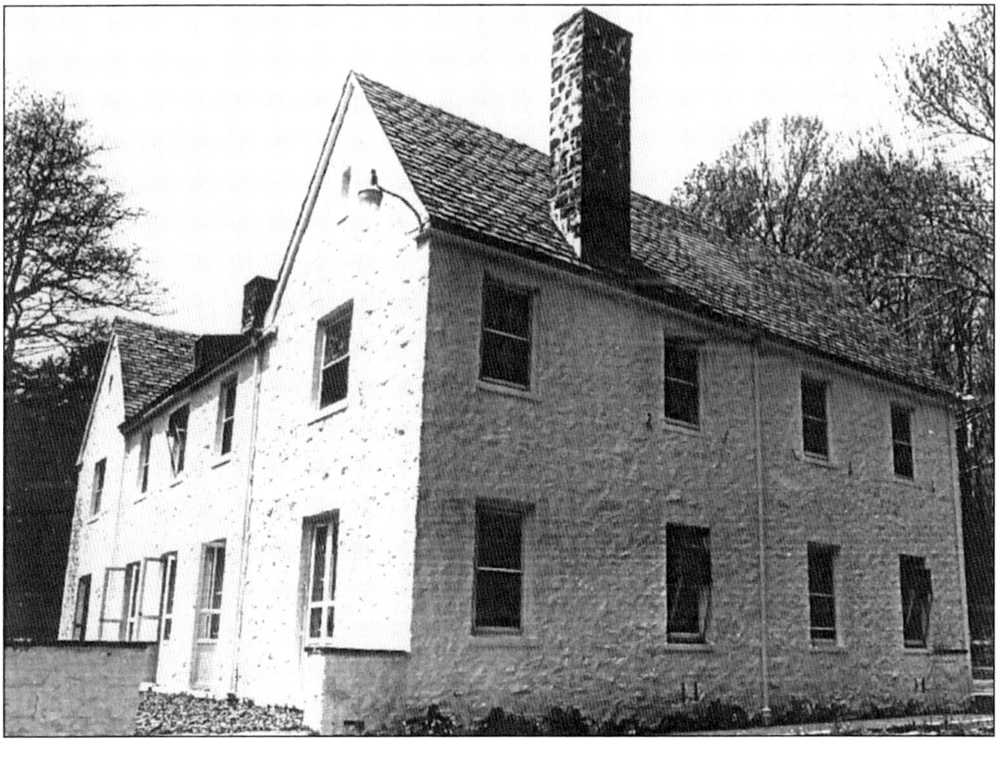

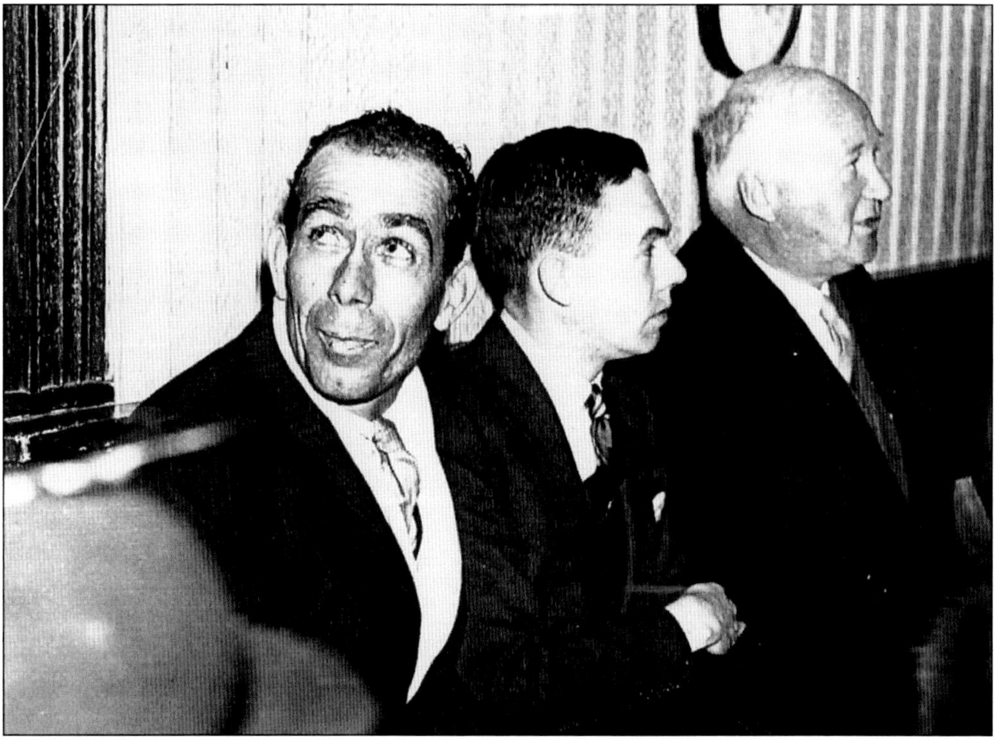

Millard Whited, a Lambertville lumberman, was a witness at the trial. He said he saw the defendant near the Lindbergh home about the time of the kidnapping. (Hunterdon County Democrat photo.)

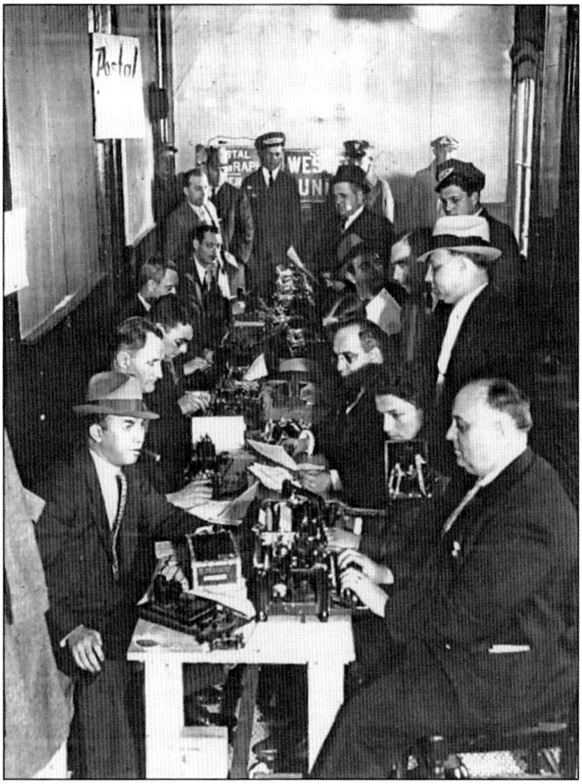

Flemington's Union Hotel, across the street from the court house, provided a press room in its basement. Telephones were at a premium as reporters phoned each detail of the trial to their newspapers. (Hunterdon County Democrat photo.)

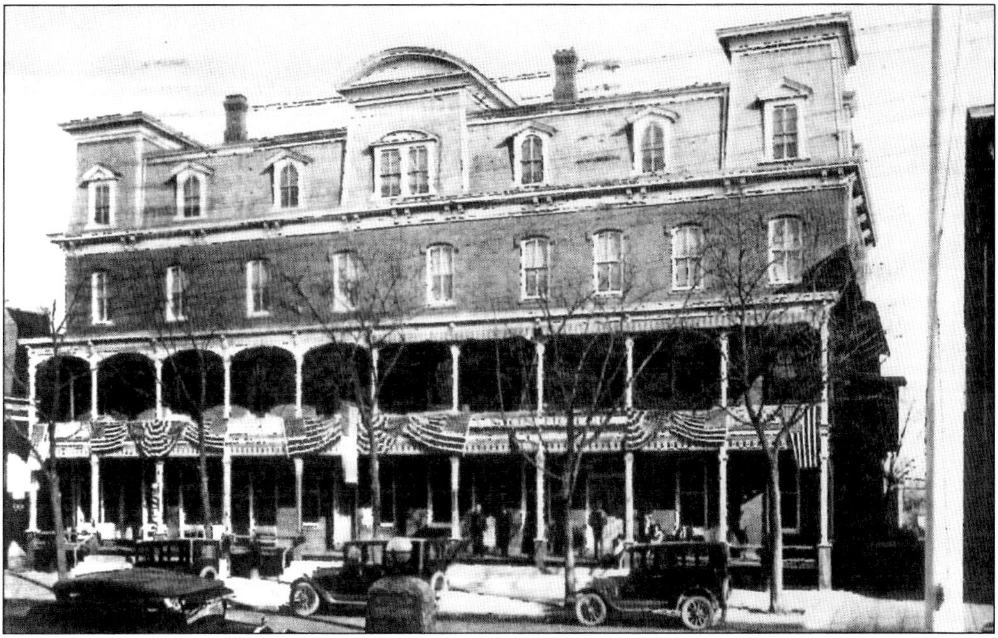

Famous writers and radio commentators who stayed at the Union Hotel included Damon Runyon, Walter Winchell, Lowell Thomas, Edna Ferber, and Fanny Hurst. Dorothy Kilgallen and Gabriel Heatter were also on the scene.

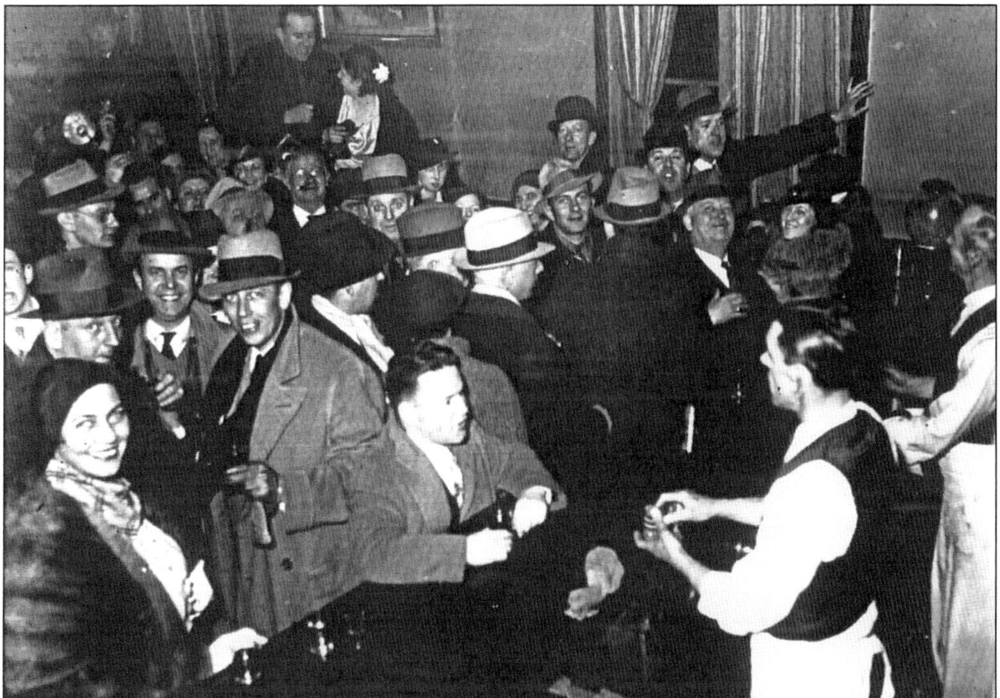

At the trial's end on February 13, the crowd celebrated in the Union Hotel bar. Hauptmann was electrocuted on April 3, 1936. Fifty years later, his wife was still protesting his innocence. (Hunterdon County Democrat photo.)

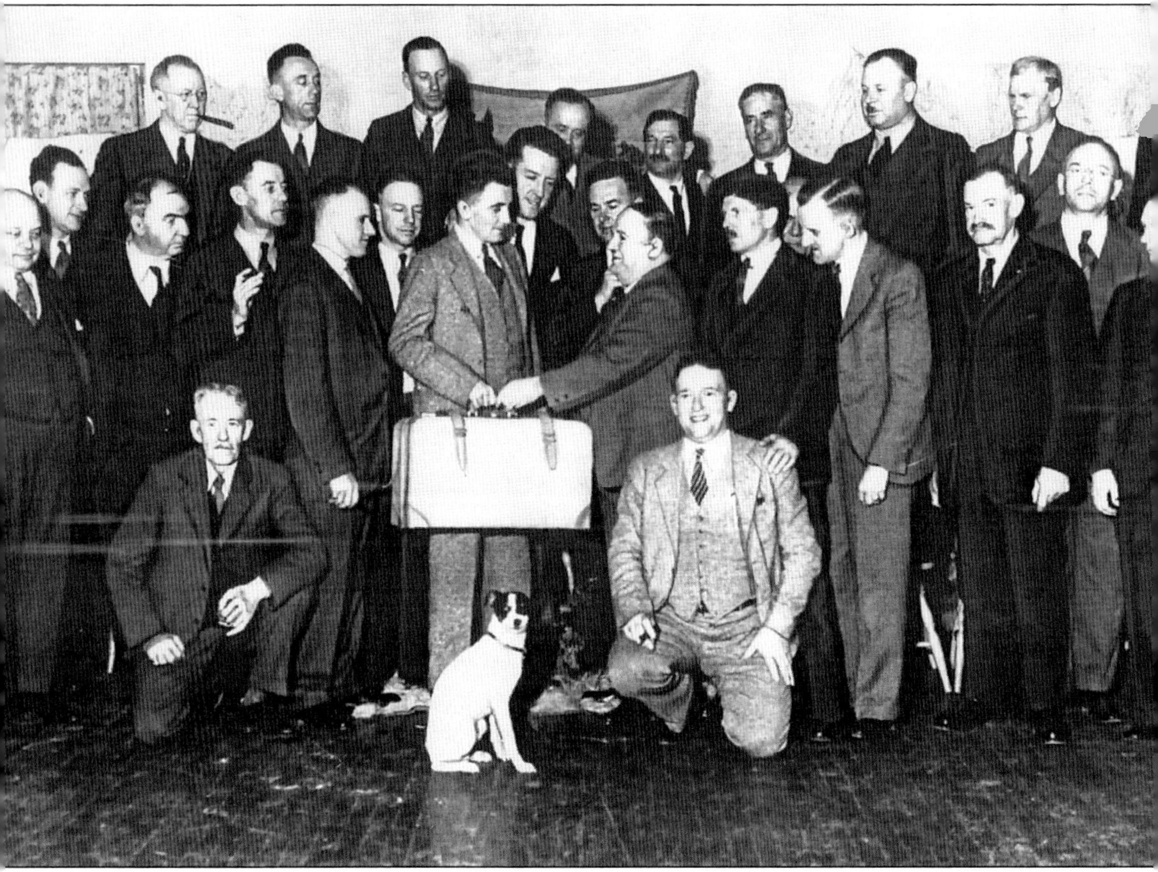

A month after the end of the trial, a stag party was held for County Sheriff John H. Curtiss (center, left) by the constables and special deputies who helped him keep order and the guards who watched over Hauptmann. Guests, who numbered about thirty-five, included *New York Daily News* photographers Martin McEvilly and Bob Seelig; Dr. B.S. Fuhrmann of Flemington, one of the physicians who made daily examinations of Hauptmann; and George Voorhees, a Clinton Township farmer who served on the jury. Under-Sheriff A. Keith Barrowcliff presented a travel bag to Curtiss. (Hunterdon County Democrat photo.)

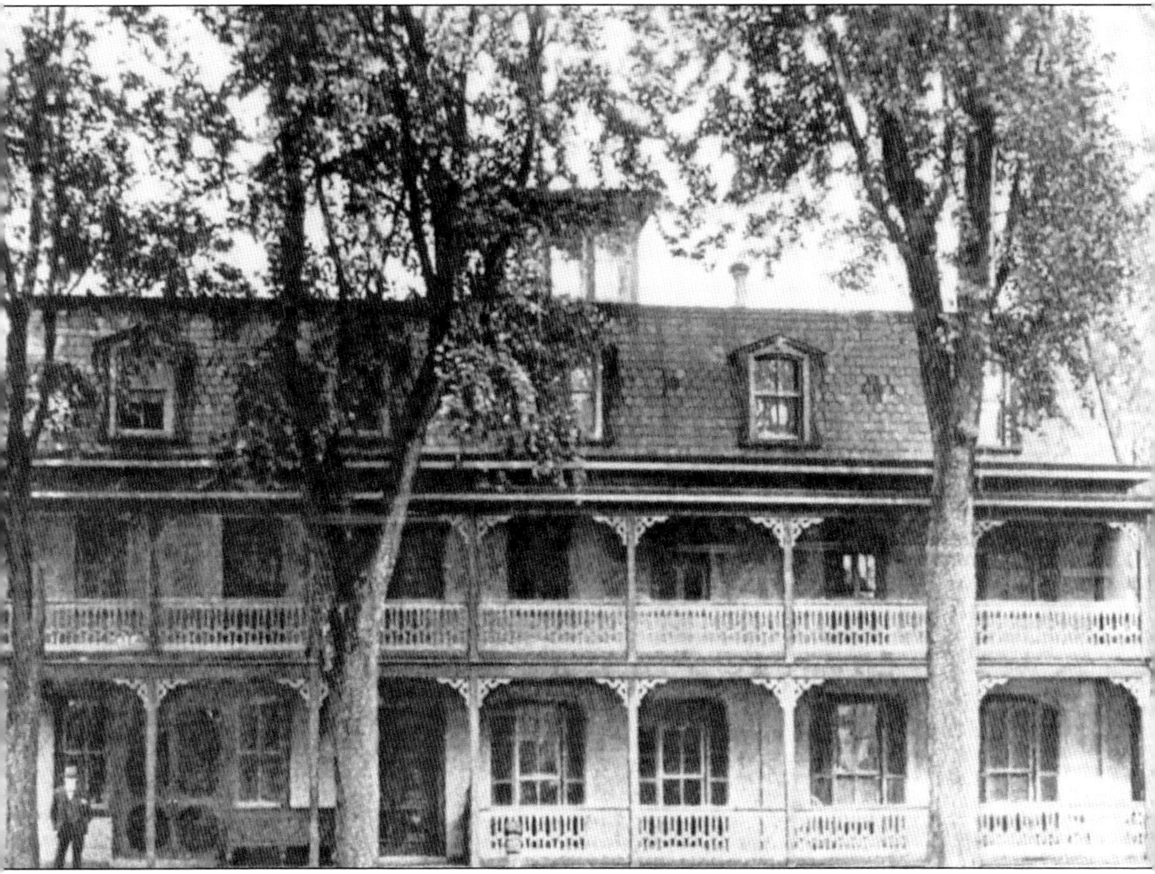

The Stockton Inn near Lambertville was an overflow hotel for reporters during the Hauptmann trial because it had telephones. Built in 1710, it had installed a bar by 1832. A garden restaurant with waterfall and wishing well were added by the Colligan family, owners between 1922 and 1983. The inn became famous when Richard Rodgers and Lorenz Hart were inspired by it to write the song, "There's a Small Hotel (with a wishing well)," and used it in the 1936 Broadway show, "On Your Toes." Dorothy Parker, Robert Benchley, and friends from New York's Algonquin Roundtable were regular patrons of the inn. (Stockton Inn photo.)

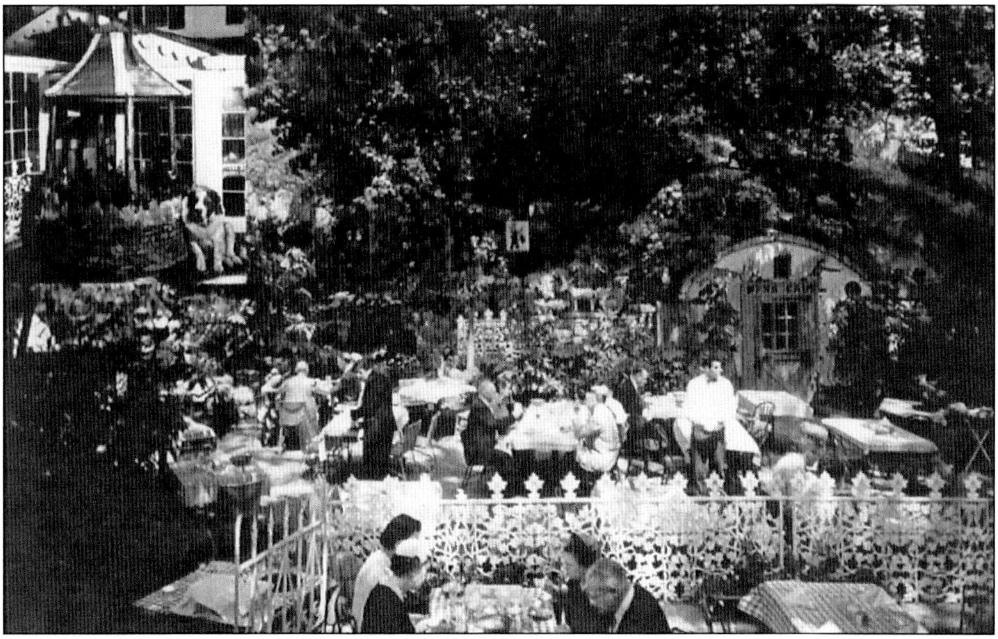

This postcard of the garden restaurant was a giveaway at Colligan's Inn in the 1950s. Today's owner, Andrew McDermott, has removed several ornaments, including the donkey (center), and added a shiny green glass globe among the trees. (Stockton Inn photo.)

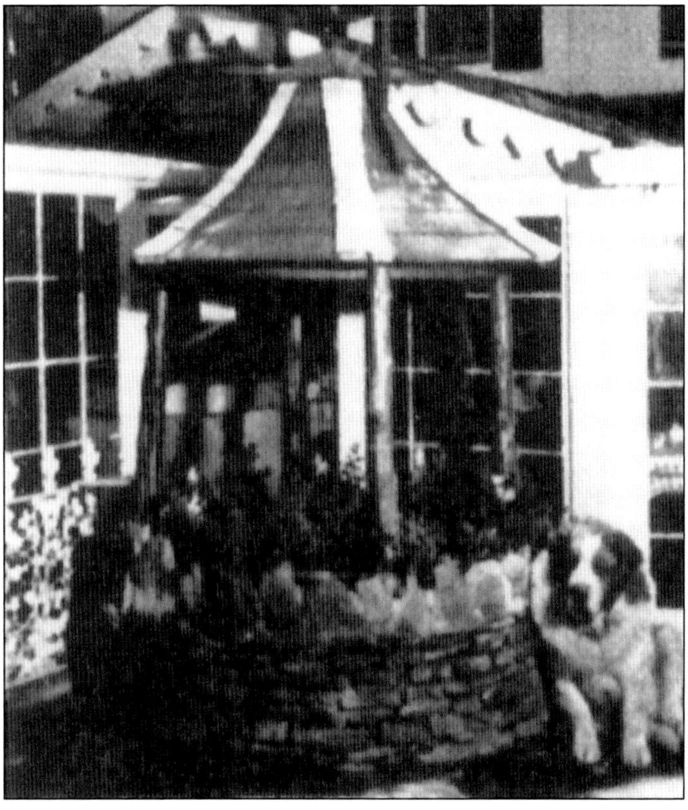

This inset from the photograph above shows the wishing well guarded by the Colligan family's pet St. Bernard. "There's a Small Hotel" was reprised in the 1940 musical, "Pal Joey." (Stockton Inn photo.)

Eleven

FIRE AND FLOOD

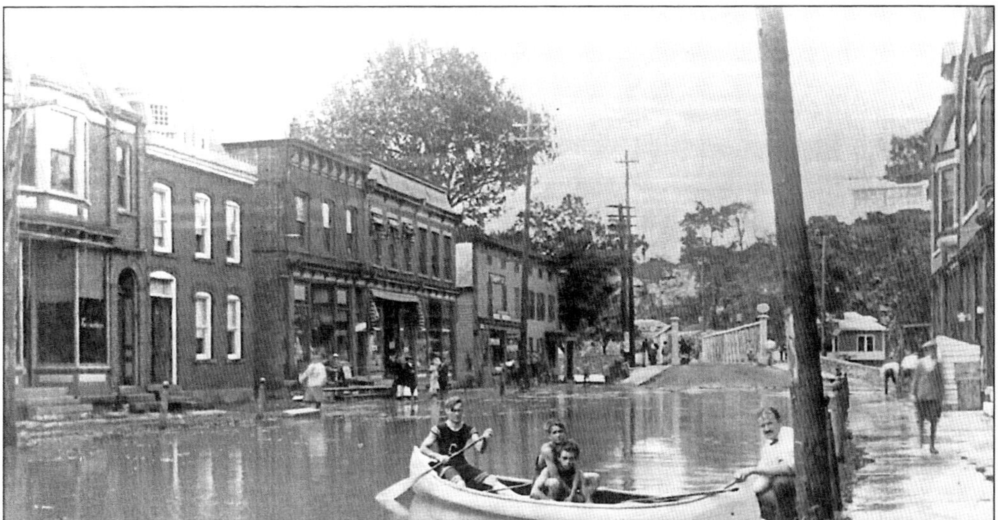

The rivers were a mixed blessing to the communities which grew up beside them. While they provided transportation, jobs, food, and recreation, they could also cause trouble when they flooded. Residents learned to cope, just as they coped with another disaster: fire. Fire fighters battled flames, first as volunteer brigades and later as established companies. In floods, though, everybody pitched in. Clinton's floods, caused by the fact that the west end of Main Street was lower than the mill dam, were ended by damming Spruce Run Reservoir in the 1950s. (Clinton Historical Society photo.)

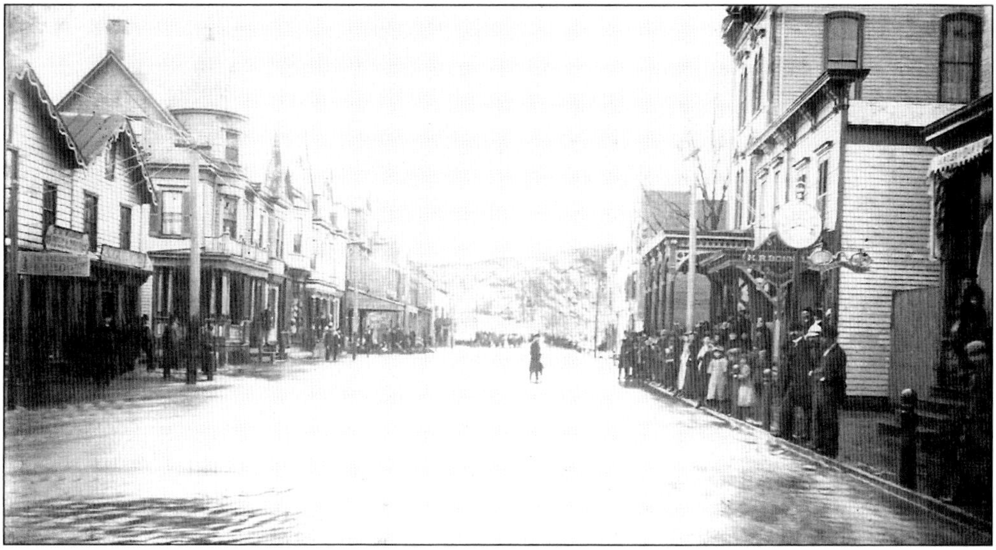

A flood in 1896. Clinton merchants had just gotten Main Street rebuilt and operating after the 1892 Great Fire when they were hit by a major flood four years later. Everyone turned out to see the water rippling down the street. (Clinton Historical Society photo.)

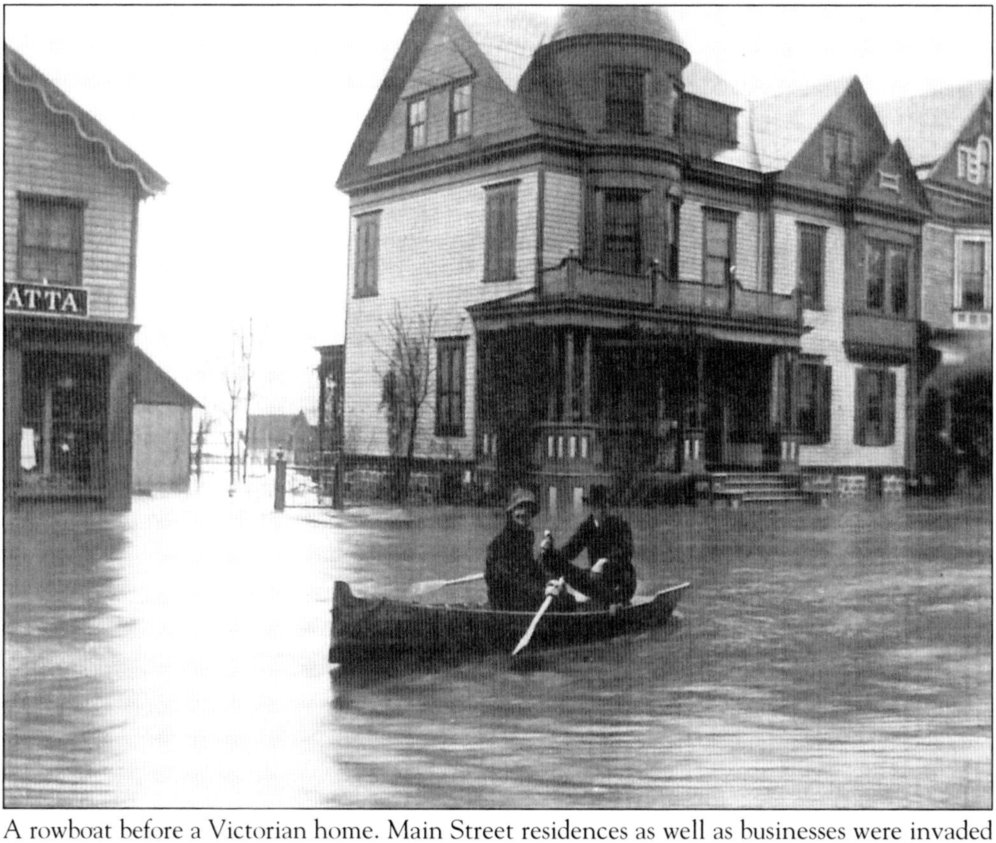

A rowboat before a Victorian home. Main Street residences as well as businesses were invaded by flood waters in 1902. This home belonged to William Baker, pharmacist and sometime mayor. (Clinton Historical Society photo.)

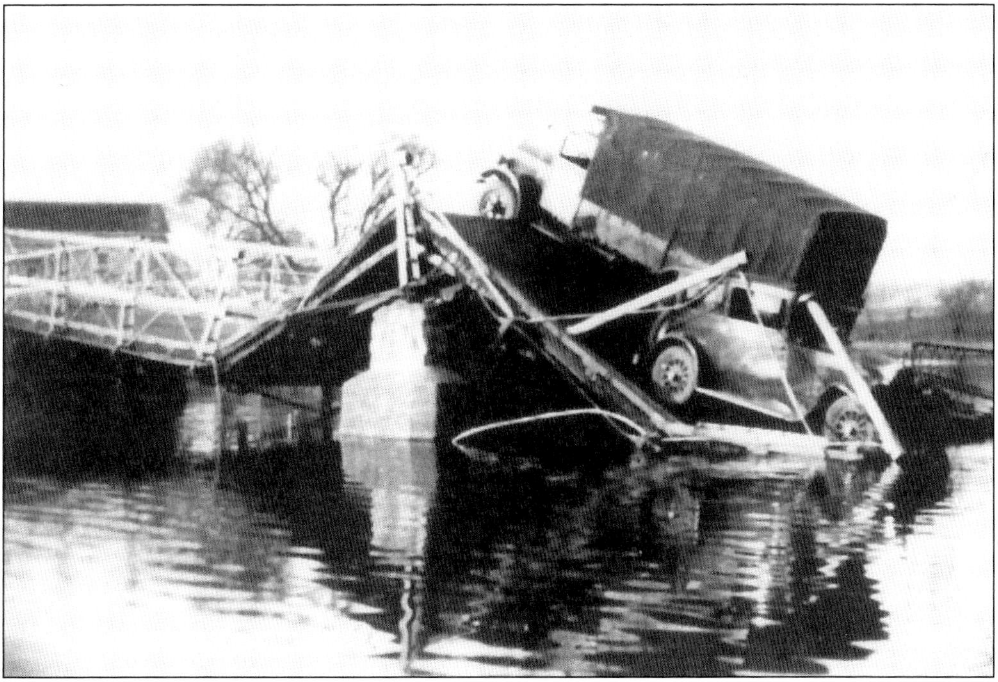

Bridge collapse. In the April floods of 1931, Clinton's Main Street bridge was weakened and finally collapsed. A truck and a car were on it at the time. (Clinton Historical Society photo.)

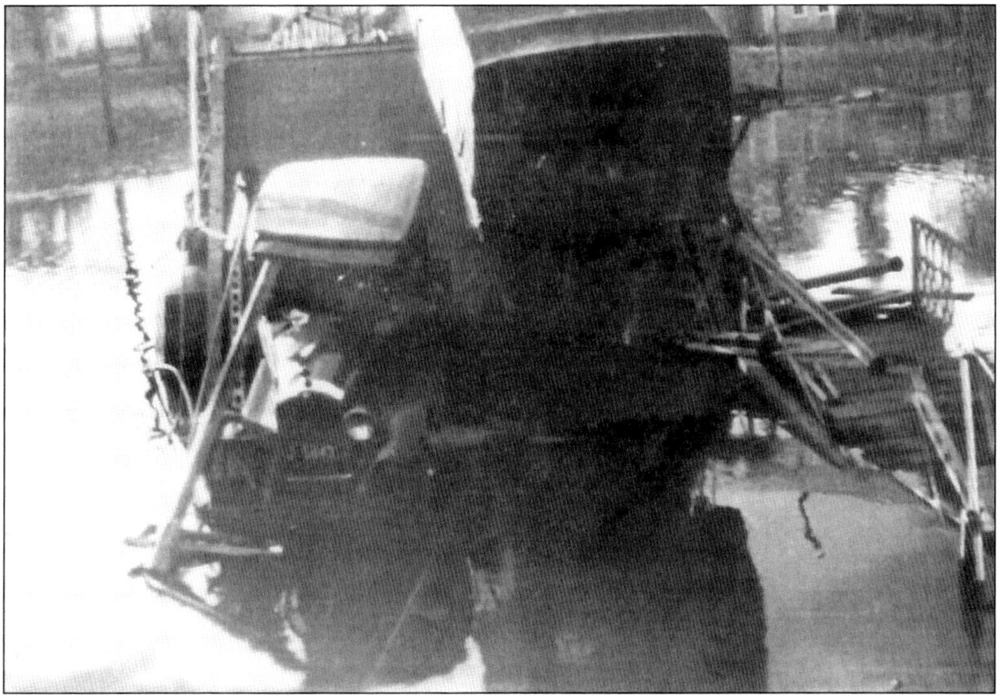

Another view of the bridge collapse. While the bridge was out of commission, people could cross the river in rowboats, but vehicles had to go around to another bridge. (Clinton Historical Society photo.)

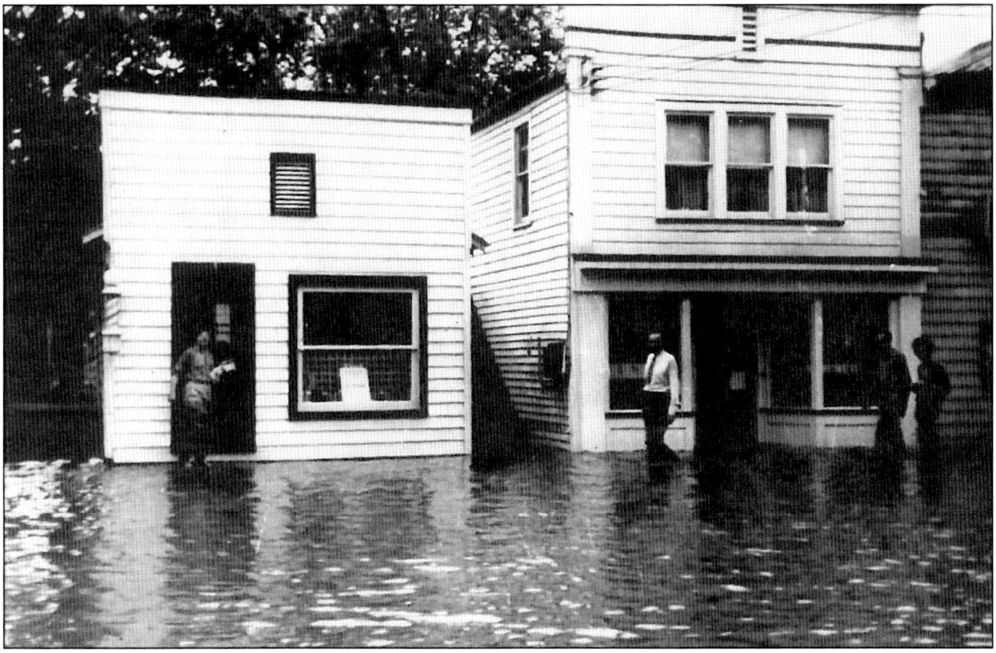

Clinton shopkeepers must have been irate when they came to work one day in 1945 to find the waters of the South Branch of the Raritan lapping at their doorsills. (Clinton Historical Society photo.)

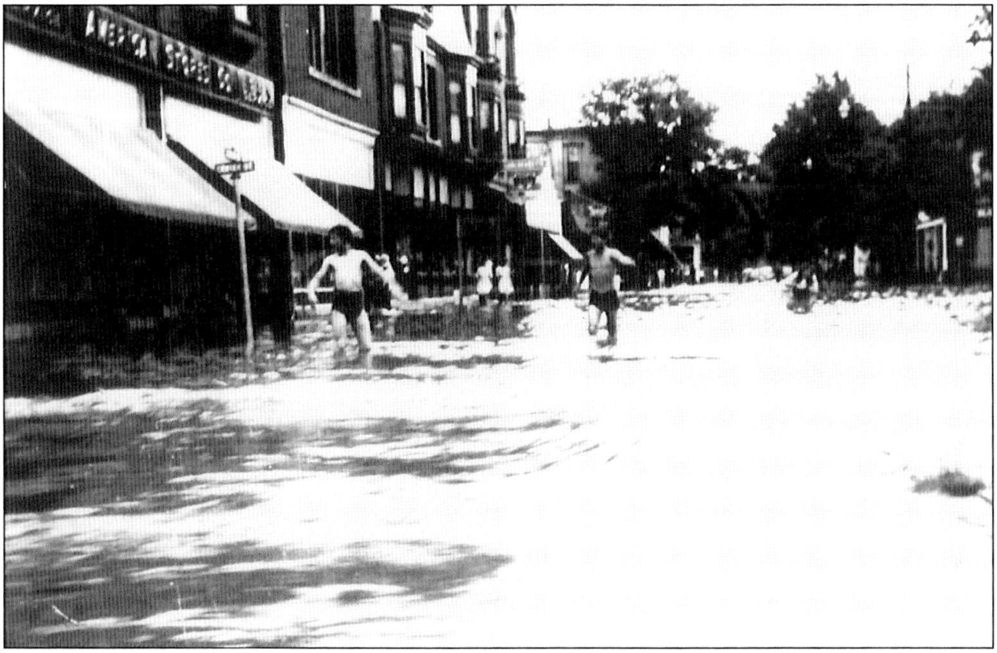

But these youngsters were no doubt ecstatic—especially when the grocer in the store on the left offered them a nickel for each watermelon they retrieved as it bobbed away from his outdoor display. (Clinton Historical Society photo.)

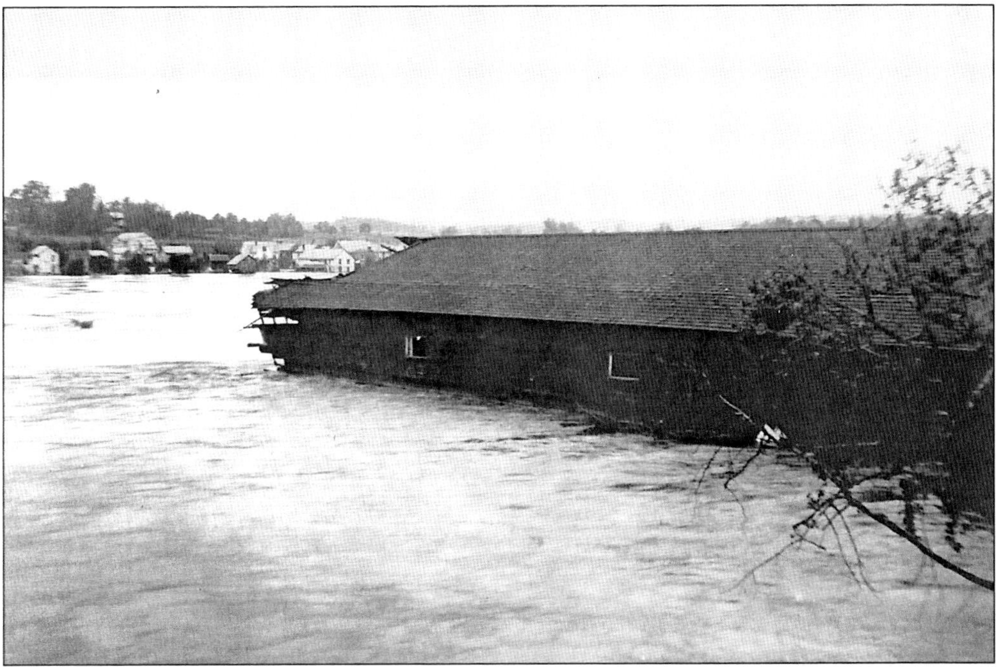

The Delaware did its share of flood damage, destroying Lambertville's second covered bridge on October 11, 1903. The first, completed in 1814, was washed away in 1841. (Lambertville Historical Society photo.)

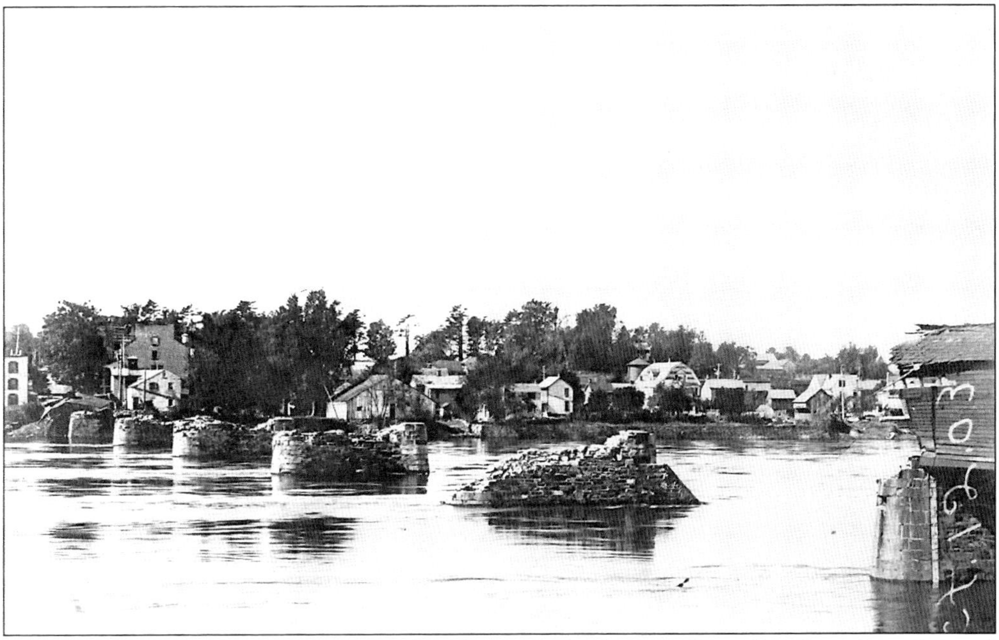

The bridge pilings were left standing after the 1903 flood in Lambertville. Note the splintered end of the covered bridge on the right. The present steel bridge replaced this wooden one. (Lambertville Historical Society photo.)

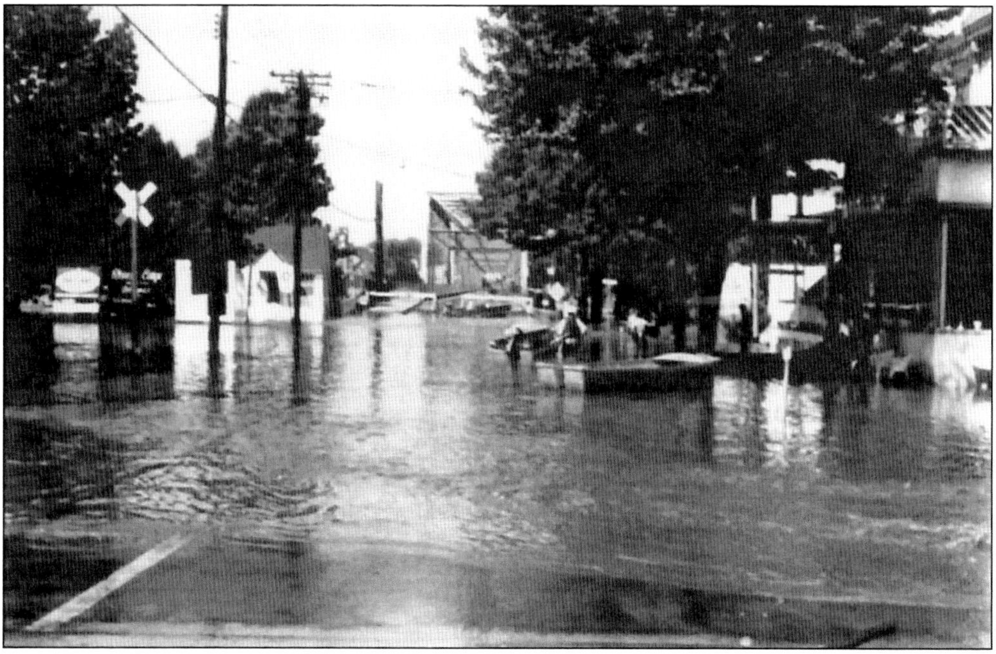

An August downpour caused this 1955 flood in Lambertville. This Bridge Street photograph shows that the steel bridge withstood the river's onslaught. (Lambertville Historical Society photo.)

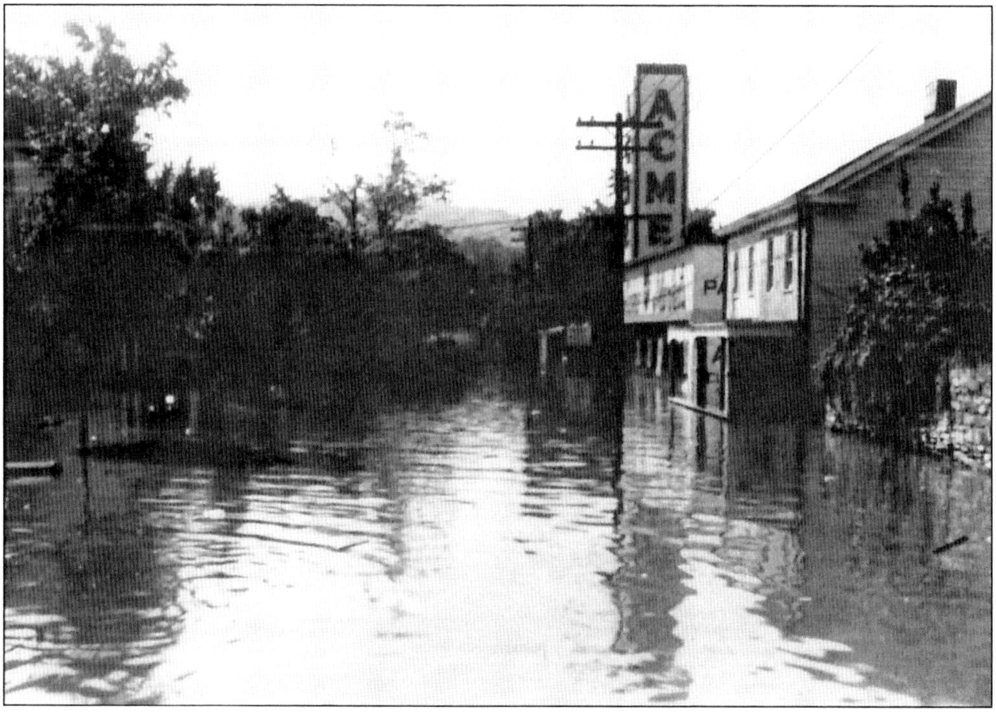

Lambertville storekeepers on South Union Street shared Clinton storekeepers' distaste for floods, and so did householders, who couldn't get to the grocery store for supplies while the river was up. (Lambertville Historical Society photo.)

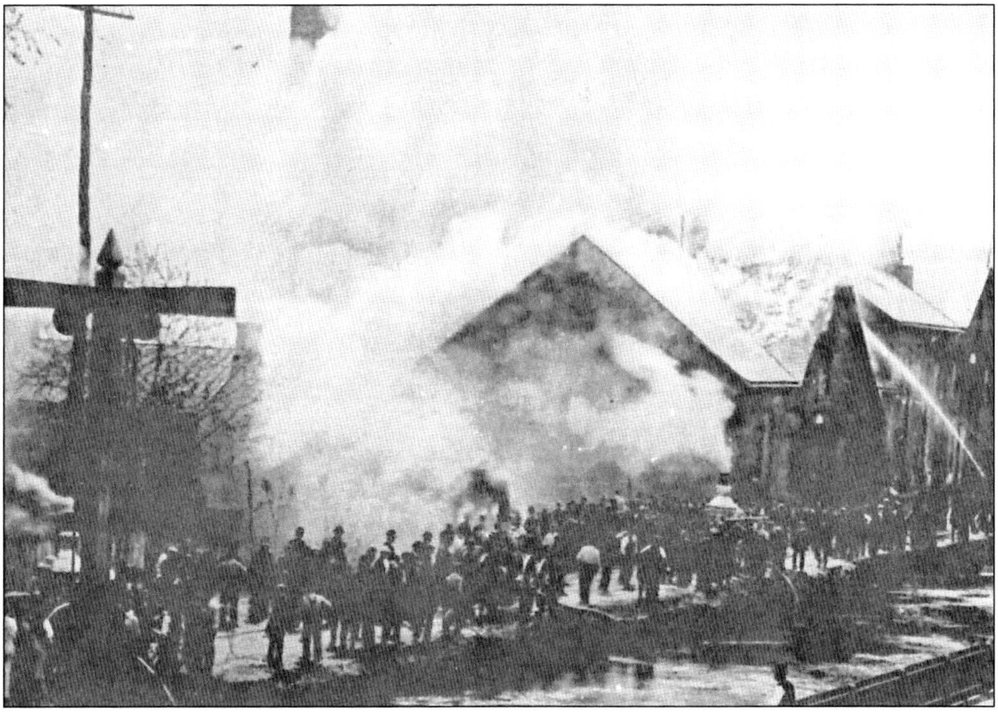

Fire brought further disruption of daily life, but also further excitement. William McReady owned the Perseverance Paper Mill on South Union Street, Lambertville, which burned in 1906. (Lambertville Historical Society photo.)

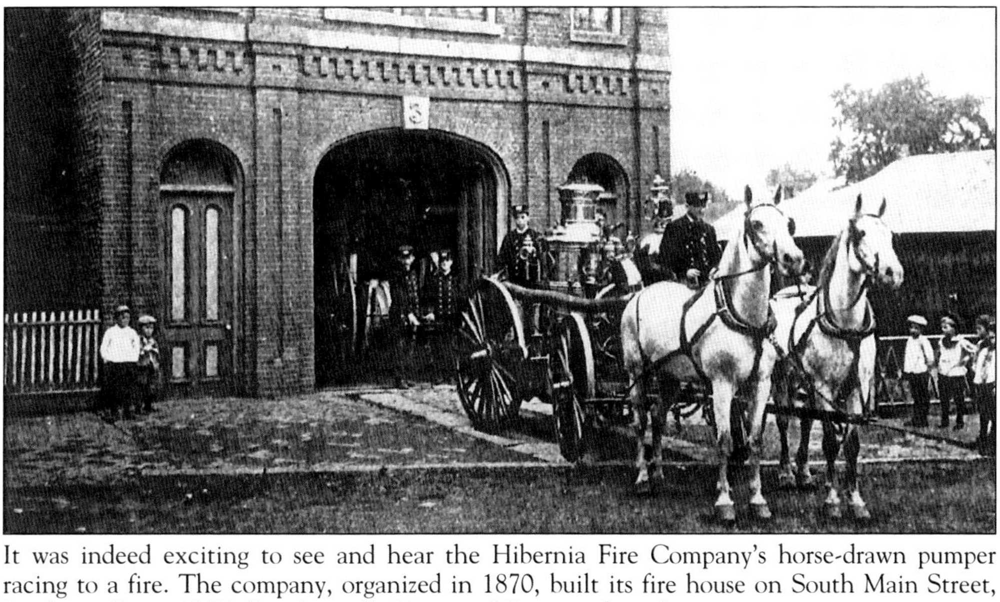

It was indeed exciting to see and hear the Hibernia Fire Company's horse-drawn pumper racing to a fire. The company, organized in 1870, built its fire house on South Main Street, Lambertville, in 1885. (Lambertville Historical Society photo.)

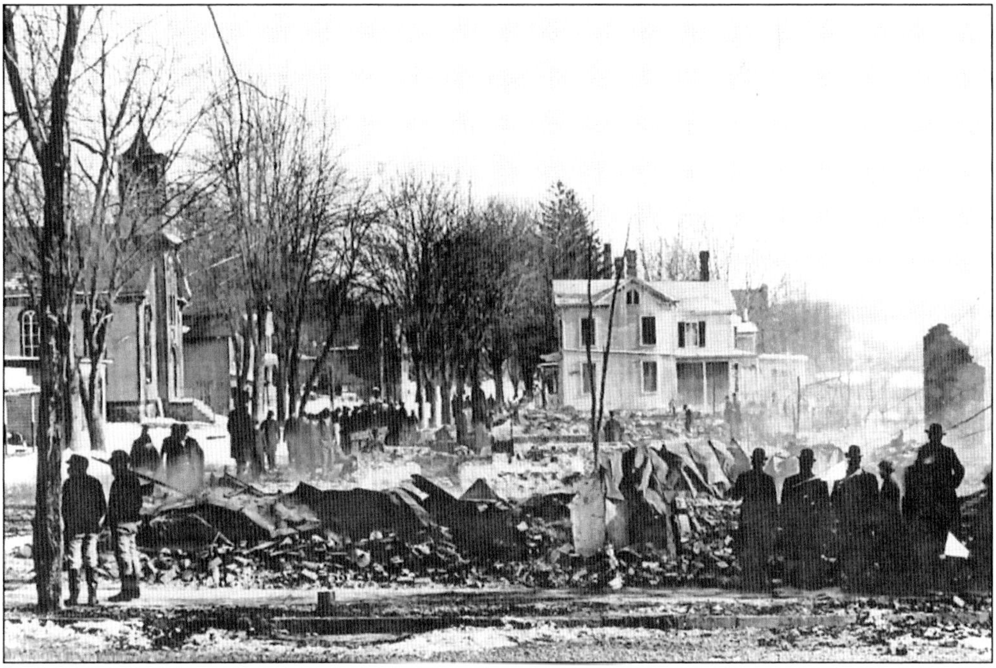

A Stockton fire in early days left only rubble for townspeople to brood over and for a photographer to record. (Lambertville Historical Society photo.)

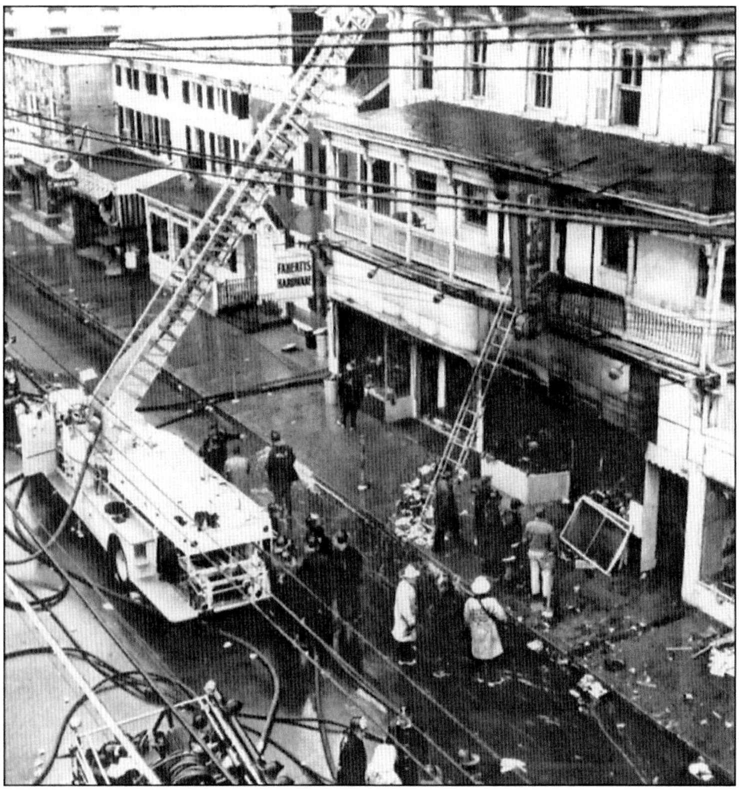

An extension ladder and other modern equipment made it easier for fire fighters to work in 1959, but Lambertville's Mackler Building on North Union Street still couldn't be saved from its fire. (Lambertville Historical Society photo.)

Twelve

CELEBRATIONS

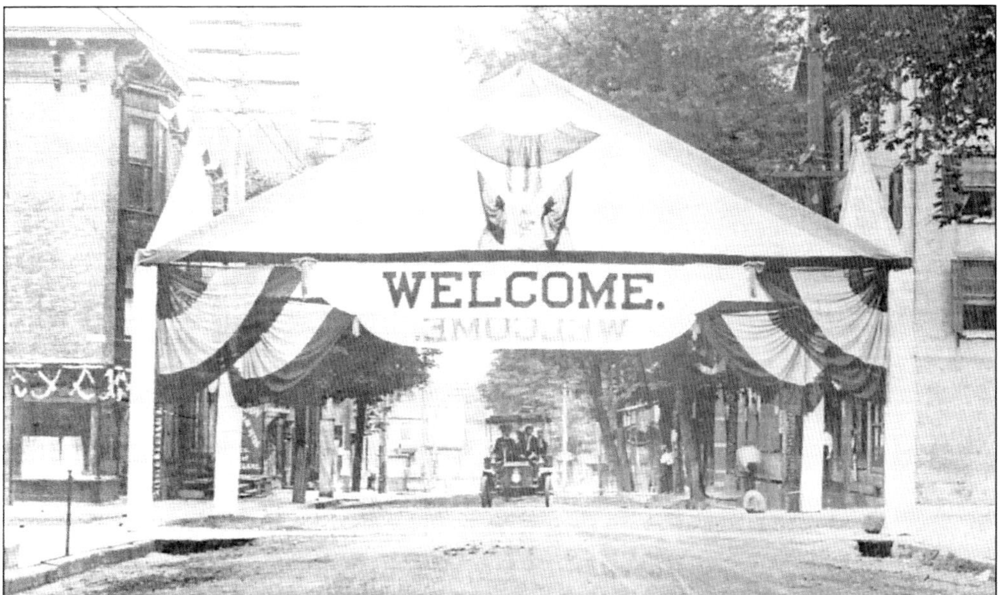

All of the Hunterdon County communities loved a celebration. No one was gayer than the people of the Gay Nineties when it came to decorating for parades and turning out in droves for a carnival or a fair. Yards of bunting in fanciful fans decked this Lambertville street sign at the corner of Union and Bridge Streets to welcome the people who came in from area farms to watch the 1904 Labor Day parade. (Lambertville Historical Society photo.)

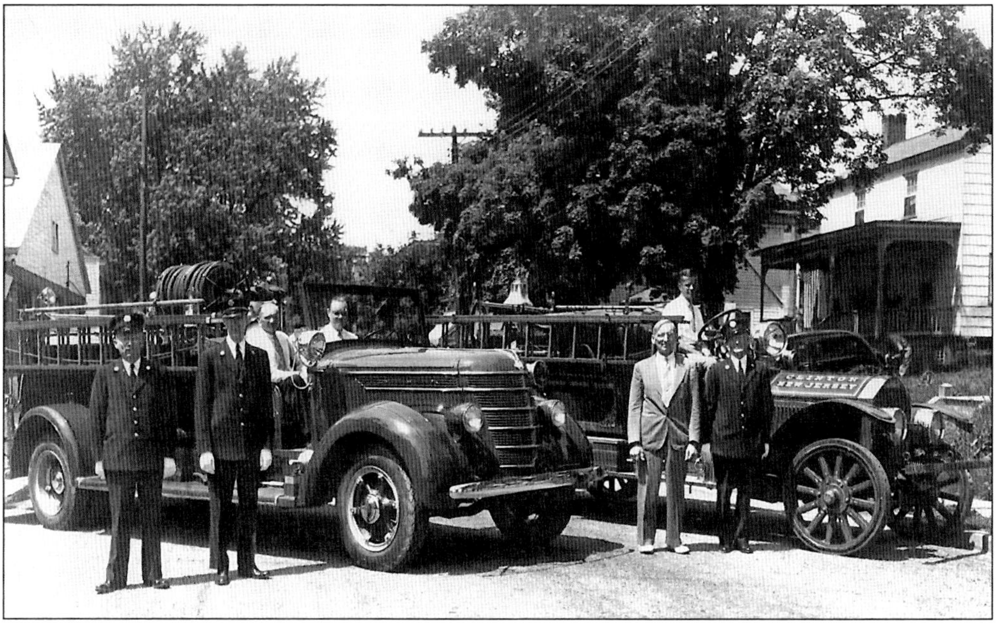

Parades invariably included bands and fire trucks. The Clinton Fire Company, formed by volunteers in 1892 after the Great Fire, shined up its equipment for the 1945 Fourth of July parade. (Clinton Historical Society photo.)

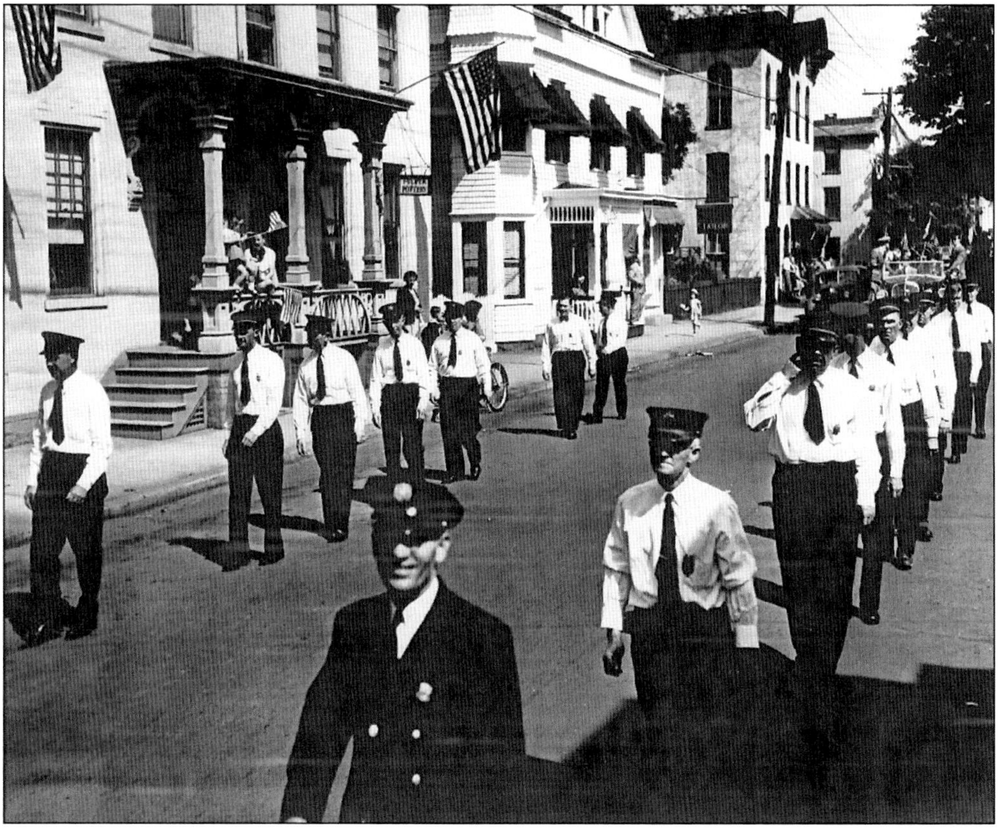

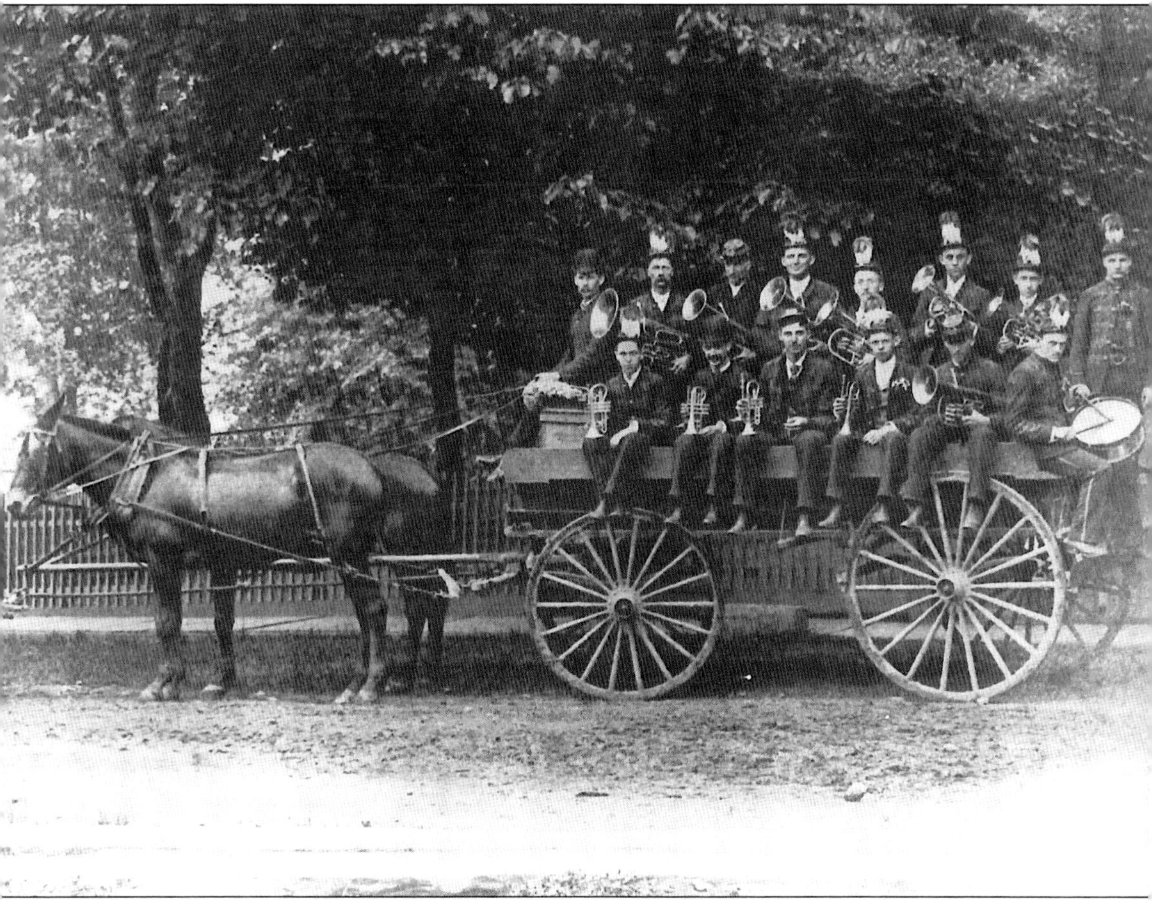

Clinton's band rode in 1890 parades in a horse-drawn wagon driven by William Harm. The musicians included: (back row, from left) William Auks, William Trimmer, John Yawger, Raymond Gary, Grant Haver, Sam Jones, and Irvin Robinson; (front) Dr. Lesaver, William Wilson, Ase MacPherson, George Rittenhouse, George MacPherson, and Charles Trimmer. The lilting marches they played kept time for the feet of both parade participants and onlookers.

Opposite: Members of several Lambertville fire companies combined forces and marched together in parades. This parade marked Memorial Day, 1946. (Lambertville Historical Society photo.)

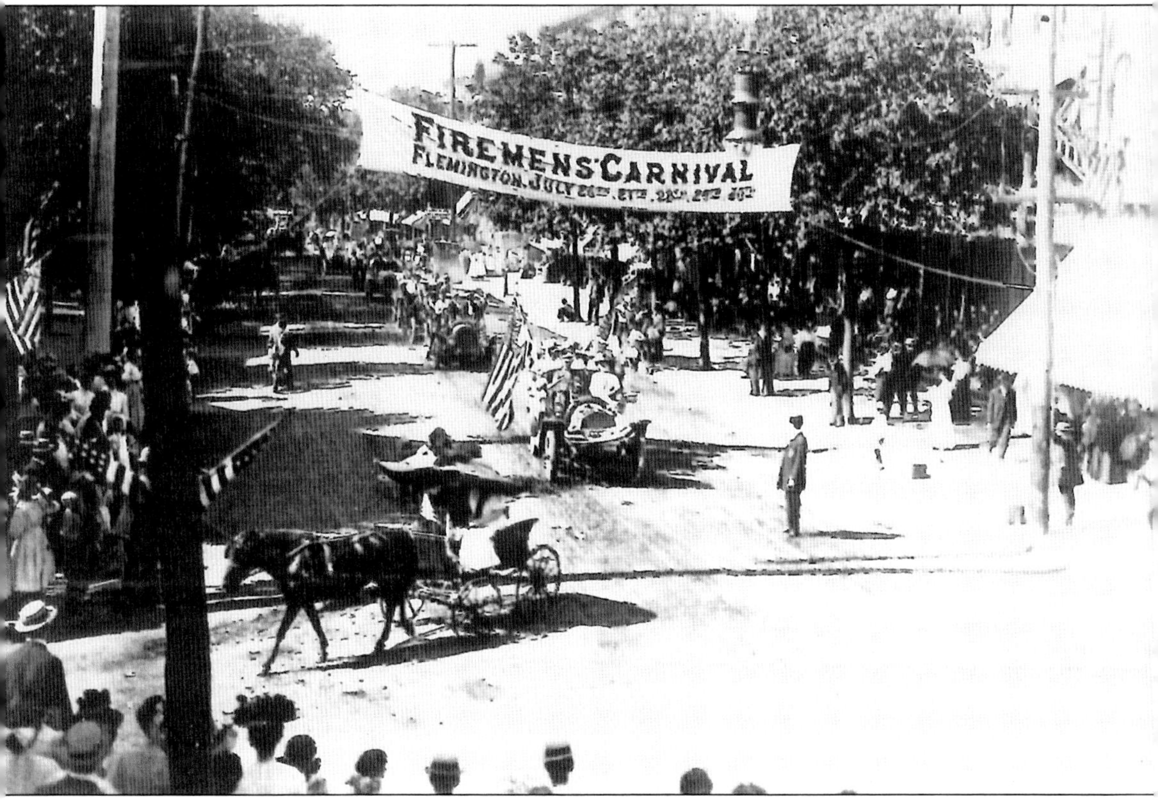

The best parade of all for Flemington children was the one which led them to the Firemen's Carnival each July. Bands, floats, marchers, and certainly shiny red fire engines were all part of the big parade's fascination. But at the end of the parade was the carnival, with merry-go-round and Ferris wheel, cotton candy and hot dogs—what could be more fun? Children's behavior undoubtedly took a turn for the better just before the carnival, as it did just before Santa's arrival during the celebration of Christmas.

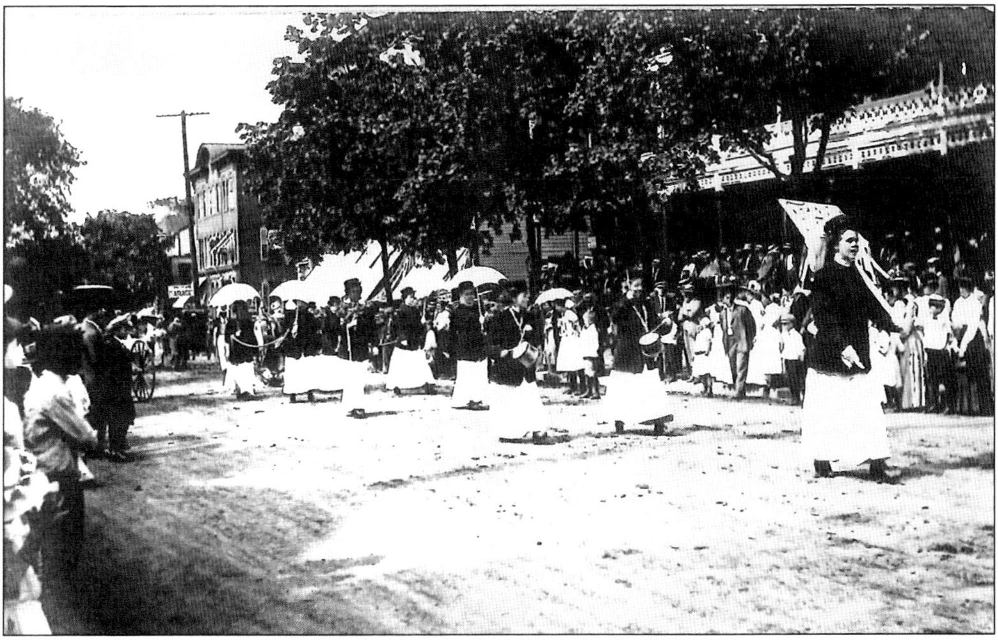

This photograph of women marching with parasols was one of eight taken at the Flemington Firemen's Parade and Carnival one year at the turn of the century and made into postcards which are now part of a Flemington collection.

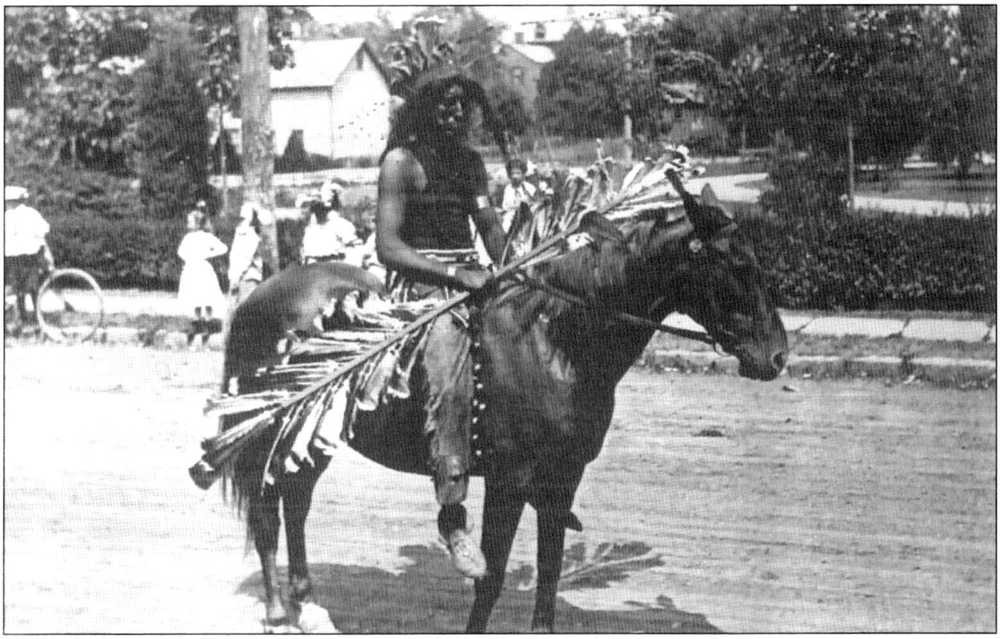

A real, honest-to-goodness American Indian on horseback no doubt was a thrilling sight to Flemington children in the Firemen's Parade.

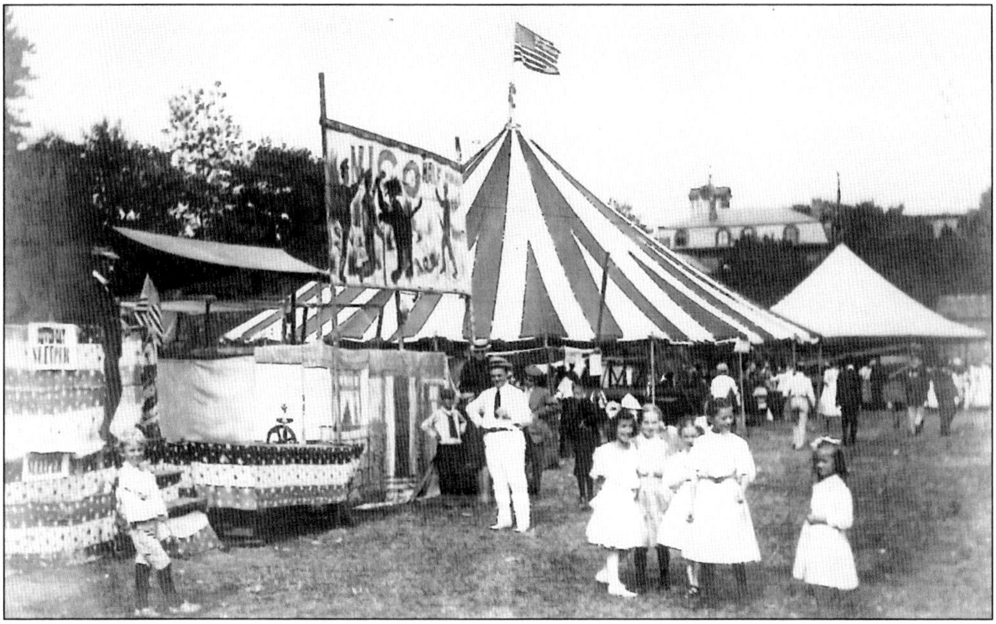

Little girls wore their best white dresses and hair bows to go to the Firemen's Carnival. Little boys at least started out with clean shirts and slicked-down hair, but likely got grubby very quickly in the dust of the carnival grounds.

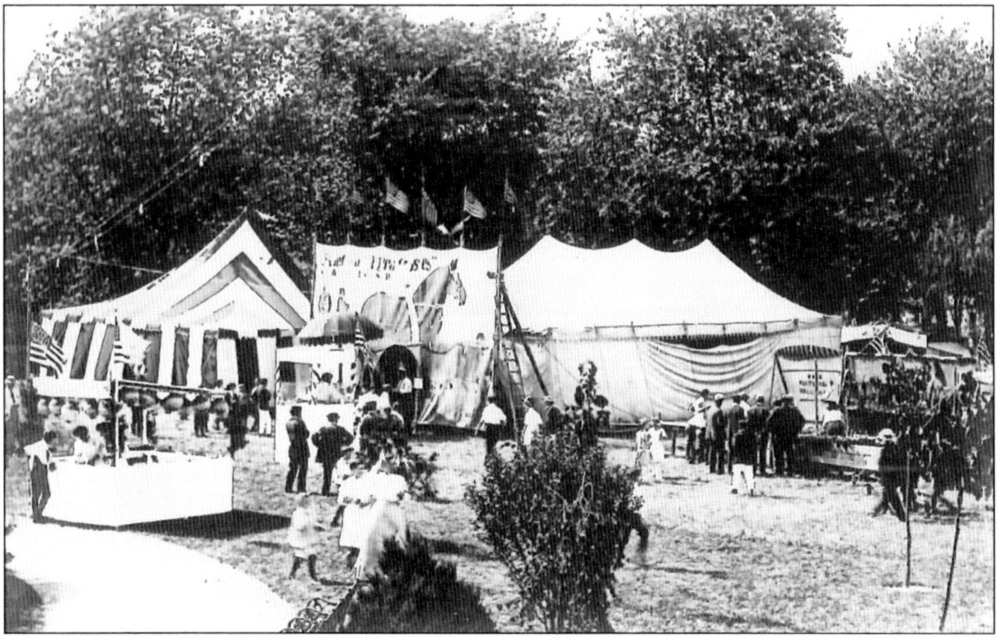

The carnival's gay striped tents could hold all sorts of marvels—like tigers and lions, the fat lady and the thin man, or games where you could hit a wooden pin with a baseball and win a prize to take home.

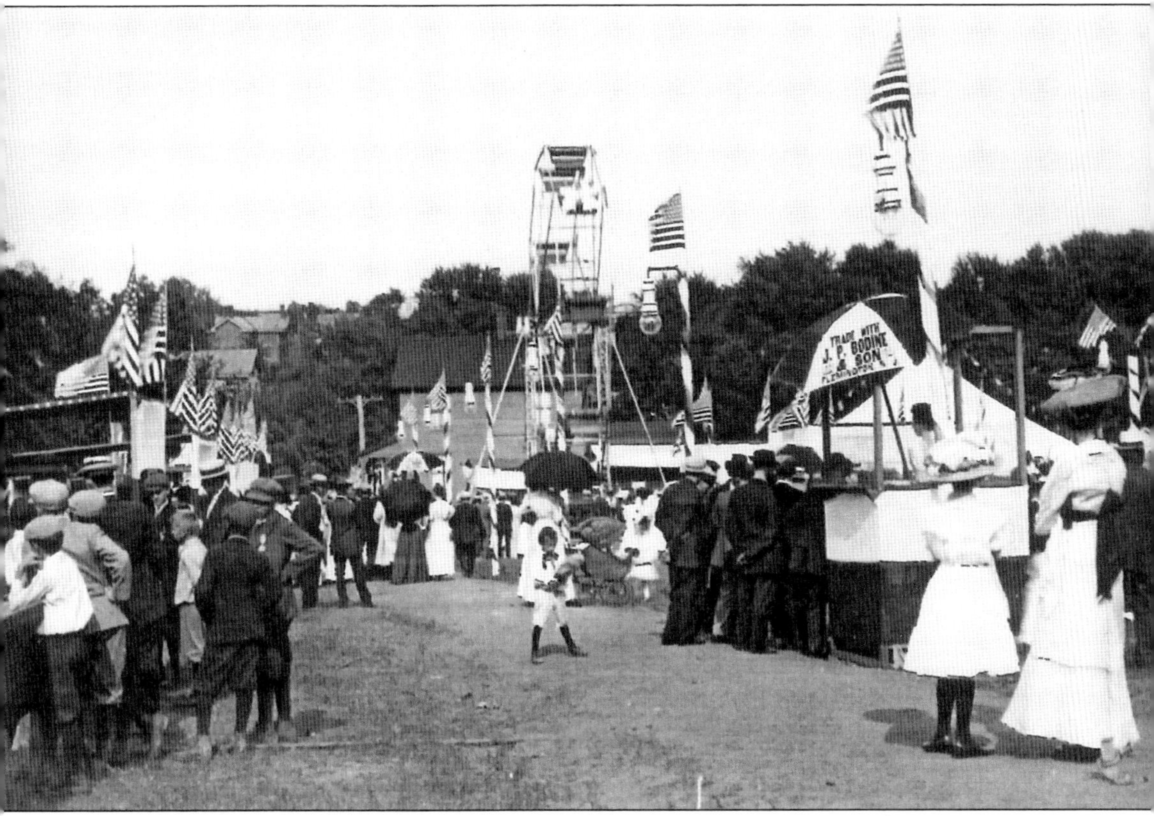

Looking back on it all, we see life as a lot more simple in those early years when excitement could mean a ride on a Ferris wheel. But we can't forget that the farmers and townspeople of Hunterdon worked hard for their moments of pleasure. Farm work began at dawn and was never done. Town shops had to be kept stocked and polished, and often failed despite the owners' best efforts. Building a road with shovels and picks was a lot harder than with today's advances. So was washing clothes, preparing meals, and coping with illness. Those people earned the right to celebrate their continuing existence. From our vantage point in the late twentieth century, we salute them wholeheartedly.

ACKNOWLEDGMENTS

This book could never have been completed through my efforts alone. I want to thank all those who allowed their treasured photographs to be copied for the book—and took their time to give me information and come along to the printers—because of their love for Hunterdon County and their desire to have the old pictures in their care made available to the people of their communities. They include David Breslauer, director of Clinton Historical Society, and his staff members, Jean Daly and Patty Hoff; Yvonne Warren, docent at Lambertville Historical Society; Donald Freiberg, director of Califon Historical Society (a special thank-you to the owners of Rambo's store, who let me interrupt Freiberg's work repeatedly!); Mr. and Mrs. George Melick of Oldwick; Jay Langley, editor, and Olivia Dorfman, librarian, of the Hunterdon County Democrat, and Andy McDermott, owner of the Stockton Inn. They also include a member of the Washington Crossings Postcard Collectors' Club who provided many Flemington pictures but wishes to remain anonymous. Finally, I thank my husband, Arthur Freedman, for his help with my data entry and word processing.

Also I want to thank all the people of Hunterdon County I encountered who expressed enthusiasm for the book while it was in process. I had the privilege of living in Tewksbury Township (near Frederick Philhower's stone bridge on Longview Road) and working as a volunteer at Clinton Historical Museum for seven years—from 1984 to 1991—and I literally loved every minute of that time. Please forgive my errors.